# Teaching and Learning
with Computers

□□□□□□□□□□□□□□□□□□

*Barry Heermann*

# Teaching and Learning with Computers

*A Guide for College Faculty and Administrators*

Jossey-Bass Publishers

San Francisco  •  London  •  1988

TEACHING AND LEARNING WITH COMPUTERS
*A Guide for College Faculty and Administrators*
by Barry Heermann

Copyright © 1988 by: Jossey-Bass Inc., Publishers
350 Sansome Street
San Francisco, California 94104
&
Jossey-Bass Limited
28 Banner Street
London EC1Y 8QE

**Library of Congress Cataloging-in-Publication Data**

Heermann, Barry.
  Teaching and learning with computers : a guide for college faculty
and administrators / Barry Heermann. — 1st ed.
    p.   cm. — (The Jossey-Bass higher education series)
  Bibliography: p.
  Includes index.
  ISBN 1-555-42084-2 (alk. paper)
    1. Education, Higher—United States—Data processing.  2. Computer
-assisted instruction—United States. I. Title. II. Series
LB2395.7.H44   1988
378'.179445—dc19                                        67-30962
                                                        CIP

Manufactured in the United States of America

The paper in this book meets the guidelines for
permanence and durability of the Committee on
Production Guidelines for Book Longevity of the
Council on Library Resources.

JACKET DESIGN BY WILLI BAUM

FIRST EDITION

*Code 8749*

*The Jossey-Bass*
*Higher Education Series*

# Contents

Preface     xi

The Author     xvii

1. Computers for Teaching and Learning:
   Promises and Problems     1

   **Part One: Enriching Instruction with Computers**

2. Deciding When and How to Use Computers
   in a Course     20

3. The Computer as Teaching Machine:
   Enhancing Informational Skills     46

4. The Computer as Simulator: Developing
   Problem-Solving and Integrative Skills     57

5. The Computer as Resource: Fostering
   Investigative Skills     70

6. The Computer as Tool: Improving
   Analytical Skills     85

7.  Acquiring and Implementing Educational
    Software                                                    103

        Part Two: Creating an Environment for
            Computer-Enriched Instruction

8.  Planning an Institutionwide Computer
    Environment                                                 125

9.  Overcoming Resistance and Building Support
    for Computer Use in Instruction                             148

10. Organizing and Managing Academic Computing
    Programs                                                    168

11. New Technology and the Future of Teaching
    and Learning with Computers                                 185

    Resource A: Glossary of Common Computer
    Terms                                                       199

    Resource B: Sources of Information and
    Assistance for Academic Computing                           217

    References                                                  225

    Index                                                       235

# Preface

Analysts have estimated that by the end of this decade, over half of all white-collar workers (thirty-five million people) will routinely use a personal computer on the job ("Personal Computing . . . ," 1985). This widespread adoption of computers in American society has already had an impact on both students and institutions of higher education. Marleen McDaniel of Sun Microcomputers estimates that 20 universities each have an annual computing budget (including both hardware and software) of between $25 million and $50 million, and an additional 100 institutions commit $20 million every year (Turner, 1987d). This notable expenditure reflects a growing demand, coming from both inside and outside higher education institutions, for integration of computers into the teaching and learning process. The question has become not whether computers will be used in higher education instruction but how they should be used. This book is intended to help faculty members and administrators answer this question.

## The Purpose of This Book

The personal computer offers remarkable promise for aiding instructors and students in the teaching and learning process. It can speed and simplify performance of routine tasks, leaving more free time for personal interaction and exploration

of academic subjects in depth. It can make learning more exciting and increase opportunities for independent, creative exploration and experimentation. Computer use in education today, however, has hardly begun to realize that promise. Indeed,
students, instructors, and administrators have encountered
many problems while attempting to integrate computers into
existing instructional curricula.

One reason for these problems is that computer incorporation in higher education institutions frequently has been addressed strictly from a technological rather than a pedagogical
standpoint. The goals of teaching and learning have been lost in
discussions of hard disks, megabytes of memory, modems, and
other matters of computer hardware. Educators have tended to
overlook the fact that computers, no matter how sophisticated,
in themselves can do nothing to further student learning. If computers are to truly enhance education, methods for incorporat-
ing them must be determined first and foremost by educational
considerations, not technological ones.

This book will address the use of computers in higher
education instruction from a pedagogical point of view. In
other words, as its title suggests, it will explore the possibilities
of teaching and learning with computers. It is not primarily a
theoretical work, however. Rather, it is intended to be a concise
handbook that will guide faculty members and administrators
through practical steps by which they can integrate computers
into instruction in ways that will fulfill the technology's promise and avoid its problems.

This is a book for educational practitioners, including faculty members, administrators (academic vice-presidents, pro-
vosts, deans, educational computing directors, and department
heads), faculty development specialists, teaching and learning
specialists, and instructional technologists assisting educational
administrators and faculty. It can be useful to both the experienced and the novice computer user, but it particularly addresses
the needs of instructors or administrators who are unfamiliar
with the educational uses of computers. It will not teach them
how to operate a computer; rather, it will help them explore the
far more important questions of how—and why—to use computers to help students learn.

The first part of this book addresses the concerns of faculty members who are trying to decide how (or whether) to integrate instruction involving computers into existing courses. It attempts to answer such questions as these:

- How are computers being used in higher education instruction today? What has been the result of those uses?
- What learning objectives, intellectual skills, and teaching styles can be enhanced by computers? How can computers help in achieving instructional goals?
- In what ways (modes) can computers deliver instruction? When and how should each of these modes be used?
- In what types of assignments can computers be used? How can they be used?
- How can an instructor analyze an existing course to determine the best way or ways to use computers in it?
- How can an instructor find out what types of software (programs) are available and evaluate that software for possible use in instruction?

The concerns of administrators in higher education institutions are the focus of the second part of this book. This part is intended to help answer such questions as the following:

- What experiences have higher education institutions had in introducing computers into instruction on an institutionwide basis? What lessons can be learned from these experiences?
- How can administrators find out how computers are currently being used in instruction in their institution and what additional uses faculty members would like to explore?
- How can administrators develop and gain support for a coordinated, institutionwide plan for introduction of computers into instruction?
- What education and other forms of support will be needed by faculty and staff using computers for teaching and learning? How can those forms of support best be provided?
- What organizational structures are possible for administration of an academic computing program? What are some advantages and disadvantages of each type of structure?

This book attempts to take the mystery out of computer use in higher education instruction. By placing the concerns of teacher and learner at the center of its focus, it helps education professionals avoid the pitfalls that arise when the computer is seen either as a panacea or as a mechanical monster that threatens to eliminate instructors and turn students into robots. It works to reveal the computer for what it is, a useful tool that can greatly enhance the timeless goals and techniques of education.

## The Organization of This Book

This book is organized into two major parts, which are preceded by a prologue (Chapter One) and followed by an epilogue (Chapter Eleven). Chapter One provides an overview of the promise and problems inherent in the use of computers in higher education today. It briefly describes four modes of instructional delivery by computer and examines the effects of computer use on instructional design, interpersonal aspects of learning, and the higher education institution as a whole.

Part One, which primarily addresses the concerns of faculty members, consists of Chapters Two through Seven. Chapter Two is designed to help instructors analyze existing courses to determine how best to add computerized instruction to them or whether even to use such instruction at all. It describes and explores relationships among four kinds of learning objectives, four kinds of intellectual skills, four kinds of teaching styles, and four modes of computer delivery of instruction. It also looks at different types of course assignments in which computers can be used and briefly describes how faculty can go about finding out what hardware and software are available for enhancement of instruction. It concludes with a questionnaire/worksheet that instructors can use in analyzing their courses to determine whether it is advisable to incorporate computer teaching into them.

Chapters Three through Six consider in more detail the four modes of computer delivery of instruction, giving many examples of current practice in the use of each mode as well as a sampling of relevant off-the-shelf software. Chapter Three describes the computer as teaching machine; Chapter Four describes the computer as simulator; Chapter Five describes the computer as resource; and Chapter Six describes the computer as tool. Each chapter concludes with a checklist designed to help instructors evaluate software used in that mode of instructional delivery.

Chapter Seven explores the actual implementation of computer-related activities in teaching. It gives general guidelines for evaluating existing educational software and also discusses the possibility of creating custom software for particular pedagogic needs. It describes techniques for preparing students to use computers in their coursework and helping them get the most out of computerized instruction. Finally, it considers questions of evaluation, both of student work with computers and of the computer-related activities themselves.

Part Two, comprising Chapters Eight through Ten, is addressed to administrators of higher education institutions. Chapter Eight shows administrators how to apply use and needs assessments to develop a vision of institutionwide academic computer use. It discusses ways of gaining support for the vision both inside and outside the institution and then goes on to guide administrators through the process of preparing an action plan to turn the vision into a reality.

Chapters Nine and Ten consider two important aspects of an academic computing program, its support environment and its organizational structure. Chapter Nine considers such aspects of support as education (faculty development programs and the like), incentives, technical support, and group support. Chapter Ten discusses formal and informal organizational structure, different types of authority (line and staff, centralized and decentralized), and different centers of control. Both chapters give a number of examples of current practice and draw useful lessons from each.

Chapter Eleven, the epilogue, concludes the book with a look at the future of academic computing. It considers technological advances that are likely to occur during the next decade and examines ways they are likely to change not only the forms of computer-related instruction but the very structure of higher education delivery itself. It also points up the basic aspects of instruction that computers will *not* change.

Two resources give further aid to education professionals

dealing with computers. Resource A is a glossary of computer-related terms that are used in this book or are likely to be encountered by educators exploring the uses of computers in instruction. Resource B lists associations, networks, books, magazines, and other sources of information about computers in instruction and educational software.

## Acknowledgments

As I reread the final manuscript I became aware of how much my ideas were influenced by Morris Keeton. I am grateful to him for suggesting possibilities for teaching and learning that caused me to stretch and, more important, to take action to create educational programs that would serve learners.

My appreciation to all those who offered insights during the development of this book, including Shirley Allen Zoernig, Benjamin Davis, and Barbara Dougherty. Special thanks to Kenneth Rothe, who challenged me to suspend my judgment about the dehumanizing effects of technology long enough to see how computers really could empower learners. My path in writing this book was also illuminated by the visions of Richard Van Horn, Richard Cyert, and Raymond Neff, by Judith Axler Turner's timely reports on relevant issues and events, and by John Walker's and Sonja Kirkwood's helpful and cordial responses to my needs for information.

I particularly thank Lisa Yount, who contributed significantly to the strengthening of the final draft. My thanks, too, to the staff at Jossey-Bass for their wonderful support.

Any contribution that I have made to teaching and learning has come out of my commitment to my family, and to learners generally, especially my daughter, Jennie, who will next year venture off to college with a sense of vision and a computer to use in translating that vision into action. Finally, I owe much to my wife, Susan, a brilliant educator, who supported my efforts to create and recreate the vision of this book throughout its development.

*Yellow Springs, Ohio*                                            Barry Heermann
*January 1988*

# The Author

Barry Heermann has been committed to helping instructors and learners design and structure learning projects that contribute to their lives and to the world.

Heermann is the executive director of the Higher Education Management Institute (HEMI) in Yellow Springs, Ohio. HEMI serves as a resource to colleges and universities seeking to use computers in educational programs. He received A.A. and A.S. degrees from Sinclair Community College in Dayton, Ohio; a B.S. degree from Bowling Green State University; an M.B.A. degree from the University of Dayton; and a Ph.D. degree from Ohio State University (1971) in higher education.

Heermann served as a dean of public services and as a director of alternative education programs at a large urban two-year college in Ohio (the Experience-Based Education Department of Sinclair Community College). He also was a dean and vice-president of the Union for Experimenting Colleges and Universities in Ohio. Heermann has edited several Jossey-Bass books, including *Personal Computers and the Adult Learner* (1986).

# Teaching and Learning
# with Computers

# 1

░░░░░░░░░░░░░░░░░░░░░░░

# Computers for Teaching
and Learning:
Promises and Problems

"Nicholas Armington, a senior at Dartmouth College in Hanover, N.H., says he has 'never written a paper onto a piece of paper.' Instead, he has done his writing on the word processing terminals scattered around the campus. Armington has also used computers to study philosophy, create random geometric patterns in a course on art and technology, and brush up on his French. To keep up with current events in a banking course, he spent $20 an hour for an electronic clipping service, and while studying statistics he used computers to verify the probabilities of such large-scale events as flipping coins thousands of times. 'The computer lets you run through a large sample you could never generate yourself,' he says" (Fiske, 1984, p. 40).

Nicholas Armington may be an extreme example, but he definitely represents a trend. A decade ago, a key item in many a college freshman's luggage was a shiny new typewriter; today's freshman is likely to bring a personal computer instead. It is estimated that of the three million students who enter colleges and universities every year, about 750,000 own personal computers (Turner, 1987d). About 13 percent of *all* students own personal computers, ranging from 14 percent of students in private colleges and universities to 7 percent of those in two-year

1

colleges, according to a 1987 study of computer use in 211 colleges and universities (Turner, 1987c).

Institutions of higher education are installing computers just as eagerly—to the tune of $100 billion spent annually. From 1985 to 1986, colleges and universities more than doubled the number of personal computers they owned, according to a survey by the Computation Center at the University of Texas, Austin (1986). On the average, colleges and universities have one personal computer for every 16.7 students and faculty members. When student- and faculty-owned computers were factored in, the ratio dropped to 5.3 students and faculty members for each computer. Students and faculty members have access to institution-owned computers for an average of 3.3 hours per week (Turner, 1987c). A small but increasing number of institutions, such as Philadelphia's Drexel University, either require all their students to own personal computers or provide computers for all students (Turner, 1985).

Higher education's current preoccupation with computers is driven by both pedagogical and technological forces. The pedagogical force is suggested by Dressel and Marcus (1982, p. 202), who assert that a fundamental purpose of teaching and learning is "to make each learner as independent as possible." The computer opens up many possibilities for helping students to become more independent and effective learners. The technological force is reflected in computers that are constantly becoming cheaper, smaller, and better: able to handle larger amounts of information, easier to operate, and employing increasingly useful and sophisticated software (much of it first developed commercially for business and scientific use). *Forbes* analysts predict that in the next ten years personal computers will increase in power tenfold and decrease in price by 20 percent ("Personal Computing . . . ," 1985).

But will advances in computer technology necessarily translate into increased student efficiency and instructional effectiveness? Harvard President Derek C. Bok, in his 1985 annual report to the Harvard Overseers, pointed out, "There is still little proof that the new devices [personal computers] yield lasting improvements in learning. . . . Thomas Edison was clearly wrong in declaring that the phonograph would revolutionize education. Television met a similar fate in spite of glowing predictions" (McCarthy, 1985).

## Promises and Problems

Obviously, the ultimate value of computers in higher education will depend on how the machines are used by both students and instructors. Computers can be merely sophisticated typewriters, calculators, and notebooks—or they can be much more, producing evolutionary changes in the way learning takes place. Finding the best way to realize the potential of these new tools understandably confounds many educators, however. There are agreed-on traditions for using such familiar tools of teaching and learning as books, chalkboards, pens, notepaper, typewriters, and pocket calculators. No such traditions exist for computers.

The promises of computers are manifold. They can give each student a tireless electronic combination of secretary, mentor, and research assistant. Potentially they can allow students to work more independently and to do both more and better work. Carnegie-Mellon President Richard M. Cyert has predicted that the computer could permit students to complete a bachelor's degree in three years ("Three-Year Bachelor Degree . . . ," 1984).

Nonetheless, many problems with using computers have arisen. Many academicians, like Bok, remain unconvinced of the value of the new technology, and research has also suggested that it is not at present as useful as its supporters would like to believe it is. For example, students and faculty at Dartmouth College both believed computers to be useful in instruction, but studies did not corroborate this (Mac Committee, n.d.). Students said their grades would suffer without computers, but in twenty-one out of twenty-four introductory courses, no differences in grades were found between the students who used computers and those who did not.

This chapter will consider both the promise and the problems presented by computer use in four vital aspects of higher education. The aspects covered include instructional delivery, instructional design, the interpersonal aspects of learning, and institutional concerns related to computer use.

## Instructional Delivery

The computer can help an instructor deliver instructional content and develop student skills in a number of ways. It can act as a teaching machine, a simulator, a resource, or a tool. Each of these modes of instructional delivery presents its own promise and problems, which we will discuss briefly here. The uses of these four modes of instructional delivery will be considered in more detail in Chapters Three through Six.

*The Computer as Teaching Machine.* The best-known use of the computer in instruction is as a "teaching machine." This use is commonly referred to as computer-aided instruction or CAI. CAI can give step-by-step presentation of principles and theory, provide practice in applying those principles, test comprehension, give immediate feedback, and assign instruction based upon student responses. It can gear presentation and exercises to a student's proficiency level, providing extra help to those who need it. It allows each student to set a comfortable pace, yet ensures that instruction will remain uniform from student to student. It can also help instructors keep track of student performance. Good CAI designed for today's computers is enlivened by sound and high-resolution color graphics and allows considerable interaction between the student and the computer. CAI will be discussed more fully in Chapter Three.

The PLATO system, first introduced in 1959, was a pioneering tool in the development of CAI (Hofstetter, n.d.). PLATO was originally designed for use with a mainframe, but it has more recently been adapted for personal computers. Using PLATO and other systems, programmers and educators developed CAI for tutorial and drill-and-practice purposes in a variety of academic disciplines. It has also been used for training in industry and the military and as an educational tool in the home and elementary and secondary school markets. Off-the-shelf CAI programs, as well as programs developed by universities or individual faculty members using authoring systems, are increasingly used as supplements to instruction in undergraduate higher education. In the next decade, CAI programs may expand to include video presentations with which students can interact.

CAI has proven to be especially useful for teaching such structured and drill-oriented subjects as mathematics, sentence structure, spelling, and grammar. Computerized writing labs guide students through writing drills and check papers for incorrect usage. The personal computer used as a teaching machine can be a powerful addition to instruction because of its self-pacing and uniformity of presentation. The student can take as much time and receive as much repetition and practice as he or she needs, aided by a mechanical "teacher" that never becomes impatient or tired.

CAI can also prove invaluable to the instructor. By scoring tests, coaching students in preparation for classroom sessions, and providing routine instruction and drill, it saves time and frees the instructor to engage students in exploring more sophisticated or advanced aspects of the discipline.

In spite of its potential usefulness, CAI has never taken on much importance in mainstream undergraduate education. This is in part due to CAI's lack of responsiveness to diverse student learning styles. Research has shown that many students learn better through nonsequential and experiential ("learning by doing") processes than through the sort of logical, linear ones in which CAI excels. Gueulette (1982) reports, "Recent research has indicated that perhaps as much as one half of the population has the sort of cognitive structure that resists acquisition of knowledge from the highly linear and orderly process of the computer. . . . CAI programs may favor those learners who have the ability to quietly concentrate, pay attention to details, memorize facts, and stay with a single task until its completion. Extroverts (or perceptive learners), on the other hand, may not fare so well" (p. 181). It should be noted that uses of the computer for instructional delivery other than CAI rely much less strongly on the "linear and orderly process" that Gueulette criticizes.

Use of the computer as a teaching machine also does not fit well with some teaching styles. Some faculty members fear the loss of control of the teaching process that CAI seems to imply, for example. Others fear its potential for diminishing teacher-student contact.

Many of today's CAI programs are quite limited, both pedagogically and technologically. CAI is far from the only method for using the computer to aid in instructional delivery, however. The computer may also be used as a simulator, a resource, and a tool.

*The Computer as Simulator.* The computer as simulator models physical or social phenomena. It promotes understanding of the interrelationships of the parts of a model to each other and to the whole by permitting students to manipulate individual parts and observe the effects of their actions on the rest of the model. At the same time, the computer as simulator helps students develop problem-solving skills. Computer simulations will be discussed more fully in Chapter Four.

A classic example of this mode of computerized instructional delivery is the flight simulator. In such a simulator, students manipulate controls much like those on a real airplane and see the results on a video screen—including a realistic "crash" if mistakes are serious enough. Simulations may also be used in economic, scientific, political, or other contexts.

Computers are uniquely suited for delivering simulations. Every time a student makes a change in the model, the computer responds by changing all the other parts of the model that are affected. Color, shape (often in three dimensions), and movement allow the student to see the interrelationships of parts to whole in a way that would not be possible without (or sometimes even with) direct contact with the phenomenon being studied.

So far, computer simulations have been used mostly in mathematics and science classes. For example, an Annenberg/Corporation for Public Broadcasting project funded through the University of Nebraska used computer simulations with videodisks in introductory physics, biology, and chemistry laboratory courses. In a chemistry lesson on titration, students turned a "stopcock" at various speeds and saw the results on video as color changes in the liquid undergoing titration. A physics lesson on energy transformations used different types of bicycles to illustrate problems in the physics of rotational motion. Students attempted to solve the problems and saw the results on the video screen (*Videodisc Science Laboratory Simulations,* 1985).

Computer simulations are equally useful in humanities and social science courses. At Stanford University, for example, *Hamlet* can be staged through a computer simulation of actors, props, and scenery. The student can position these elements of the play on a simulated stage, portrayed on the computer monitor screen, and observe the interaction of the parts of the play in producing a whole (Turner, 1986e). Similarly, at the Massachusetts Institute of Technology, a computer simulation teaches German by providing a dormitory room with some typical objects and a German-speaking "poltergeist" with whom the student can converse. The student must follow rules of German grammar and usage in the conversation. If the poltergeist does not "understand" a directive, it may suggest grammatical or spelling changes, thus providing feedback for the student (*The Athena Language Learning Project,* n.d.).

The promise of the computer used as a simulator lies in allowing the student to have a close facsimile of direct experience with realities to which actual exposure would be impossible due to cost, time, safety, geography, or other factors. Through simulation, students can tour the inner reaches of the human body, manage a nuclear power plant, or mastermind a plan for world peace. Simulations allow students to take a much more active role than is usually possible with traditional classroom instruction.

Of course, even the best simulation is not the same as the reality it represents. The complexities of, say, ecological relationships can be only hinted at, not fully represented, in a simulation. Unpredictable factors that often have important effects in real situations usually do not appear in simulations. Students' confusion of simulation and reality can cause erroneous assumptions based on oversimplification.

Another problem is that the principles and assumptions on which a simulation's design is based usually are not made obvious to students (or even to the instructor). Questioning or evaluating those assumptions is therefore difficult, and students may unconsciously accept ideas that should be critically examined. Finally, finding a simulation consistent with the instructional intentions of a particular course, let alone building an original simulation "from scratch," can be extremely expensive, time consuming, or both.

*The Computer as Resource.* The computer used as a resource makes available a supply of information and a means of communication that students can use to complete many kinds of learning projects and research. It helps students strengthen their investigative skills. Via computer networks, students can "meet" or leave messages with other students, with faculty members, and with authorities in their field. Data bases accessed by computer can increase students' contact with literature, research, and other sources of information in their field. Technologically, use of the computer as a resource may involve the university library, a departmental local area network, an institutionwide network of computers and data bases, and/or the use of communications software and devices (modems) to reach beyond the institution. Uses of the computer as a resource will be described more fully in Chapter Five.

Uses of the computer as a resource are diverse. Dartmouth offers a large social science data base, which helps students conduct inquiries and carry out investigative projects (FIPSE Technology Study Group, n.d.). The University of Illinois developed a computer-based "textbook" in pathology that is very much like a data base and serves as both a resource for continuing education and an up-to-date information base for medical students doing research in this field (Balestri, Cochrane, and Thursh, 1984).

The Electronic University Network, sponsored by Telelearning in collaboration with a diverse set of colleges and universities, delivers on-line credit and noncredit courses to homes and businesses ("A Wizard's Plan . . . ," 1984). It combines use of the computer as a resource with elements of CAI. Use of the computer as a resource offers great time and space flexibility to students, permitting them to study at home, at work, in the dormitory, or at other locations at convenient times while maintaining most of the interactivity of a classroom course. As the network's catalogue notes, "Electronic University Network Forums allow you to discuss specific course subjects just as you would in a live classroom. Debate a hot topic. Review or critique a case study. Discuss a hypothetical problem. All of these capabilities are possible under the direction of your instructor" (*The Electronic University Network*, 1986). Unlike students taking traditional correspondence courses, who may have to wait weeks to find out answers to questions or scores on homework assignments, students taking Electronic University Network courses get responses from their instructors within forty-eight hours.

The promise of the computer used as a resource is a great increase in student efficiency in securing and sending information for academic purposes. This computer use directly facilitates communications—that is, getting data (bibliographic sources, facts and figures, literature, messages to faculty, faculty evaluations and assignments, and so on) from one place to another.

One disadvantage of using the computer as a resource, however, is that the technology involved can be hard to use. Students must become familiar with the protocol involved in calling up data or in communicating with an instructor or another student via computer. Some conferencing, bulletin board, and data base services are anything but "user friendly."

Another important problem in the use of the computer as a resource is cost. Despite recent economies and a decline in fees, the costs for the telephone and computer time needed in accessing on-line data bases and some computer conferences places these uses of the computer out of the reach of most middle-class students attending community colleges or urban universities. The cost to institutions, too, is often prohibitively high. Some campuses cannot afford a local area network for a department or building, let alone a communications network for the whole institution. The alternative of providing modems and communication software for students' own computers may be cheaper but is not always easy to implement. These problems impede use of the computer as a resource in higher education today.

A final problem lies in what these uses of the computer do *not* do. Accessing information through on-line data bases does not teach students how to sort or evaluate that information. Computer conferences are only pale imitations of face-to-face meetings, lacking the important signals in facial expression, vocal intonation, "body language," and so on. Students may come to rely on the computer too much, assuming that the machine will take care of thinking or social interaction for them.

*The Computer as Tool.* The computer can be an effective tool to enhance development of writing, analytical, computational, and other learning skills. This use of the computer usually involves readily available, inexpensive, highly sophisticated off-the-shelf software. Much of this software was originally developed for business and scientific applications. As Adeline Naiman notes, "Data base programs now come with templates in social studies up and down the grade levels. Spreadsheets are being applied to the teaching of mathematics. Fast graphing routines have revitalized algebra, and computer graphics support both Euclid and transformational geometry" (1987, pp. 199–200).

Computer software "tools" that can be useful in higher education include word processing, spreadsheet, accounting and financial, data base, graphing, decision support, statistical, outlining, and "idea generation" programs, as well as "integrated software" packages that combine several of these applications. All these application programs help students manipulate data: numbers, words, concepts, and images. In addition to aiding academic work, learning how to use many of these kinds of tools (word processors and spreadsheets, for example) will prove useful to students later in their working lives. "Tool" software will be discussed more fully in Chapter Six.

Properly used, software tools can greatly increase student efficiency. Such tools can save students time, help them organize their thoughts better, and lead them to discover relationships they might never have noticed on their own. Word processing programs help students compose and revise essays and reports. Spreadsheet programs help them analyze mathematical relationships among data. Accounting and financial programs help them manipulate and classify financial data. Data base programs help them categorize and discover meaningful relationships in data. Graphing and other graphics programs help them use visual representation to make relationships clearer. Decision support or project management programs help them analyze alternative scenarios to arrive at an optimal decision or plan of action. Statistical and mathematical programs help them perform calculations to solve complex problems. Idea generation and outlining programs help them brainstorm possibilities and then outline or arrange these ideas into a meaningful pattern.

At Drexel University, where all freshmen are required to have access to a personal computer, students use computers as tools in a variety of ways. Economics students use spreadsheet programs to construct "what-if" models of changes in the money supply, balance of payments, or currency exchange rates. All papers and lab reports of engineering students, including drawings, charts, tables, and graphs, are generated on computers. Psychology students analyze survey data and reproduce classic experiments on the computer. Sociology students prepare models of social organizations; nutrition students use computers to analyze diets; design students sketch costumes and explore design concepts on their computers; and chemistry students use spreadsheets to determine equilibrium points of chemical reactions (*Drexel University . . .*, n.d.).

Problems with the use of the computer as a tool may include difficulty in learning the commands and functions of some programs; each program has a unique "learning curve" that reflects the ease with which the program can be mastered (Green, 1985). Some complex programs require ten to twenty hours of instruction before students can effectively employ them in learning projects. (On the other hand, some extremely effective programs can be learned in fifteen to twenty minutes—and user-friendly programs are becoming more common.)

Yet another problem involves the "fit" of off-the-shelf programs to the particular demands for analysis that apply in various disciplines. For some disciplines and some kinds of analyses, expensive custom software may be required.

Some instructors also see a problem in the very feature that many students like best about these programs: the drudgery they save. The programs minimize or eliminate the performance of routine tasks such as calculation of complex formulas (spreadsheet programs), identification of spelling errors (spelling checker components of word processing programs), or selection of the most appropriate alternatives for solving a case or resolving a problem related to a simulation (decision support programs). Instructors fear that students will not learn the logic of these tasks if they never have to do them manually. They also see the discipline involved in the completion of such work as essential to a successful academic experience.

Similar criticisms arose when pocket calculators were first introduced into schools. Many instructors expressed concern about how these aids would affect students' understanding of the underlying logic of mathematical processes. There is an important learning gain in performing computational tasks without the assistance of a calculator. But there is also value, after basic skills and their underlying logic have been mastered, to freeing students from the limitation of pencil-and-paper calculations.

The same logic can be used regarding application programs on the computer. Instructors need to decide when students are best served by using the computer to complete routine academic tasks and when they are not. If the work time needed for, say, writing an essay is expected to be greatly decreased by use of the computer, instructors need to decide whether to require higher standards for essays, assign more essays, or make some other adjustment in course requirements.

A related problem is perhaps most serious of all: the assumption by students (or even instructors) that the programs will do much more than they really can. "Tool" software can help students develop skills, but it does not teach those skills, nor will it substitute for them. Doing an assignment faster is not the same as doing it better. A word processor cannot make a student a good writer, nor can a spreadsheet make a student a business analyst. These tools can facilitate the process of teaching and learning, but they can never replace it.

## Instructional Design

The computer's potential for giving students increased autonomy and heightened effectiveness in completing certain learning tasks can have considerable effects, both positive and negative, on instructional design. These effects go far beyond the need to design the computer assignments themselves. When computers are introduced into a course, the design of non-computer instructional components will also change.

Some instructors fear such changes, but they need not do so. Changes in instructional design brought about by computers can actually permit faculty to place greater emphasis on critical thinking skills, affective education, group interaction, and inquiry into issues and problems related to a course of study. This promise arises both from the student and faculty time computers can free up for personal interaction and from the increased complexity of intellectual exploration that computers can make possible.

There is no doubt that the introduction of computers into a course will force an instructor to answer some difficult questions. For example, consider the following:

- How can a course be restructured to deal with the fact that students and instructors no longer have to be in the same place at the same time in order to "meet"?
- How should homework or class assignments done on the computer be evaluated?
- How should the traditional "three credit hours" be redefined to take into account the effects of the computer on students' work efficiency?
- How should group-based classroom processes be related to independent activities involving the computer?

In many institutions, finding the best answers to these questions is made even harder by bureaucratic inertia that locks faculty into the static instructional milieu of textbooks, established class meeting times, and fixed classroom locations. Hardware incompatibility, lack of appropriate software, and scarce resources can also cause frustration. Nonetheless, pioneering faculty in a number of institutions are beginning to meet the challenges that integrating the computer into instructional design presents. Aspects of integrating computers into the instructional design of a course will be considered further in Chapter Seven.

What may appear to be the greatest problem in integrating the computer into a course's instructional design is in fact the computer's greatest promise. Deciding how to use computers in a course often forces an instructor to rethink the basic purposes and instructional approaches of the course. The result of this reconceptualization is often beneficial to all concerned. Harvard President Derek C. Bok affirms, "As more people begin to use technology for educational purposes, they are bound to think more carefully about the best ways to help students absorb new knowledge and master new intellectual skills" (Turner, 1985, p. 26).

## Interpersonal Aspects of Learning

Changes caused by the introduction of computers into a course are not limited to materials and instructional approaches. The roles and relationships of the people involved in the course —both students and teachers—may be greatly altered as well. This change in role dynamics results from a variety of factors, the two most critical of which are increased student autonomy and increased student efficiency in completing learning tasks.

When computer-aided instruction was first introduced, some instructors feared that the computer would create a new student dependence and alienation. They had an Orwellian vision of endless stretches of programmed instruction, of impersonal technology controlling and dominating passive student victims. In workshops that I conduct on computers in instruction, the most frequently expressed fear is still that the computer will "depersonalize" education.

This tendency toward depersonalization can in fact appear when computers are used by educators who are insensitive to the human and affective dimensions of learning. It can also appear when the computer is used to the exclusion of other experiences, as a complete, stand-alone package of instruction rather than as a supplement to other instruction in an integrated course plan.

Computers need not depersonalize education or alienate students, however. To begin with, the computer can decrease student dependence on libraries, classrooms, and faculty, allowing learning to take place at times and in spaces convenient to the learners. Because of this increased autonomy, computers potentially can increase students' sense of identity and self-esteem.

The promise of increased student autonomy also carries problems, however. Students vary greatly in their appreciation of and need for structure and supervision. Some will not be able to handle greater autonomy. Younger students, in particular, sometimes lack the motivation and self-discipline necessary for contract learning or independent study projects.

Motivation can also be a problem when the computers used by students are located in a computer laboratory. To ensure that students make the trip to the laboratory, the computer work in a course either must be heavily weighted toward the final grade or must make learning considerably easier, more effective, or more enjoyable.

Some instructors as well as some students see the increased student autonomy made possible by computers as a threat. These instructors fear the effects of no longer having students under their direct supervision. In fact, far from "replacing" teachers, computers make instructor guidance of the learning process more essential than ever. Furthermore, they can save time for faculty as well as students (by providing routine practice and automatic grading of simple assignments, for example), thus freeing instructors for more meaningful individual and group interaction with students.

Dustin Heuston provides this vision of the way the computer could simultaneously save an instructor's time and give a student more individual help than would normally be possible:

"A student would take his paper to a writing center, where he would be asked by a terminal to type in his name and the title of his paper. . . . The computer screen will then ask him to input the first symbol that the faculty member has written on his paper. Here the student might type in CS [for comma splice] or rule #42, and the screen would then say, 'John, this is the third time you have missed a comma splice. . . . I am going to explain it to you once again, give you some drill and practice until you have mastered it, and then urge you not to make this mistake again.' There would then ensue a quarter to half an hour of drill and explanation on comma splices until John can satisfy the computer program that he has mastered the concept. . . . The student is receiving personal instruction in precisely the areas where he needs help without the teacher being present" (1986, p. 45).

Computers can increase students' interaction with their peers as well. A common stereotype pictures the computer-using student as a socially isolated "nerd." In fact, however, a Drexel University study found that computer-using students were more likely to be involved in extracurricular activities than those who did not use computers (McCord, n.d.). By increasing work efficiency, the computer gives students more time for socialization. It also gives them a subject for interaction as they learn to use hardware and software and then work together on computer-based group projects. Creative instructors can use the computer to encourage and facilitate student dialogue about academic problems, either in person or through computer communication.

In addition, because the computer can let students handle routine instruction and drill privately, it can free classroom time for more group processes, dialogue, and interpersonal exchange with both faculty and peers. Computer conferencing can also increase student dialog with faculty and other experts.

The full realization of the computer's promise in increasing student independence and efficiency would result in an "ideal world" in which students would learn at their own pace, independently, but come together in groups to discuss problems and to synthesize and share their experiences. All students would master the subject matter to roughly the same degree, yet each would use exactly the amounts of time, energy, and insight appropriate for his or her individual needs. The instructor would support and guide students in the learning process, facilitating group discussion and advising individuals on particular plans for application of what they have learned.

The way to avoid possible depersonalizing effects of the computer is to keep the learner at the center of the instructional process. What Carl Rogers (1969) called "person centeredness" ought to be a guiding principle in any reconfiguration of instruction that involves the computer. In all good teaching, decisions about the use of educational media—including, and perhaps especially, the computer—are based on the nature and needs of the students. The use of personal computers in instruction must always have the person at its heart.

## Institutional Concerns

The resources, policies, and politics of colleges and universities inevitably affect the instruction they produce. This is particularly true of the use of computers in instruction. Today, many universities and colleges are evaluating alternative organizational and managerial actions involved in the introduction of computers to be used in instruction. In this area, too, both promise and problems are being encountered.

In recent years there has been a shift in views of the way computers should be used in higher education, and with that shift has come a shift in organization. Only a few years ago, students—if they were concerned with computers at all—"learned about" computers. Basically, this meant learning to program. Such a course of study emphasized the mastery of computer languages such as COBOL and FORTRAN and was usually taken in preparation for a career in computing or data processing. It was taught by the faculty of a discrete computer science department.

Today, however, the emphasis has shifted to "learning with" computers, a form of learning that can be part of just about any academic discipline. This shift reflects the increasing use of computers in a wide variety of careers and for a wide variety of functions in the society at large, a change that in turn has been produced by the increasing availability of small, inexpensive personal computers and easy-to-use software. As a result of these changes, the group of students who want to learn how to use computers effectively has become both much larger and much more heterogeneous.

During the early stages of this shift in attitude, the computer science department usually remained in control of computer resources, often aided by continuing education staff who taught "computer literacy" to adult learners. As both the need for and the meaning of "computer literacy" continued to change, however, the demands on many computer science departments far outstripped the departments' ability to respond. Furthermore, although the computer science staff were unquestionably the most knowledgeable about the technical aspects of computers, they often had limited experience with the instructional issues involved in the educational use of the machines.

It became increasingly clear that an institutionwide organizational approach to the introduction and use of computers in instruction was called for to meet the institutionwide need. Planning needed to be systematic and carefully thought out. All kinds of problems arose when, as was all too often the case, such systematic planning did not occur. These included splintered and unpublished experimentation within different departments, decentralized computer labs, and "fiefdoms" or protected sanctuaries of power within the university (for example, the college of engineering and science often had primary "rights" to computers on campus).

To meet the need for institutionwide planning for the use of computers in instruction, many of the most forward-looking higher education institutions have developed an organizational unit, sometimes called Academic Computing, that is solely committed to facilitating the use of the computer throughout the curriculum. Such a unit can greatly help in adapting the computer to an institution's particular educational program, student needs, and fiscal realities. This kind of organizational unit, as well as other considerations involved in institutionwide planning for use of computers in instruction, will be discussed in detail in Part Two of this book (Chapters Eight through Ten).

There is as yet no consensus on the effectiveness of computers as tools for teaching and learning in higher education. According to Turner, writing in the *Chronicle of Higher Education*, "only a handful of researchers are looking at [this] subject, and most of them are in the data-gathering phase" (1987a, p. 28). Only time will lead to true evaluation, including consideration of the "Hawthorne effect" that makes so many new programs and techniques effective—as long as they are new. Similarly, there is no consensus on the best way to use computers to maximize learning, including the process's affective and interpersonal as well as its intellectual aspects. Yet these are issues that no thoughtful faculty member or institutional administration can afford to ignore.

The remainder of this book will be devoted to helping instructors and administrators plan how to incorporate computers into existing curricula in ways that will help to realize the great promise of the computer as an aid to teaching and learning and at the same time minimize the problems that have become associated with computer use. The first of the book's two major sections, consisting of Chapters Two through Seven, is intended to help faculty members enrich their courses by integrating the computer into them in any or all of its four modes of instructional delivery: as a teaching machine, as a simulator, as a resource, and as a tool.

# 2

■■■■■■■■■■■■■■■■■■

# Deciding When and How
# to Use Computers in a Course

Exchanges of ideas and feelings between people have always been and will always be at the heart of teaching and learning. As Joseph Lowman states in his book, *Mastering the Techniques of Teaching,* "In contrast to approaches that focus on . . . technological innovations, my perspective rests squarely on the assumption that college teaching is and should be interpersonal, that it is above all an enterprise involving human beings and their personalities, and that it is incapable of being reduced to mechanical cause-and-effect relationships" (1984, p. 2).

Similarly, Stanford Ericksen, in his book, *The Essence of Good Teaching,* affirms, "The passage of time and technological inventions have not changed the human dimensions of teaching. Students will always benefit from 'earthworm professors whose impact derives from the enthusiastic commitment to the enduring value of the substance of their subject-matter specialty, their insistence that material be thoroughly learned, and their precept and example" (1984, p. 11).

## Integrating the Computer with Other Teaching Methods

Computers will not change the fundamental importance of human interaction in teaching and learning. They also will not change the instructor's central role in the process. Lowman observes, "College classrooms are fundamentally dramatic arenas

20

in which the teacher is the focal point, just as the actor or orator is on stage" (1984, pp. 11–12). The computer is not an understudy, eager to replace the human teaching "star"; rather, it is (or has the potential to be) a very useful prop in the instructor's performance.

Similarly, traditional teaching techniques will continue to be important in courses into which computers have been integrated. Lectures by instructors, for example, will continue to be a primary means of stimulating student emotions and intellectual activity. Chet Meyers asserts, "Lectures are appropriate, perhaps the best, means for stimulating interest by raising questions and presenting problems, providing information not available in texts or supplementary readings, clarifying difficult concepts through example or analogy, summarizing main points of discussion, and demonstrating through example how teachers engage in critical thinking" (1986, p. 57). Computers in no way change the truth of that assertion.

Computers also will not affect the need to balance lectures with group interaction and inquiry. As Meyers points out, "The main problem with lecture as a primary mode of teaching is the disallowance of any time for students to interact with and process subject matter. Furious note taking may appear to be a form of interaction, but it is no substitute for processing information by thinking out loud, restating concepts in one's own words, discussing issues with fellow students, or challenging a teacher's assumptions and conclusions" (p. 57).

The computer can, however, enrich lectures, group processes, and other traditional teaching techniques when used as a supplement to them. Lowman suggests that "technology-based individual teaching is best used in tandem with more traditional lecture-discussion formats" (1984, p. 161). Ericksen also affirms, "It is important to integrate instructional technology with the live presentation and the other resources for teaching" (1984, p. 31).

The key to effective use of the computer in teaching and learning is the proper integration of this new technology with more traditional teaching methods. Such integration takes careful thought and planning. This portion of the book (Chapters Two through Seven) is intended to help instructors ask themselves the kinds of questions and make the kinds of plans that will allow computers to be incorporated into their courses in the most enriching and least disruptive way.

The first step in planning for integration of computers into a course is thinking carefully about the nature and purposes of the course as it presently exists. This chapter will describe a number of factors that an instructor should consider when deciding how best to integrate computers into a course (or whether to do so at all). For the instructor's convenience, these factors are summarized in a questionnaire-worksheet at the end of the chapter. Groups of factors to be considered include the following:

- Learning objectives
- Intellectual skills
- Teaching styles
- Modes of computer delivery
- Types of assignment
- Available hardware and software

Items in the first four of these groups of factors have been found to bear a certain general relationship to each other. This relationship can be summarized in a four-cell matrix that will be pictured and described in the sections that follow. In this matrix, factors involved in teaching and learning are plotted along two dimensions: other-directed (the "other" being a teacher, a computer, or other resource) learning versus self-directed learning and applied versus theoretical learning. An excellent discussion of this latter distinction is provided by Thomas Ewens (1979), who describes the difference between knowing by discovery and knowing through instruction.

Faculty intent on fostering self-directed learning actively support students in creating their own learning experience; faculty who encourage other-directed learning design the process so that students receive carefully sequenced and organized presentations of the discipline, with students taking notes, completing exams, and following prescribed instructions and assignments (Knowles, 1975). Faculty who stress theoretical learning focus on student mastery of the abstractions, theory, and principles of the discipline; faculty biased toward applied learning emphasize involvement with the realities being studied, either through direct experience or through simulations of that experience (Keeton, 1976; also see Ewens, 1979 for an excellent analysis of theory and practice in the liberal arts curriculum).

## Learning Objectives

The first set of factors an instructor needs to consider in deciding whether and how to use computers in a course is what he or she wants students to learn—that is, what kind or kinds of knowledge students should have at the end of the course. Classification of the outcomes of student learning has been debated by educational philosophers and practitioners for decades. Several of the most popular taxonomies are those of Bloom (1956) and Gagne (1965). The simplified taxonomy presented here is drawn from several educational philosophers (Ryle, 1949; Broudy, 1961; and Soltis, 1968). It divides learning objectives into four categories: "knowing that," "knowing how," "knowing where," and "knowing what and why." The place of these objectives on our matrix is shown in Figure 1.

**Figure 1. Learning Objectives.**

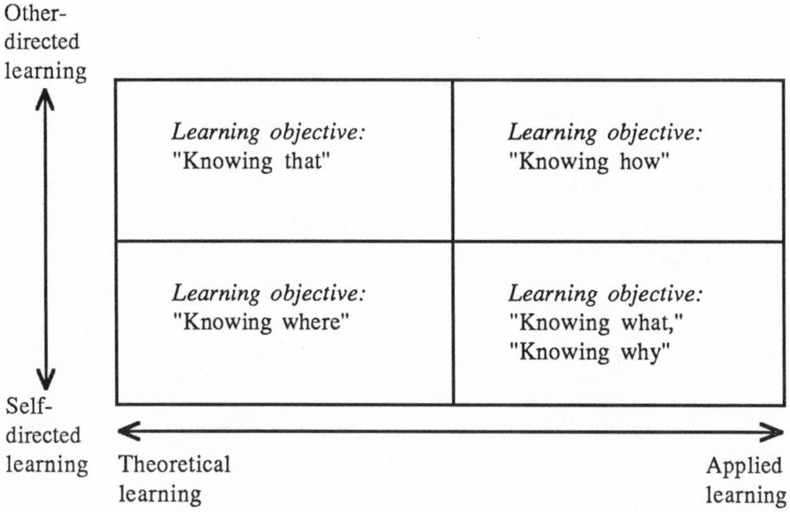

Other-
directed
learning

| | |
|---|---|
| *Learning objective:* "Knowing that" | *Learning objective:* "Knowing how" |
| *Learning objective:* "Knowing where" | *Learning objective:* "Knowing what," "Knowing why" |

Self-
directed
learning

Theoretical
learning

Applied
learning

*"Knowing That."* Ryle (1949) asserted that there are essentially two kinds of knowledge, represented by "knowing that" and "knowing how." Examples of "knowing that" include knowing that George Washington was the first President of the United States and knowing that quartz is a type of mineral. This sort of factual knowledge can also include principles, theories, and concepts. As Figure 1 shows, the objective of "knowing that" is most likely to be achieved by other-directed, theoretical learning. This objective will be discussed more fully in Chapter Three.

*"Knowing How."* "Knowing how" is the result of applied learning. Because such learning is usually guided by an experienced person, it is also a form of other-directed learning. According to Ryle, knowing how to play the bassoon or knowing how to debate the merits of an issue such as racial integration in schools is quite different from knowing that the bassoon uses a double reed or knowing that the Supreme Court ruled that school segregation was unconstitutional in 1954. Neither kind of knowledge guarantees the other. A student may know all kinds of facts about the bassoon and still have little or no ability to play the instrument, or he or she may be an excellent musician in practice but have very little theoretical background. The objective of "knowing how" will be discussed more fully in Chapter Four.

*"Knowing Where."* Soltis (1968), modifying the taxonomies of Ryle (1949) and Broudy (1961), characterizes this form of learning as discovering the "locus" of information. The category as used here encompasses the locating and gathering of information from which theories and ideas might be extracted. An example might be using reference works or data bases to locate literature relevant to a certain research topic. "Knowing where" is an objective of self-directed, theoretical learning. This objective will be discussed more fully in Chapter Five.

*"Knowing What and Why."* Harry S. Broudy in his essay, "Mastery" (1961), discusses two types of knowledge that, for present purposes, can be combined into one category. By

"knowing what," we mean what Broudy calls "classificatory knowledge"—an ability to distinguish among different types of information and data. "Knowing why," as used here, means finding or exploring theoretical understanding or conceptual knowing. (Note the distinction between being presented theory and concepts, which results in "knowing that," and discovering relationships and formulating theories, which results in "knowing why.") A chemistry student who arrives inductively at a rule for formation of salts from acids and bases as a result of experiments has achieved the objective of "knowing why," for example. "Knowing what and why" are objectives of self-directed, applied learning. These objectives will be discussed more fully in Chapter Six.

## Intellectual Skills

Just as different kinds of knowledge can result from learning, so different kinds of intellectual skills can be developed to acquire certain kinds of knowledge. The kinds of skills an instructor wants students to develop are a second important group of factors to consider in determining the best uses of the computer in a course. The grouping of intellectual skills described here was derived from classical theory regarding the purposes of education, specifically Phenix's *Realms of Meaning* (1964) and Dressel's *College and University Curriculum* (1968). Several competence-based education programs, such as those of Alverno College in Wisconsin (Alverno College, 1973) and Grand Valley State College in Michigan (Grand Valley State College, 1973), incorporate these skill areas explicitly in their educational processes, and the same skill groups are implicitly developed in the curricula of many other institutions. Certain courses stress some kinds of intellectual skills more than other kinds, but many courses are designed to help students develop all four groups of skills to some extent. Figure 2 shows the placement of intellectual skills in our four-cell matrix.

*Informational Skills.* These skills allow the mastery of the factual information, principles, and theories important to a discipline or course of instruction. Use of the skills results in "know-

Figure 2. Intellectual Skills.

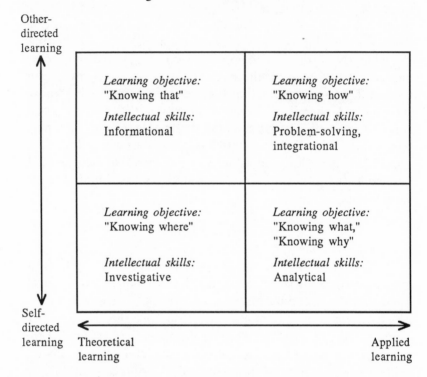

ing that." Informational skills are most often used in other-directed, theoretical learning. A student reading a textbook chapter or reviewing lecture notes is primarily using informational skills. Development of these skills will be discussed more fully in Chapter Three.

*Problem-Solving and Integrative Skills.* Problem-solving skills allow a student to find the best outcome for situations in the real world or in simulations. Integrative skills allow a student to see relationships among individual things or among parts of a whole. These intellectual skills are also fundamental life skills. They are the basic tools needed to acquire any kind of applied knowledge. The use of problem-solving and integrative skills results in "knowing how." Students are often helped by others to acquire these skills, as when a teacher or a computer program presents a mathematics problem for solution. Development of these skills will be discussed more fully in Chapter Four.

*Investigative Skills.* These skills enable a student to locate and access information and ideas. These may be the opinions of peers, faculty members, or authorities in a field, or they may be information or ideas derived from a discipline's literature. Investigative skills are often important in the preparation of research projects, essays, papers, and other scholarly studies. Use of these skills results in "knowing where." Students often develop these theory-oriented skills during independent work. Development of investigative skills will be discussed more fully in Chapter Five.

*Analytical Skills.* These skills involve interpretation, evaluation, and examination of subject matter in order to arrive at basic or general truths: in other words, inductive reasoning. Such skills may be developed by, for example, textual analysis of a work of literature or mathematical analysis of the results of experiments in chemistry or physics. Analytical skills are most often developed through independent work in applied learning. Their use results in "knowing what and why." Development of these skills will be discussed more fully in Chapter Six.

## Teaching and Learning Styles

Instructors may play many roles before their students. Sometimes they are teachers, giving information to passive student listeners. Sometimes they are facilitators, guiding students in group interaction or problem-solving activities. Sometimes they are mentors, helping students sort through a welter of data to find what is relevant. Sometimes they are brokers, encouraging students to experiment and apply knowledge to discover concepts independently. A single instructor may well play all four of these parts during the "drama" of a course's presentation, becoming a teacher when lecturing, a facilitator during seminar or laboratory sessions, and a mentor or broker when helping students handle out-of-class assignments. Nonetheless, an instructor is also likely to have a favorite role among the four, a teaching style that he or she feels most comfortable with and uses most often.

Teaching styles, both as personal characteristics and as tools to use in different parts of a course, should be considered when an instructor decides how best to integrate computers into his or her teaching. Also, as many instructors are aware, each teaching style implies a learning style; that is, students with different interests and degrees of independence respond best to different styles of teaching. The instructor thus will also want to consider the predominant learning style of his or her students.

The four teaching styles of Teacher, Facilitator, Mentor, and Broker are shown on our matrix in Figure 3. The following sections will further describe these teaching styles and the learning styles they imply.

*The Teacher.* The Teacher disseminates factual information through highly structured lectures and reading assignments. This role is important and valuable in almost any course, particularly in the undergraduate curriculum (Dressel and Marcus, 1982). It is consistent with the "pitcher and mug" metaphor of education, wherein passive students are "filled" with knowledge by instruction. Instructors who prefer this style are likely to be biased toward theoretical learning and to desire firm control over their students. They stress the learning objective of "knowing that."

Students respond to the Teacher by taking notes, studying textbooks or other assigned readings, or answering questions on examinations—in other words, by using informational skills. The Teacher is most effective with students who are stimulated by theory, principles, and abstractions and who learn best by receiving structured presentations of information and ideas. Many undergraduates fit into this category; they are reassured by structure and are too uncertain of their abilities to be comfortable with extended independent work. Use of the computer by instructors with the preferred teaching style of Teacher will be considered in Chapter Three.

## Figure 3. Teaching Styles.

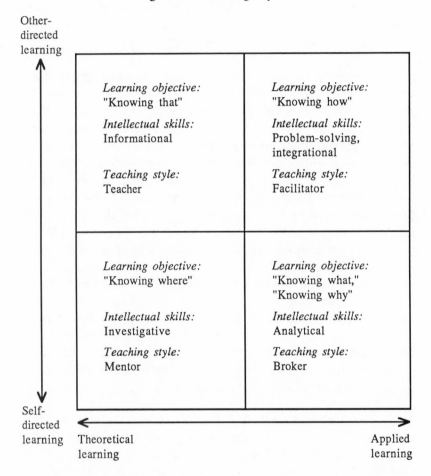

Other-directed learning

Self-directed learning

Theoretical learning

Applied learning

*Learning objective:*
"Knowing that"

*Intellectual skills:*
Informational

*Teaching style:*
Teacher

*Learning objective:*
"Knowing how"

*Intellectual skills:*
Problem-solving, integrational

*Teaching style:*
Facilitator

*Learning objective:*
"Knowing where"

*Intellectual skills:*
Investigative

*Teaching style:*
Mentor

*Learning objective:*
"Knowing what,"
"Knowing why"

*Intellectual skills:*
Analytical

*Teaching style:*
Broker

*The Facilitator.* An instructor playing the role of Facilitator plans and closely monitors learning activities that involve students as directly as possible in the phenomena being studied. If actual experience with the phenomena is not practical, the Facilitator may use simulations. Instructors who prefer this teaching style are likely to be biased toward applied learning and to see "knowing how" as the primary objective of learning. They emphasize the development of problem-solving and integrative skills in their students. The Facilitator is most effective with students who respond to direct involvement with realities but who prefer to be supervised during that involvement. Use of the computer by instructors with the preferred teaching style of Facilitator will be considered in Chapter Four.

*The Mentor.* The Mentor organizes readings, group processes, and presentation of theory and principles in such a way that students choose the experiences they need to master the discipline at their own pace, on their own terms. To an instructor who prefers this teaching style, the classroom is a catalyst rather than a source for learning activities. Such an instructor may encourage independent study projects that require considerable outside reading of materials selected by the students themselves. Such projects develop investigative skills and lead to the learning objective of "knowing where." The skillful Mentor elicits student responses, provides feedback, stimulates group discussion, poses provocative questions and answers, suggests roles for students to act out, and extends learning beyond the level of required reading assignments (Richards, 1986). The Mentor is most effective with students who enjoy learning theory and principles and who are both willing and able to take direct responsibility for mastering those abstractions. The use of the computer by instructors with the preferred teaching style of Mentor will be considered in Chapter Five.

*The Broker.* The Broker, like the Mentor, encourages students to direct their own learning through independent study projects. The Broker's orientation, however, is practical rather than theoretical. Thus the Broker is likely to encourage a physics or biology student to perform experiments and analyze their results rather than to critique the experiments of other scientists. In a literature class, the Broker would probably have students analyze works of literature themselves rather than survey the opinions of critics. An instructor who prefers the Broker teaching style will encourage students to develop analytical skills through direct experience, with the objective of "knowing what and why." The Broker is most effective with students who prefer to initiate or create their own learning activities and who prefer activities that emphasize doing rather than knowing. The use of the computer by instructors with the preferred teaching style of Broker will be considered in Chapter Six.

## Modes of Computer Delivery

An instructor trying to decide how best to use computers in a course will want to think about the different ways in which computers can be used. Different modes by which computers deliver instruction or facilitate learning are appropriate for achievement of different learning objectives, development of different intellectual skills, and supplementation of different teaching styles. The mode of computer use can be an important factor in determining whether and how computers should be used in a particular course or part of a course.

The four modes of computer delivery (first presented in Chapter One), and their relationship to learning objectives, intellectual skills, and teaching style are shown in Figure 4. These modes and their uses will be discussed in detail in Chapters Three through Six and described briefly in the following sections.

*The Computer as Teaching Machine.* This mode of computer delivery supports the acquisition of basic factual or theoretical knowledge in a particular subject area. An example might be a CAI program that offers a drill in the vocabulary and grammar of foreign language or a tutorial program that helps geology students learn to distinguish among different types of rocks. The computer as a teaching machine aids students in developing informational skills and achieving the learning objective of "knowing that."

An instructor with the preferred teaching style of Teacher might use this mode of delivery to supplement lectures and textbooks, letting the computer direct the students' learning just as the Teacher does in the classroom. CAI is likely to particularly benefit students who prefer structure and who need factual learning delivered in small increments, interspersed with frequent questioning and feedback. Chapter Three is devoted to the use of the computer as a teaching machine.

Figure 4. Modes of Computer Delivery.

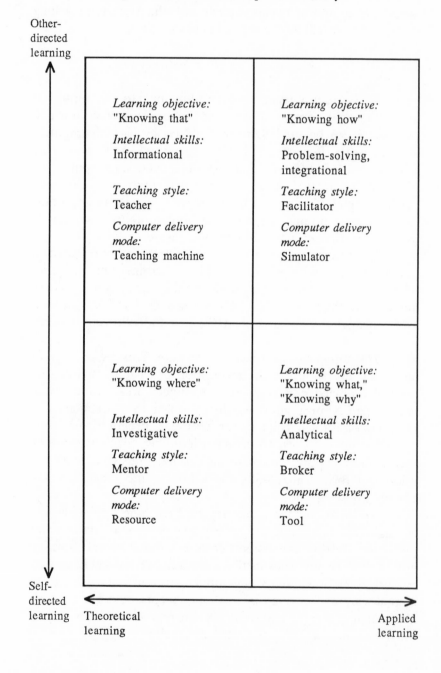

Other-
directed
learning

*Learning objective:*
"Knowing that"

*Intellectual skills:*
Informational

*Teaching style:*
Teacher

*Computer delivery
mode:*
Teaching machine

*Learning objective:*
"Knowing how"

*Intellectual skills:*
Problem-solving,
integrational

*Teaching style:*
Facilitator

*Computer delivery
mode:*
Simulator

*Learning objective:*
"Knowing where"

*Intellectual skills:*
Investigative

*Teaching style:*
Mentor

*Computer delivery
mode:*
Resource

*Learning objective:*
"Knowing what,"
"Knowing why"

*Intellectual skills:*
Analytical

*Teaching style:*
Broker

*Computer delivery
mode:*
Tool

Self-
directed
learning

Theoretical
learning

Applied
learning

*The Computer as Simulator.* In the simulator delivery mode, the computer promotes the development of problem-solving and integrative skills by allowing students to manipulate parts of a model of reality and observe the effects on the rest of the model. Examples might be a role-playing game in which students in a political science class act the parts of diplomats representing various countries, or a simulation in which medical students pretend to be epidemiologists trying to find the cause and cure of a deadly infectious disease. By allowing "practice" with realities not otherwise available for experimentation, the computer as simulator helps students apply their learning and achieve the learning objective of "knowing how."

An instructor with the preferred teaching mode of Facilitator might use computer simulations to supplement a laboratory course in science or to give history students a feeling of what it was really like to live and work in an ancient culture. Because it is self-contained and operates according to a limited number of rules, a computer simulation allows such an instructor to maintain the relatively firm control over student learning that he or she desires. Simulations can particularly benefit students who like grappling with realities but need a fairly large amount of guidance and feedback during the experience. Nontraditional students in an urban community college might be an example of such students. Chapter Four will be devoted to the use of the computer as a simulator.

*The Computer as Resource.* The computer acting as a resource connects the student with a network of people and/or data via a communications device or link. It hones investigative skills by allowing students to ferret out information in data bases or consult peers, instructors, or experts through teleconferencing or bulletin board messages. As a result, the students gain an understanding of theory and fulfill the learning objective of "knowing where."

An instructor with the preferred teaching mode of Mentor might assign biology students to consult a data base while preparing reports on recent developments in genetic engineering, for example. In teaching a social science class, this kind of instructor might have students consult with each other and experts in the field via computer during a group project that evaluates alternatives for integrating the mentally ill into the community. Students who are well organized, independent, and very interested in finding out about the thoughts and experiences of others will benefit most from using the computer as a resource for self-directed learning. Chapter Five will be devoted to the use of the computer as a resource.

*The Computer as Tool.* Students can use computers as tools in many kinds of learning tasks, but common "tool" programs such as idea generators and spreadsheets are particularly well suited to aid students in developing analytical skills. Generating graphs or performing statistical analyses with the help of a computer, students working independently on practical problems can concentrate their time and energy on achieving the learning objectives of "knowing what and why."

An instructor with the preferred teaching style of Broker might use computers in the "tool" mode by directing students in an economics class to draw conclusions about the financial health of the electronics industry after applying spreadsheets or financial analysis software to data about stocks of selected electronics companies. Students especially likely to benefit from using the computer as a tool are those who have considerable desire and ability to direct their own learning and who prefer to apply that learning in direct interaction with real-world situations. Chapter Six will be devoted to the use of the computer as a tool.

Like all models, the model presented in Figures 1 through 4 is a simplification of reality. The categories it describes may overlap, and the relationships it suggests do not always hold true or prove mutually exclusive. For example, some CAI programs develop problem-solving skills as well as informational skills. The same students who use a data base to acquire information for a report may use a word processing program when writing the report. Furthermore, as has been noted, all of the learning objectives, intellectual skills, teaching styles, and modes of computer delivery described in the model may well apply at some point or to some degree in a single course. Nonetheless, the model can be useful in helping an instructor visualize ways to use the computer to further particular learning objectives, intellectual skills, and teaching styles.

## Types of Assignments

Another set of factors that an instructor should consider in deciding how to use computers in a course is the types of assignments used in the course. Computers can be used in connection with any of the traditional categories of assignment: classroom work, short homework assignments, more extensive out-of-class projects, and independent study.

In some cases, an instructor may decide to modify existing assignments to allow for the requirement or possibility of computer use. Students might be encouraged or required to consult a computer data base in addition to or instead of traditional library reference works when doing a bibliographic paper, for example. (Some computer uses, such as the use of a word processor to compose an essay, may require no modification of the assignment and can be left to the students' discretion.)

In other cases, the instructor might want to rethink assignments more radically or even prepare new assignments to take full advantage of the computer's promise. A group research project involving computer conferencing might replace a term paper, for example. A number of sessions with a computer simulation or role-playing game might replace a group of traditional homework assignments.

The following sections briefly discuss ways that computers can be used in different kinds of course assignments. Just as with traditional assignments, the types of computer assignments that are appropriate for a given course will depend on the nature and objectives of the course, the teaching style of the instructor, and the learning needs and degree of independence of the students.

*Classroom Work.* If workstations or terminals are available, students may use the computer in the same classroom in which lectures or other course-related activities take place. This situation allows an instructor to oversee and advise students engaged in, say, a group activity involving a computer simulation.

More often, however, the classroom in which computer activities take place is likely to be the computer lab. Applications in this setting must be capable of being used with a minimum of outside direction, either because of the structured nature of the program (a CAI tutorial, for example) or because of the independence and previous training of the students (use of modems to access data bases or computer conferences). Use of the computer lab as an "alternate classroom" can free up regular class time for greater personal interaction, group projects, and the like. However, it may also cut down on traditional class meetings; for example, a typical three-credit-hour class that formerly met for three hours a week might meet two hours a week in conjunction with one weekly session of computer lab work or one weekly hour of participation in a computer conference on a theme or project assigned by the instructor.

Students may also be encouraged to use computers to augment special forms of class work. They might use small, portable "laptop" computers to take notes and record data during lectures, laboratory experiments, or field trips, for example.

*Short Homework Assignments.* In some cases an instructor may require that a homework assignment be completed on the computer. A session with a CAI drill program might be an example. More frequently, students will use "tool" software such as spreadsheets or word processing programs on their personal computers, at their own discretion, to complete assignments in their dormitory rooms or at home. If students are being encouraged but not required to use computers, the instructor should plan to discuss with them the computer uses that are appropriate to a particular assignment.

*Out-of-Class Projects.* A level of student autonomy beyond that needed for short homework assignments is involved in focused out-of-class projects that use the computer. These activities are more extensive and creative than simple homework and may account for a significant part of the course grade. Use of the computer (either the student's own or an institutional computer to which the student has access) would be required rather than optional in these projects, but students might be given quite a bit of latitude in determining the exact strategies of computer use. An example might be groups of students participating in a community service project. They might use an electronic bulletin board to communicate with each other during the project and use spreadsheets, statistical programs, and/or graphing software to analyze the project's results.

*Independent Study.* Students may also use computers in independent projects that they design themselves, in consultation with their instructors. In this kind of project, the student may select the ways of using the computer as well as the purposes for which it will be used. For example, in a political science independent study project a student might decide to search a data base for literature regarding the voting patterns of communities of a certain size, plot trends and characteristics with a graphing program, and prepare an annotated bibliography with a word processor. Instructors can aid students in planning for this kind of study by discussing a range of possible computer uses with them and making sure they know what kinds of software are appropriate and available.

Stand-alone courses delivered entirely on computer, such as those produced by the Electronic University Network (see Chapter One), represent a different kind of independent study. Students taking such courses have little or no control over course structure, unlike students working on self-designed independent study projects. These students are independent, however, in that they are completely freed from the need to meet with instructors in person. The "classroom" for these stand-alone courses is wherever student and computer terminal happen to be. Students taking this kind of course leave reports, assignments, and other communications in the computer "mailboxes" of assigned instructors, who respond with evaluative feedback and suggestions that are also delivered electronically. In on-campus versions of stand-alone courses, students might meet in the computer lab for a certain number of hours each week to take the course.

## Available Hardware and Software

In an ideal world, an instructor would need to consider only pedagogical factors when trying to decide how to integrate computers into coursework. Reality, however, makes other factors important as well. The sad truth is that funds for acquiring computer equipment and commercial software, as well as time and expertise for developing custom software, are severely limited in most higher education institutions. In addition, some software will not work with some kinds of computers. An instructor's choices, then, are inevitably limited by the hardware and software existing in the institution or obtainable within time and budget limits. Thus it is important to find out just what is available.

An instructor should begin a search for information with a visit to computer experts in his or her own institution. These may be members of the computer science department, academic computing department, or computer center, or they may be other professionals such as librarians or other faculty members in any discipline who have frequently used computers in their courses.

To start with, the instructor should find out what hardware the institution owns or is planning to purchase in the near future. Hardware includes not only computers but peripheral devices used with them, such as modems (communication devices) and printers. The instructor should learn how many of each kind of device will be available to students, where the devices are, and what scheduling arrangements are involved in their use.

Even more important than learning the brand name of the institution's computers is learning the "family" the computers belong to, which is determined by the operating system they use. An operating system is a program that controls the operation of a computer. The kind of operating system determines the kinds of software that "run on" (can be used on, are

compatible with) that computer. For example, IBM PC computers and the many brands of "clones" that are "PC compatible,"
such as Compaq, Tandy/Radio Shack, and Leading Edge, run an
operating system called MS-DOS. The Apple Macintosh uses a
different operating system. This means that software that runs
on an IBM PC will not run on a Macintosh, and vice versa.
(Some kinds of software exist in different versions for different
operating systems, however.)

The instructor should also learn what software the institution currently owns or will soon own. If possible, the instructor should arrange for a demonstration of software that is of
interest and/or should "play with it" on his or her own. He or
she should learn how many copies of the software are available
or can be made legally for students (see note in Chapter Eight
on software piracy and intellectual property rights). If an instructor is thinking about developing software, he or she should
also ask what authoring systems or other software development
tools (if any) the institution owns. (The option of developing
courseware is further discussed in Chapter Seven.)

The next stop in the information search should be a visit
to an administrative official who has knowledge or control of
the budget that the instructor would draw on if he or she purchased new software. The instructor will need to know how
much money (if any) is available for software purchase and
what the procedure is for requesting such purchases. Administrators can also give an instructor information about release
time or other compensation and support available to faculty
members who develop custom software or new instructional
uses of the computer. Finally, and perhaps most important, administrative officials can describe the plans that are being made
for academic computer use in the institution as a whole.

If an institution does not own software suitable for an instructor's needs, the instructor should investigate software that
is available "in the public domain." This software can be copied
legally without cost. Computer communication networks and
bulletin boards often carry public domain programs or information about them, and the programs can be easily "downloaded"
to the instructor's or institution's computer. Many simple utility

or "tool" programs can be acquired in this way, and some educational software (mainly CAI programs or simple simulations) may also be in the public domain. A related category, also available through networks and bulletin boards, is "shareware." There are no restrictions on copying shareware, but the authors of the programs request voluntary payment of $10 to $75 if the software is used regularly. Public domain software and shareware can be useful, but instructors should not expect it to equal commercial software in complexity or sophistication.

Interinstitutional clearinghouses of educational software, such as those listed in Resource B, are good sources of information about software developed by and/or used in higher education institutions. Visits to faculty members of institutions actively engaged in developing new software or uses of the computer in instruction may prove enlightening. Computer conferences devoted to educational software, such as those sponsored by EDUCOM, can also be helpful.

If free or low-cost software is not suitable for an instructor's needs and funds for software purchase are available, the instructor will want to consider purchase of off-the-shelf (commercially produced) software. In addition to faculty members at one's own and other institutions, clearinghouses, communication networks and bulletin boards, and users' groups and other support groups (see Chapter Nine), sources of information about commercial software include reviews in computer magazines, announcements by software manufacturers, on-line data bases, and indexes and directories. Many of these sources are listed in Resource B.

General guidelines for evaluating software are given in Chapter Seven. In addition, specific tips for evaluating software involved in particular modes of instructional delivery by computer (teaching machine, simulator, resource, and tool) are given at the ends of Chapters Three through Six.

As this chapter has shown, many factors are important in determining the best use or uses (which may mean no use at all) for the computer in a particular course. Ultimately, however, the factor with the most fundamental importance is the students: their relationship to the instructor, what the instructor wants them to learn, how he or she wants them to learn it, what help they need to learn most effectively, and how that learning can enrich their lives. As Ericksen reminds us, "As an aid for instruction, the book, visual image, or computer program is important insofar as it elicits active responses from students, to help them find meaning within themselves" (1984, p. 33).

## Worksheet/Questionnaire for Planning Computer Integration

Exhibit 1 presents a worksheet/questionnaire based on the teaching and learning factors discussed in this chapter. It is designed to help an instructor organize his or her thoughts when analyzing a course for possible incorporation of computer work. Answers and comments on the worksheet will probably be added to or modified as planning proceeds and new information is obtained. For example, an instructor is more likely to have ideas about specific computer applications for a course after having read Chapters Three through Six of this book. He or she may be able to answer the questions in Part VI of the worksheet only after having talked with representatives of the academic computing department and the institutional administration and having done some outside research to discover what kinds of off-the-shelf software exist.

### Exhibit 1. Worksheet/Questionnaire for Planning Computer Integration into an Existing Course.

Course being considered: _____

I.  Learning Outcomes

    A.  List the course's five most important learning outcomes (things students should know or be able to do at the end of the course).
        1.
        2.
        3.
        4.
        5.

(continued on next page)

**Exhibit 1. Worksheet/Questionnaire for Planning
Computer Integration into an Existing Course, Cont'd.**

B.   Note the parts or aspects of the course, if any, in which each
     of the following categories of learning objective is important.

"Knowing that":

"Knowing how":

"Knowing where":

"Knowing what or why":

C.   Rank the following categories of learning objectives in order
     of their importance to the course as a whole (1 = most im-
     portant).
     _____ "Knowing that"
     _____ "Knowing how"
     _____ "Knowing where"
     _____ "Knowing what or why"

D.   In what ways, if any, might computers help students attain
     the learning objectives for this course?

II.   Intellectual Skills

A.   Note the parts or aspects of the course, if any, in which you
     expect students to develop or use each of the following cat-
     egories of intellectual skills.

Informational skills:

Problem-solving and integrative skills:

Investigative skills:

Analytical skills:

B.   Rank the following categories of intellectual skills in order
     of their importance to the course as a whole.
     _____ Informational skills
     _____ Problem-solving and integrative skills
     _____ Investigative skills
     _____ Analytical skills

C.   In what ways, if any, might computers help students devel-
     op the intellectual skills needed for this course?

### Exhibit 1. Worksheet/Questionnaire for Planning Computer Integration into an Existing Course, Cont'd.

III.  Teaching Styles

    A.   Note the parts or aspects of the course, if any, in which you use each of the following teaching styles.

        Teacher:

        Facilitator:

        Mentor:

        Broker:

    B.   Check the teaching style you prefer to use in this course as a whole.
        _____ Teacher
        _____ Facilitator
        _____ Mentor
        _____ Broker

    C.   In what ways, if any, might computers supplement the teaching style or styles you use in this course?

IV.  Modes of Computer Delivery

    A.   Note the parts or aspects of the course, if any, in which you would consider using each of the following modes of computer delivery of instruction:

        Computer as teaching machine:

        Computer as simulator:

        Computer as resource:

        Computer as tool:

V.  Types of Assignment

    A.   Place a check in the left column for each of the following types of assignment or activity that you currently use in this course. Place a check in the right column for each type that you would consider modifying to incorporate computer use or adding as a computer-related assignment.

*(continued on next page)*

**Exhibit 1. Worksheet/Questionnaire for Planning
Computer Integration into an Existing Course, Cont'd.**

| | | |
|---|---|---|
| Lectures | _____ | _____ |
| Demonstrations | _____ | _____ |
| Assigned readings | _____ | _____ |
| Class discussion | _____ | _____ |
| Small group work in class | _____ | _____ |
| Simulations, role playing | _____ | _____ |
| Laboratory experiments | _____ | _____ |
| Short homework assignments | _____ | _____ |
| Term papers, essays, written reports | _____ | _____ |
| Out-of-class group projects | _____ | _____ |
| Independent study projects | _____ | _____ |

B.  What specific assignments or teaching techniques in this
course might you modify to incorporate computer use or replace with computer assignments? What modifications or
new assignments might you make?

VI.  Available Hardware and Software

A.  List the specific kinds (including brand names and operating systems) of institutional hardware (computers, printers,
modems, and so on) to which students of this course will
have access.

B.  Where is this hardware located?

C.  What time constraints, if any, limit student access to insti-
tution-owned computers?

D.  List the specific kinds (including brand names) of software
to which students of this course will have access.

E.  About what proportion of your students are likely to have
their own computers? About what proportion of your students are likely to have had experience in using computers?

F.  About how much money, if any, will your institutions make
available to you for purchase of new software for this
course?

**Exhibit 1. Worksheet/Questionnaire for Planning
Computer Integration into an Existing Course, Cont'd.**

G.  About how much time, if any, can you devote to creation of custom software for this course?

H.  To what authoring systems or other tools for creating custom software, if any, do you have access?

Do you have any experience in using these tools?

I.  List here any off-the-shelf programs you think would be particularly useful in this course.

J.  If you could have any kind of software you wanted (presently existing or not) for use in this course, what would you like?

# 3

□□□□□□□□□□□□□□□□□□□□

# The Computer
# as Teaching Machine:
# Enhancing Informational Skills

The ultimate aim of higher education is to help students think critically—to evaluate and analyze the factual and conceptual material of a discipline. "Regardless of the discipline," notes Chet Meyers, "it [is] the nature of the college educational experience for students to question, examine, prod, poke, dissect, and explicate" (1986, p. 8). Before students can do these things, however, they must learn the facts and concepts that they will later analyze. This chapter will discuss the importance of informational skills, which lead to achievement of the learning objective of "knowing what." It will then explore ways in which the computer as teaching machine can help students develop these skills. Computer uses that can help students develop higher-order intellectual skills will be considered in subsequent chapters.

## The Importance of Informational Skills

Informational skills are those skills used in the mastery of factual information and its underlying conceptual framework. Understanding of facts and basic concepts provides a vital foundation for making sense of higher-order concepts, solving problems, making decisions, and analyzing options.

Informational skills are not limited to memorization of isolated facts. They can also help students master the concepts

46

that underlie and give relevance to those facts. This use of informational skills becomes extremely important in our present "information age," in which students, like many people in the society at large, often feel they are about to drown in a sea of unrelated and meaningless data. Critical to the mastery of factual material, according to Ericksen (1984), is the notion of "figure-ground relationship"—the placing of facts within some larger frame of reference or context (relating the figure to the ground). Often, when students have trouble remembering factual material, the problem proves to be that their background has given them no context for this information. They therefore have no reason to find the information memorable or valuable.

Part of an instructor's job is to supply the context, the "ground" into which the specific "figures" of a discipline's facts may be set. This conceptual context, Ericksen says, consists of "theory, methods, and values that give meaning within a discipline to the factual body of knowledge" (p. 20). Success in academic, personal, and career life depends on the use of these concepts. As Ericksen points out, concepts help students connect one experience with another (pp. 75-76).

## The Computer as Teaching Machine

The computer as teaching machine can help students develop informational skills. It can present factual material in an organized way that helps students remember and give meaning to those facts. In addition, it can help students grasp the sort of higher-order concepts that can be represented easily by a name, label, or symbol. However, it usually is not very successful at presenting concepts that are more abstract or difficult to characterize. Noncomputer instructional methods or other modes of instructional delivery by computer work better in teaching these. The computer as teaching machine is better at dealing with surface structures than with deep ones.

The process of teaching and learning typically includes three phases:

1. *Instruction*—student participation in activities designed to transmit factual information and concepts.

2. *Practice and evaluation*—the opportunity to try out what has been learned so that degree of mastery can be determined.
3. *Assessment*—student reflection on the meaning or relevance of the information and concepts that have been learned.

Instruction using the computer as a teaching machine also includes these three phases. Some CAI programs focus on one or another of these phases particularly, however. The following sections will describe examples of CAI or "teaching machine" programs that have been used in higher education to focus on each of the three phases of instruction.

*Instruction-Centered Programs.* Instruction-centered programs concentrate on presentation of information and concepts. A novel example of an instruction-centered program, "An Introduction to Nuclear Arms Issues," is used at Rhode Island's Brown University. It is one of a number of instructional projects created at Brown as a "sampler" to demonstrate to faculty the possibilities of educational software.

The nuclear arms issues program features illustrations, animations, and textual information, such as trajectories of MIRV missile warheads, maps and charts, tables, and excerpts of letters such as Einstein's 1939 letter to Franklin D. Roosevelt expressing concern about the use of nuclear power. Historical topics dealt with by the program are organized along a timeline.

Students using the program select "information filters" that allow them to focus on particular topics presented along the timeline, such as technology, arms control, or other specific issues or events. After a selection is made, text and graphic material relevant to the chosen topic appear in "windows" on the computer monitor's screen. Students also can select any or all of four types of supplementary material associated with each theme: an annotated bibliography, a glossary of terms, a list of selected research topics, and a list of references used for the program. The different types of supplementary material also appear in the monitor "windows." Questions, followed by feedback, are provided periodically to encourage students to apply their learning (Yankelovich and others, 1985).

This program is used as part of a political science class. Its purpose is to give students quick background information, thus assisting them in the preparation of research papers and also freeing class time for thoughtful discussion of nuclear arms negotiations. A textbook or other assigned outside reading could have conveyed some of the same information, but it could not have made the selection of particular topics so easy or provided the "windows" that let students see several aspects of a topic at once. It could not have been immediately modified to filter out extraneous information and focus on a single event. It could not have given feedback along with questions to help students check and integrate their learning. As with a textbook, the main disadvantages of this kind of program are that students may rely on it too much, rather than seeking out other sources of information, and that its treatment of topics may be too limited and superficial.

A variation on instruction-centered programs is being pioneered at Brown University by Norman Meyrowitz, the head of the Intermedia Project, using what he calls a "hypertext/hypermedia system." Hypertext provides "links" between pieces of information that let students move from one piece to another in a branching or weblike rather than linear way. Similarly, hypermedia encompasses graphics, animation, sound, and video to create multimedia webs of information. Students select the information they want by using a "mouse" or similar pointing device to indicate particular icons (simple pictorial symbols) on the computer screen. For example, an English literature student studying Robert Browning can choose one icon to get a picture of Browning, another to get a timeline of his writings, another to get a biographical sketch, and so on. Additional choices branch out from each piece of information selected. Hypertext allows students to trace an individualized path through a web of information, selecting only the items that are relevant to their interests or to a particular assignment, rather than having to plow linearly through information, selected by someone else, that may or may not be relevant (Osgood, 1987).

*Practice and Evaluation-Centered Programs.* One of the most exciting possibilities for the computer as teaching machine, one that bridges the gap between "knowing that" and "knowing how," is the practice- and evaluation-centered program. CAI programs of this type differ from instruction-centered ones in that practice- and evaluation-centered programs devote most of their time to offering students a chance to apply the facts and concepts that the programs teach. Popularly known as "drill and practice," programs of this type are among the most prevalent forms of CAI. Typically they provide an opportunity for a student to test recall of information or practice a certain skill. They then offer feedback, telling the student whether each response was correct. Sometimes they give explanations, or offer "hints" and allow the student to try a question again, if a response is wrong. Finally, they present additional practice exercises, frequently chosen by the computer to remedy the weaknesses revealed by the student's performance on the first group of exercises.

Another component of the Brown University "sampler" provides an interesting example of a practice-centered program. The program, called "A Linguistic Approach to Writing," uses a model that represents linguistic structure as having two levels, semantic and informational. The semantic section describes a method for understanding and diagramming the "deep structure" of sentences, while the informational section focuses on emphasis and meaning and explores the importance of word order and context.

In addition to presenting the terminology associated with each linguistic level, the program gives students numerous sentences to diagram, thus teaching them to identify structural ambiguities. Often one "window" on the computer screen presents verbal explanations at the same time that another shows visual examples (diagrams) and a third offers practice exercises (Yankelovich and others, 1985). The strength of this program lies in its simultaneous presentation of several teaching modalities: verbal examples, visual examples of diagramming, and practice exercises. It also provides students with immediate and private feedback and allows them to repeat exercises they have had trouble with.

Another example of a drill-and-practice CAI program is "Program CAdE," used by North Carolina Central University to teach basic factual information and concepts to students in an introductory sociology course. The program presents randomly selected multiple-choice questions based on the textbook used in the course. If a student answers a question incorrectly, the computer responds, using the student's first name, with a hint or prompt about the correct response. Students who respond incorrectly again are provided with the number of the page in the textbook where the correct answer is located.

Research was conducted to determine whether students using this program learned the text material any better than students who simply read the text and did standard homework assignments. Researchers randomly assigned 115 students of moderate to low academic ability, characterized as "passive learners," to control or experimental groups. The experimental group did better than the control group on a final test, the difference in mean test scores being significant at the .05 level. These "passive learners" particularly benefited because they "were forced by the nature of the exercises to concentrate and become involved" in the material (Robinson, 1985, p. 37).

Many drill-and-practice programs are primitive in design. Nonetheless, they have the advantages of offering immediate feedback, self-pacing, and a certain degree of interactivity. They can help students focus their energy on the mastery of basic information and concepts. They can also save an instructor the time that would otherwise be needed to correct "pop quizzes" or homework exercises, since the machine usually corrects the material or helps the student do so.

The disadvantage of these programs is that their highly linear, "lock-step" approach is suited only to the presentation of certain kinds of information (facts and simple concepts) and to certain learning styles. This kind of program may be a real boon to students who need help in focusing their attention or who learn best by having information presented to them in small, highly structured increments, but more independent or creative students may find the program irritatingly "mechanistic" and impersonal.

*Assessment-Centered Programs.* Assessment-centered programs differ from practice- and evaluation-centered programs in that assessment-centered programs pose questions about values, beliefs, and attitudes rather than about facts. Such questions do not have "right" or "wrong" answers. They help students reflect on the emotional and ethical meaning of information and concepts encountered in a course rather than demonstrate mastery of subject matter. In these programs, students assess themselves rather than being assessed by the computer.

Ferris State College in Big Rapids, Michigan, uses one module of a thirteen-module management diagnostic and training program called "Thoughtware" (produced by Thoughtware, Inc.) in Basic Management, an undergraduate business course. Completion of the program is just one part of the eclectic set of experiences that make up the course, which includes group activities, written exercises, case studies, and videotaping of class projects. For example, students work in teams to create a management training video that focuses on a key concept taught in the course, such as motivation or leadership.

The "Thoughtware" module used in the Ferris course allows students to self-assess attitudes and behaviors that might affect their future effectiveness as managers. The students place themselves along various dimensions of managerial skills such as ability to work with others, leadership, and motivation, and then compare their responses with those of actual managers across the nation. Students use printouts of their assessment results to develop an action plan (a workbook activity completed away from the computer). The module also poses probing "thought questions," to which students respond in the workbook.

"The computerized module presents material in a lucid, attractive, and straightforward manner," an instructor using the program observed. "Since the order of the concepts covered in class and [that] in the training exercises are the same as those assessed . . . the learner simultaneously examines each concept, trains or is trained on it, and completes a computerized instrument to examine personal strengths and weaknesses in that area" (Warfield, 1986, p. 31).

Unlike other kinds of CAI programs, assessment-centered programs involve students in higher-order thinking skills. At the same time, these programs retain the CAI advantage of giving feedback immediately and privately. Even so, any assessment program, computer-based or not, runs the risk of causing students to focus on isolated behavioral elements and thus lose track of the true complexity of human behavior. Such programs also may carry explicit or implicit value judgments with which some students or instructors may disagree.

### Commercially Available Programs: Some Examples

"CHEMICAL REACTIONS" (COMPRESS, $50; runs on IBM PC and compatibles with color monitor). This program is one of a series designed for a freshman-level "introduction to chemistry" course. It gives students the opportunity to write and balance equations for combination, decomposition, replacement, and ionic reactions. Over 150 problems are provided. In some problems, names and formulas of all reactants and products are provided, and students are asked to enter appropriate coefficients; in others, students must enter formulas as well as coefficients when given the names of reactants and products; and in still others, students must predict the products and balance the equation when given the names of the reactants ("Computer Software . . . ," 1987e).

"MOZART" (Kinko's Academic Courseware Exchange, $13; runs on Apple Macintosh). "MOZART" is designed for use in music theory and composition courses. It permits students to experiment with various musical arrangements, tempos, and articulations. Students compose a minuet from one of six predefined two-measure phrases. This music can be played on the built-in speaker, printed as hard copy, or both ("Computer Software . . . ," 1987b).

"CAPER: Computer-Assisted Program for Economic Review" (Harcourt Brace Jovanovich, College Division, $19.95; runs on IBM PC and compatibles). This program is intended for use in conjunction with the textbook *Economics: Principles and Policy*, by Baumol and Blinder, in a course on the principles of economics. The program provides tutorials on economic concepts that can be shown in graphs, such as elasticity of demand.

It also provides diagnostic tests to help students find out how well they are mastering this material ("Computer Software . . . ," 1987a).

"MATH/PC LIBRARY" (IMSI Sales Division, $420; for IBM PC and compatibles). This program, designed for use in courses in calculus and differential equations, provides students with mathematics subroutines for differential equations and integration, Eigensystem analysis, error functions and gamma functions, interpolation, approximation, smoothing, linear algebraic equations, optimization, and vector matrix arithmetic ("Computer Software . . . ," 1987d).

"LESSONS IN THE HISTORY OF WESTERN CIVILIZATION" (COMPRESS, $750; runs on IBM PC and compatibles with color graphics card and color monitor). This program, designed for an introductory western civilization course, presents twelve lessons that cover periods from antiquity to the nuclear age. Each lesson features maps and pictures of important historical figures associated with the period being covered. Lessons also include drill-and-practice routines and educational games that help students master key information, such as dates ("Computer Software . . . ," 1987f).

"LATIN FLASH DRILL" (Centaur Systems, $95; runs on Apple II series and on IBM PC and compatibles). This program uses drill and practice to teach students Latin forms and endings. It also provides a reference section of reading materials that clarify specific points of grammar and usage ("Computer Software . . . ," 1987c).

"SIBEX" (North Carolina State University Software, $20; runs on Apple II series). This program, which can be used effectively in basic statistics courses, teaches complex statistical concepts by breaking them down into small steps. For example, standard deviations are constructed from individual deviations, from the means of their squared values, and from the average of the original deviations ("Computer Software . . . ," 1986).

### Evaluating Software for the Computer as Teaching Machine

The first step in determining which part of a course, if any, might be enhanced by the use of the computer as a teaching machine is to analyze the course, as described in Chapter Two. Once an instructor has determined that this form of computer use is appropriate to a course, he or she most likely will want to analyze existing programs (commercially available or custom created) to determine whether any of these meet the course's needs.

It is most practical to begin analysis with programs already available in the institution. If none of these is suitable and acquiring new software (by purchase or by arrangement with institutions that have developed it) is possible, the instructor can go on to consider other available programs. (Chapter Two suggested some ways to find out what is available.) If no existing software seems to meet a course's needs, the possibility of developing custom software should be considered. This process is discussed in Chapter Seven.

The following checklist is intended to help instructors evaluate existing software designed for use in the computer as teaching machine. In addition to consulting these guidelines, the instructor should consider the general criteria for evaluating software that are presented in Chapter Seven.

- What facts and concepts does the program present? Are they appropriate and up to date? Are they relevant to the overall content and aims of the course?
- Is the level of detail in the presentation sufficient for the purposes of the course?
- Is the material presented by the program appropriate for presentation by the computer as teaching machine? That is, does it consist of facts and of concepts that can be represented easily by a name, label, or symbol?
- How does the program present the factual material in which students are being instructed? Are graphics and sound used effectively? Is the presentation more interesting or effective than presentation by traditional methods would be?
- Are facts presented by the program organized in a way that can lead to student understanding of context or underlying concepts?
- Can students use the program independently, with a minimum of instruction or supervision?

- Does the program provide sufficient opportunities for students to recall and/or apply (practice with) facts or concepts by interacting with the program?
- Are the program's activities suitable for the ability and predominant learning style of the course's students?
- If the program tests or questions students, does it correct students' work or help them to correct their own work? Is a record of the score kept for the student and/or the instructor? If student work is not scored, how might the instructor evaluate it?
- If the program tests or questions students, what kind of feedback (if any) does it give them? Does it provide explanations or hints for students who give incorrect answers?
- If the program requires student responses, does it assign remedial exercises on the basis of student performance? Are different exercises provided for students needing different kinds of help? Does the program provide any kind of diagnostic profile for the instructor?
- If the program involves value judgments, does it incorporate judgments that students and instructor will be comfortable with?

# 4

■■■■■■■■■■■■■■■■■■

# The Computer as Simulator:
# Developing Problem-Solving
# and Integrative Skills

Stanford Ericksen observes, "Ideally, by the end of a course a student has weakened ties with the teacher and is prepared to move on alone by continuing to learn how to think independently—the most important single end product of education. . . . The prime responsibility of the teacher therefore is to help students advance from dependent memorizing to independent thinking and problem solving. This is the leading edge in educational reform" (1984, pp. 82–83).

This chapter examines ways in which the computer can help students move beyond the realm of factual learning into practical application of that learning—from "knowing that" to "knowing how." To make this leap, students need to develop problem-solving and integrative skills. The computer is best able to help students develop these skills when it acts as a simulator. This chapter will consider the importance of problem-solving and integrative skills and explore the ways in which game and simulation programs can help students develop these skills.

## The Importance of Problem-Solving and Integrative Skills

Dressel and Marcus point to the "integrative implications" of teaching and learning, asserting that students should be able to relate competencies gained from learning "into a coherent, cumulative, and somehow unified experience and to apply these competencies" (1982, pp. 55–57). Perhaps the most obvious and important form of application is the solving of problems. An American Medical Association report (Fields, 1984) urges medical schools to reduce the amount of factual information taught and emphasize instead the teaching of problem-solving skills.

Integrative thinking, or seeing relationships among things, is both preliminary and integral to problem solving. According to Ericksen (1984), the components of problem solving include the following:

- Integrating factual information, concepts, and experience into a frame of reference that is meaningful for identifying problems
- Unearthing problems and coherently defining them in terms of the frame of reference
- Determining whether inductive logic, deductive logic, or a combination of both is most useful for solving a particular problem
- Discriminating direct from inferential data
- Generating alternative solutions for the problem
- Analyzing the implications of those alternatives
- Separating prejudgments from data
- Deciding on an optimal solution.

## The Computer as Simulator

Simulations are used for many purposes, ranging from entertainment to prediction of complex climatic changes or the outcome of battles and wars. The purpose of interest here is education and training. Simulations have been used to educate students of all ages and levels of expertise, ranging from the elementary school pupil to the adult professional. In design, educational simulations may be "open ended," encouraging creative exploration of the model, or they may be carefully structured to foster the achievement of particular educational objectives.

Simulations provide models or representations of natural or social phenomena, from cells to ecosystems and from fami-

lies to international organizations. Students manipulate the behavior of parts of such a model and see the effects of their
changes on other parts and on the model as a whole. They thus
discover relationships between things (develop integrative skills).
If the simulation presents students with a problem to be solved
or a goal to be achieved, as is the case with many simulations
that are marketed as games, students also develop problem-
solving skills. They learn to explore, invent, and apply alternative modes of thinking.

Advances in software for personal computers have allowed
simulation programs to become more complex and realistic,
more responsive, and accessible to a wider audience than ever
before. Educational computer simulations exist in four major
forms:

1. *Noninteractive simulations*, which model reality and in-
   form students about the components of a system but do
   not allow student interaction with the model
2. *Interactive simulations*, which permit students to manipulate a system and observe how changes in component parts
   affect the whole system
3. *Group competitive simulations*, which portray social, economic, political, or other contexts and present problems
   to be solved by the decisions of competing teams of students
4. *Individual competitive simulations*, which engage individual students in the solution of problems and provide points
   or other incentives for mastering those problems.

The latter two forms of simulation differ from the former two in that they may have gamelike qualities. In educational simulation games, students may compete against the computer, against their own previous efforts, or against other students
or teams of students. The following sections will describe the
four kinds of simulation in more detail and will present examples of their use in higher education.

*Noninteractive Simulations.* One component of the educational software "sampler" created by Brown University (de-

scribed in part in the last chapter) is a noninteractive simulation called "Geography of the Middle East." This program instructs students not only in the geography of the Middle East but also in the ways that the region has changed over time. The program is used out of class to teach background material that is important for understanding in-class lectures. By adding a record-keeping component and disabling the program's "help" functions, instructors can use the program to test students.

Students use the program in three sessions, designated presentation, query, and labeling. (They may repeat any of these sessions as often as they wish.) During the presentation session, the program displays maps showing the Middle East and Northern Africa as they were in four different time periods (Pre-Islamic, Centuries 7-12, Centuries 12-19, and Contemporary Era). Place names on the map change through each era, and significant events that occurred at various locations during each time period are also noted.

The query session poses questions regarding geographic locations on the map. If students respond to a question by entering an incorrect location, the program poses new questions with the same answer and eventually gives the correct answer. Location names that the program does not recognize are presumed to be spelling errors. Students are given one chance to correct the error. If they do not succeed, they are given a menu of four possible choices. These two forms of help can guide even the most uncertain students through the session.

The labeling session can provide a quick review for students preparing for an exam. It gives place names and asks students to locate the places on the map (Yankelovich, 1985).

The advantages of the program include the feedback it provides to students, the chance for students to "see" the map change with time, the ease of using and reusing the program to master the subject (especially to prepare for examinations), and the program's combination of history with physical geography, which facilitates integrative thinking. Clearly, however, the program is at least as much of a CAI-type tutorial with graphics as it is a simulation. It does not have the interactive features of the best simulation programs, nor does it foster group processes in any way.

A more recent and vivid example of a noninteractive simulation is provided by another Brown program, which is used in biology courses. It makes extensive use of hypermedia (described in Chapter Three) to bring biological concepts to life. For example, it provides three-dimensional models of cells that can rotate and change scale and links them with more traditional two-dimensional drawings of cells (Osgood, 1987). Although this program is noninteractive, it does provide true simulations.

*Interactive Simulations.* In an interactive simulation, a student manipulates parts of a model and observes the resulting changes in the model as a whole. The State University College, Buffalo (New York) has developed five interactive simulation software modules for use in an environmental studies course. The modules, which are intended to illustrate the complexity of environmental systems, include "Acid Rain" and "Human Impacts on Endangered Species."

In the "Acid Rain" module, students can change six variables related to the operation of a coal-burning power plant and four variables related to the terrain surrounding a distant lake and the topography of the lake. Students thus have direct control over variables affecting air quality and the acidity of the lake. The outcomes of the students' manipulation include local atmospheric concentration of the pollutant sulfur dioxide ($SO_2$), the acidity (pH) of the lake, and the operating cost per hour of the coal plant.

The simulation in the "Endangered Species" module uses the red wolf as an example of an endangered animal. Students control the type (stage) of economic development in the region where the wolf lives, and each stage of development directly affects the wolf. The objective of the students' interaction is to maintain a balance between economic development and preservation of the red wolf's habitat (Kinsey, Wiesen, and Unertl, 1985).

The advantage of both environmental studies modules is the active role they allow students to play in affecting the key part of the simulated environment—the lake in one case and the red wolf in the other. The simulations help students see relationships among critical facts and concepts that they have been taught in the course. The modules also let students apply those concepts in a way that never would have been possible in the real world.

Because they help students grasp the delicate balance among parts of complex ecosystems, these interactive simulations are powerful and dynamic vehicles for learning. However, these and other simulations have certain disadvantages. Inevitably they oversimplify reality, both in portrayal of causes and effects and in the very idea that an individual can control such complex factors as economic development. The assumptions on which they are based cannot be discovered and examined easily. Also, this form of interactive simulation does not foster group interaction and inquiry.

Stanford University employs an interactive simulation, including video, to teach drama and theater arts. This "Theater Game" permits students to simulate the design, production, and performance of a play, using the computer as a "sketch pad" upon which settings can be placed and characters can be moved. Character movement can be synchronized with a tape recording of the play's script. Accompanying the program is a videodisk that provides an archive of theater history, including slides, filmstrips, and tutorials. Students learn to think like actors and directors as they analyze different versions of the same scene and then create their own version of the scene. They thus come to comprehend the complex physical and esthetic facets of the dramatic process, as well as the relationships among those facets, through hands-on experience (*Agenda, Academic Information Systems*, 1985; Osgood, 1987).

Advantages of this interactive simulation are its inclusion of a visual data base and its use of video as an enhancement to the learning process. This program facilitates integrative thinking and the resolution of problems related to drama production. However, it perforce omits the interpersonal dynamics involved in decisions about complex artistic elements in the real world. It also cannot fully reproduce the subtleties of production that are best experienced in a "live" theater.

*Group Competitive Simulations.* In group competitive simulations, competing teams of students make decisions that affect computerized models of phenomena relevant to a course. The business game "Cartels and Cutthroats," published by Strategic Simulations, is a good example of a group competitive simulation. The University of San Diego School of Business has found this game quite useful in some of its classes.

"Cartels and Cutthroats" simulates six companies competing in the same industry over a period of up to forty quarters. Each quarter, management (the team of students operating a "company") makes decisions about eight variables, including the quantity of raw materials to purchase, the number of units to manufacture, the price to charge for each unit, the expenditure for advertising, and the amount to be invested in research and development. Various parts of the environment in which the companies compete are simulated, including economic and labor changes. Each quarter the companies receive written financial statements and historical data that their "management" can use for decision making.

Faculty member Gary Whitney required decisions from teams to be submitted every day at 5 P.M. for two weeks. Figures describing the competitive standing of all firms in the industry were given out at 9 A.M. the next day. In addition to making the quarterly decisions, students prepared written "strategic plans" before entering the first decision period and a "strategic analysis," which critically analyzed the actions taken, after the game was completed. These written reports, assigned by Whitney to augment the game, encouraged students to come to a deeper understanding of why they planned to take or did take particular actions (Whitney, 1983).

The advantage of this kind of program is that it allows students to practice making important decisions in the safety of the college campus. It also creates a dynamic interpersonal context in which students learn to work in teams, developing cooperative and leadership skills; students must reach a consensus before making decisions. A disadvantage, as with other simulations, is that it can mislead students by oversimplifying complex realities and operating on unexamined assumptions. For example, the interpersonal dynamics involved in an organization's functioning are difficult, if not impossible, to simulate accurately.

*Individual Competitive Simulations.* These simulations involve individual students, rather than teams, in problem-solving activities that have gamelike qualities such as ways of "winning" or the awarding of points or other special incentives. They emphasize problem-solving skills more than integrative skills. Students may compete against the computer, their own previous performance, or other students in these simulations.

An individual competitive simulation designed to help students develop problem-solving skills, called "Thinking for Fun and Profit," was developed by Kamala Anandam at Miami-Dade Community College in Florida. This simulation uses video to present realistic problem situations that illustrate abstract ideas. The program branches according to the kinds of responses students make to these situations. It distinguishes between analytical thinking and automatic thinking in solving problems. Solution of problems presented by the program may involve discriminating within a series, reasoning serially, finding contradictions, drawing conclusions, finding analogies, seeking shortcuts, or some combination of these thinking skills.

Up to three students may use the program at the same time. This multiple-use feature promotes communication between students and helps them learn how their peers approach problem situations. In some instances students must agree on a solution, while in other cases individual students make decisions about a problem regardless of the opinion of their peers. In a third mode, one of the players is randomly selected and asked to respond to a problem, and the other students are then given the opportunity to agree or disagree with the first student's solution. The program keeps track of each student's progress and offers feedback on the correctness of and degree of agreement involved in each solution (Tross, 1986–87).

An advantage of this simulation is that it makes problem-solving a highly personal and involving learning process for the students. Use of video greatly increases the realism of the problem situations presented. In addition, the frequent changing of the student's role as decision-maker (as part of a group, as an independent individual, or as an individual about whose decision the group will express an opinion) provides a useful mirror of situations in the real world. The program's feedback following student responses is also useful. A disadvantage of this type of simulation is that some instructors dislike gamelike activities that match student against student, fearing that such activities will be too superficial or that the desire to be right or to "win" over other students will distract students from the true learning objectives of the course.

### Commercially Available Programs: Some Examples

"STELLA FOR ACADEME—STRUCTURAL THINKING: EXPERIENTIAL LEARNING LABORATORY WITH ANIMATION" (High Performance Systems, $150; runs on Apple Macintosh). Adaptable to a variety of courses in the science curriculum as well as courses in psychology, economics, and sociology, this program allows students to create their own simulations or models of theories, processes, and concepts in physical and social sciences by combining pieces of information represented by icons. The program automatically creates equations to simulate the process being studied. It allows students to test their models and display results as animation, a scatter plot, or a table of numeric values ("Computer Software . . . ," 1987e).

"PHYSICS SIMULATIONS I, II, III" (Kinko's Academic Courseware Exchange, $24.50 each; runs on Apple Macintosh). This three-title series, designed for introductory physics classes, provides animated simulations of problems illustrating elementary physics concepts. The first group of simulations deals with mechanics (for example, two-dimensional motion in a constant gravitational field, planetary motion, and special relativity); the second with electricity and magnetism (for example, electric field patterns); and the third with general physics (for example, the thermal motion of a particle in a one-dimensional potential, and group and phase velocity) ("Computer Software . . . ," 1987a).

"PSYCH WORLD" (McGraw-Hill, $550; runs on Apple II series or on IBM PC and compatibles). This program for introductory psychology classes provides simulations of classical psychology experiments, including graphics, and allows students to learn by manipulating the simulations. The program's fourteen modules cover such topics as split-brain syndrome, sleep and dreams, classical conditioning, operant conditioning, short-term memory, color sensation, abnormal behavior, and psychoanalysis of a dream (McGraw-Hill, telephone conversation with the author, August 1987).

"IF'S: INTERNATIONAL FUTURES SIMULATION" (CONDUIT, University of Iowa, $95; runs on IBM PC and compatibles). A "computer model of the world," this program gives students the opportunity to look at global development through the year 2030. They make projections based on more than fifty different variables in population, economics, agriculture, and energy provided by the program. Because of its multidisciplinary approach, this program could be used in a variety of courses, including courses in economics, agriculture, sociology, and history ("Computer Software . . . ," 1985).

"ELECTORAL COLLEGE SIMULATION" (Kinko's Service Corporation, $23; runs on Apple II series). This program, suitable for use in a political science course, provides a simulation of a presidential election in the United States. Based on a Monte Carlo simulation technique, the program displays month-by-month results on a color map as state primaries take place. The final outcome of the election is determined by state voting histories, month-by-month changes in trends that took place before the 1980 election, and a random normal chance factor ("Computer Software . . . ," 1987g).

"JUNIOR DRAFTER" (Learning Odyssey, $3,195; runs on IBM PC and compatibles with color graphics card and a three-button mouse). A simulation program that allows students to learn to use larger computerized design and manufacturing systems, "Junior Drafter" is ideally suited for courses in drafting or in the use of complex computerized design systems ("Computer Software . . . ," 1987e).

### Evaluating Software for the Computer as Simulator

The first step in determining which part of a course, if any, might be enhanced by the use of the computer as a simulator is to analyze the course, as described in Chapter Two. Once an instructor has determined that this form of computer use is appropriate to a course, he or she most likely will want to analyze existing programs (commercially available or custom created) to determine whether any of these meet the course's needs.

It is most practical to begin analysis with programs already available in the institution. If none of these is suitable and acquiring new software (by purchase or by arrangement with institutions that have developed it) is possible, the instructor can go on to consider other available programs. (Chapter Two suggested some ways to find out what is available.) In particular, instructors should note that many commercial simulations that are marketed as entertainment or "games" can have significant educational value. War simulation games or games such as "Balance of Power" (Mindscape), which deals with international politics, could be used in history or political science classes, for example. If no existing software seems to meet a course's needs, the possibility of developing custom software should be considered. This process is discussed in Chapter Seven.

The following checklist is intended to help instructors evaluate existing software designed for use in the computer as simulator. In addition to consulting these guidelines, the instructor should consider the general criteria for evaluating software that are presented in Chapter Seven.

- What phenomenon does the program simulate? How important is this phenomenon to the overall content and aims of the course?
- How accurate is the simulation?
- How detailed is the simulation? What aspects of the real phenomenon does it oversimplify? What aspects does it leave out?
- Upon what assumptions is the design of the simulation based? How valid are those assumptions? Do they involve political or other bias? How easy are the program's assumptions to discover and examine?
- How effectively does the program use graphics, sound, and other means to make the simulation realistic?
- What instruction does the program or its written documen-

tation provide to explain the simulation and its use? Is the level of instruction adequate for students to understand and use the simulation? Will it help them integrate the simulation with the rest of the course?

- How much time will students spend with the simulation? Are the phenomenon being modeled and the potential learning gains from use of the simulation important enough to justify spending this time on the simulation rather than on other course-related activities?

- Does the simulation permit creative, "open-ended" exploration of the model, or is it designed to achieve specific learning objectives? Is its degree of open-endedness appropriate for students' level of ability and independence and for the aims of the course?

- What parts of the simulation, if any, can students change? What other parts or aspects of the simulation change in response to student activity? What parts, if any, change without student activity? What parts, if any (the underlying data base, for example), can instructors change?

- Do students interact with the simulation as individuals or as groups? Is this form of interaction appropriate for students and course?

- What gamelike or competitive aspects, if any, does the simulation have? If there are competitive aspects, does a student compete (a) as part of a group, against other groups of students, (b) individually against another student, (c) against himself or herself (by trying to improve an earlier score, for example), or (d) against the computer (by trying to beat a time limit or counter adverse conditions set up by the computer, for example)? Is the form of competition suitable for the personalities of the students and the aims of the course?

- What facts or concepts must students integrate in order to use the simulation or solve the problem(s) it presents?

- What problem(s), if any, does the simulation ask students to solve? How relevant are these problems to the overall content and aims of the course?

- What information or other help does the simulation give students trying to solve the problem(s) it presents? Is this information adequate for the purpose?

- What steps do students take to solve the problem(s)? Is there one "right answer," or may the problem(s) be solved in more than one way? Is the difficulty of the problem(s) appropriate to students' level of ability?
- Does the program evaluate student performance in any way? If so, how? If not, how might an instructor evaluate performance?
- What feedback, if any, does the program give to students other than changes in the model? Is the feedback adequate?
- What experiences does the simulation provide that would be impossible or impractical for students to have in the real world? How useful are these experiences?
- What practical skills do students use or develop in working with the simulation? How can they apply these skills in the course as a whole? How can they apply them in the real world?

# 5

□□□□□□□□□□□□□□□□□

# The Computer as Resource:
# Fostering Investigative Skills

Engaging in meaningful intellectual inquiry depends on having access to the best thought, informed opinion, and research data relevant to the phenomena being investigated. The purpose of this chapter is to show how computers can help students develop investigative skills, specifically those aspects of investigation necessary to effectively locate and retrieve information for undertaking reports, projects, and essays. These skills help students fulfill the learning objective of "knowing where." The computer makes possible more ready access to a larger supply of data than ever before.

### The Importance of Investigative Skills

Dressel and Marcus suggest that an important part of an academic discipline is its "mode of inquiry" or investigation. In other words, investigation is fundamental to an academic discipline, and the form of investigation is different in different disciplines. Dressel and Marcus define "mode of inquiry" as the "syntactical component" of a discipline. As they explain, "The syntactical component is a set of research and organizing processes around which the discipline develops. It might be described as the grammar of the discipline. . . . A mode of inquiry is an essential element of a discipline, and the appropriate words for describing that inquiry vary with the discipline. The process includes collecting and organizing data, asserting and testing hypotheses, and relating these to broader generalities" (1982, pp. 92-93).

## The Computer as Resource

At the present time, due to cost and other problems, the computer is not often used directly by students as a resource in undergraduate education. However, the importance of this mode of instructional delivery is likely to increase in the years ahead as technological advances make on-line data bases and teleconferencing cheaper and easier to use.

The computer can be used as a resource in many ways, but the use of concern here is the gathering of data and hypotheses related to subjects under investigation in academic courses. Students using the computer in this way may be involved with either or both of two kinds of resource networks: intrainstitutional and extrainstitutional.

A department or group of departments within an institution, or sometimes the institution as a whole, may set up a so-called local area network (LAN), in which computer terminals (workstations) used by students or others are connected by cable to each other and to a "host" computer (often a larger computer, such as a minicomputer or a mainframe). Other intrainstitutional networks are accessed by individual computers through the telephone lines, using communication devices (modems) and software. An intrainstitutional network may be set up in a hierarchical way; for example, the network at the University of California, Berkeley, has individual, work group (academic department), campuswide, and off-campus levels (Neff, 1986b).

A host computer in (or run by) the campus library or computer center is often the hub of an intrainstitutional network. In addition to allowing access to library resources, the host computer can be used for problems that require more "memory" capacity than is available at individual workstations. The network allows its individual computers to access institutional data bases, send messages, and share peripheral equipment, such as a laser printer for fast, high-quality production of printouts and manuscripts. Students and faculty members can use terminals in these networks to access text, information, applications, people, and educational programs. As U.C. Berkeley's Assistant Vice Chancellor for Information Systems and Technology Raymond Neff stated about his institution's network, "We decided that connectivity for faculty, students, and staff was going to be a birthright. . . . We want to provide electronic mail for everybody [without charge to the users]" (1986b, pp. 4–5). Intrainstitutional networks provide centralized control of information processing, eliminating the complex logistics and risk of damage to equipment (especially disks) that may result when students run software individually. (See Bourque, 1985, and "An Overview of the Different Kinds of Networks," 1985, for a further discussion of different types of networks.)

Extrainstitutional resource networks usually are accessed by modem. These networks connect students to people or data bases outside their institution. In some cases students access extrainstitutional networks directly, while in other cases their access may be through their school's intrainstitutional network.

A particular kind of extrainstitutional network, which might be called the interinstitutional network, is also becoming increasingly common. The impetus for this is suggested by Douglas Gale, director of computing at the University of Nebraska, who refers to what he calls the "logical community." As Gale points out, "The chemistry department here has more in common with the chemistry department 100 miles away than it does with our own art department. . . . The logical community transcends the physical community" (Turner, 1986d, p. 28).

While Gale seemingly regrets losing the view of the university as a "community of scholars" encompassing both artists and chemists, the notion of a "logical community" joined by computer does suggest possibilities for enriched research and scholarship within disciplines. Of course, interdisciplinary conferences produce another and equally valuable kind of scholarship, strengthened by their multiple perspectives—and these may be carried on by computer equally well.

Students can use computers as resources to access either data or people. The data come from data bases of various kinds. (These "on-line" data bases differ from those created by data base programs, which will be discussed in the next chapter, in that the data in the latter are supplied by the users.) The people accessed by computer networks may be other students, faculty, or experts in various fields.

*Accessing Data.* Today there are approximately 3,000 on-line data bases in existence, covering just about every topic one can imagine (Badgett, 1987). These data bases carry information related to nearly every part of the undergraduate curriculum, including highly specialized areas of study. Most of these data bases can be accessed directly by anyone with a modem and communication software. Many are also available through commercial information retrieval services such as CompuServe and The Source. These services provide access to the data bases by means of "gateways." For example, IQuest, a "gateway" in CompuServe, provides access to over 700 data bases, including Dialog, BRS, SDC/Orbit, and NewsNet. (Individual data bases may themselves be subdivided. For example, Dialog carries 260 smaller data bases.) Because a user needs to learn only one set of commands for each "gateway," use of these programs makes data base access much easier than it would be if a user had to learn the different rules for accessing each data base directly (Bowen, 1986). Commercial information retrieval services also carry both general news services (The Source has one from United Press International, while CompuServe carries the Associated Press service) and business and financial or other specialized news services. (For further information on available on-line data bases, see Slatta, 1985, and the *Directory of Online Databases*).

Typically, information in on-line data bases consists of bibliographic entries, abstracts, and/or journal article reprints. It usually can be called up by author, title, a subject keyword, or an identifying phrase. University libraries and learning resource centers increasingly offer services that help students use such computer data bases for investigative projects throughout the curriculum. Reference librarians usually perform data base searches for students today in order to save time and money, but in the future, data base searches may become cheap and easy enough for students themselves to make.

Library catalogs themselves are increasingly being put on computer as well. Students search the collection electronically, avoiding microfiche searches and extensive browsing through library stacks.

An experiment conducted at Texas A&M University illustrates both the promise and the problems of using computers as a resource for accessing data. In the experiment, a group of 105 students enrolled in a technical writing class were offered free searches of certain on-line data bases. This course was used for the experiment because its students had to complete a research paper and because the course was required by many departments, which made its students a reasonable cross section of the student body. The experimental group was made up of five sections, averaging twenty to twenty-two students each, that were randomly selected from the forty-seven sections offered.

In the free search, students were given a bibliography of fifty references from three data bases, but not the articles themselves. Students were requested to create a list of keywords organized by concept groups. Searches requested by students were done by the library staff in half-hour blocks of time. Bibliographies were mailed to the library about one week after the search was performed, so students had to allow sufficient time for the arrival of the results of their searches. The results of the experiment were "disappointing and puzzling": only 27.6 percent of the 105 students used the searches.

Similar searches were then offered to two English classes given during the university's four-and-a-half-week summer session. This time, however, a demonstration of on-line searching was given to each class (this had not been done for the technical writing students), and the results of the searches were made available to students immediately rather than after a week's delay. This time the result of the experiment was markedly different: twenty-six of the forty-three participating students (63 percent) took advantage of the service (Dodd and Anders,

1984). This experiment shows that instruction in the possibilities of data base use and rapid availability of results are important along with free access in persuading students to use the computer as a resource for accessing data.

Byron T. Scott, Meredith Professor of Journalism at the University of Missouri, Columbia, has his journalism students make extensive use of the computer as a resource. For example, in Intermediate Writing, an advanced undergraduate course, each student must prepare four in-depth feature articles suitable for publication in magazines. Scott requires students to use on-line data bases in researching at least one of their articles. (Scott's students have access to computer communications either through their own computers or through those in the university's newsroom.) Students most often use CompuServe via the IQuest gateway, though some also use The Source, Dow Jones, or other information retrieval services.

Scott provides several class lectures on investigative skills, including the techniques of using research tools in general and on-line data bases in particular. One lecture/demonstration uses as an example an article that Scott wrote for *On Line* magazine, using the computer exclusively. Scott provides printouts showing how his work proceeded, including reference material obtained from data bases, electronic messages, on-line conferences, and drafts of the article itself.

In addition to this general instruction, Scott meets with each student individually. In the first meeting, which precedes the lectures on investigative skills, Scott and the student discuss the particular topic or theme of the student's proposed article. In a later meeting, Scott gives the student hands-on experience with Scott's own computer. He teaches the student how to access particular data bases, download files of information from the data bases to the computer the student is using (a much less time-consuming, and thus much less expensive, procedure than taking notes from the computer screen), send and receive electronic mail messages, and participate in on-line conferences.

Students may use any or all of these techniques in doing research for their articles. For example, one student used clipping morgues, Nite Rider, and other information retrieval services in preparing an article on the challenges involved in raising twins. The student also placed messages on the CompuServe Forum conference for parents, asking for contact from parents who would be willing to be interviewed for his article; several on-line interviews ultimately resulted.

The average cost for the use of on-line services in preparing one article of this type, according to Scott, was $10 to $20, which he points out is less than students would have spent to retrieve the same information by long-distance telephone. Scott maintains that the use of the computer as a resource for projects of this type requires students to think clearly when planning and carrying out their research strategies. It also fosters personal interaction in that students frequently share their on-line research information and techniques (Scott, telephone communication to the author, August 1987).

It is clear that on-line data base searches can greatly increase the amount of relevant data available to students. Nonetheless, serious problems currently prevent widespread student use of the computer as a resource for accessing data. For one thing, most data bases include only works published in the mid-1970s or later, and there is typically a time lag of a year or more before works are placed on the system. More importantly, either students themselves or the institutions that subsidize them must pay a high price for these services in the form of subscription fees, on-line uses charges, and telephone costs: the least expensive data bases cost $5 to $10 per hour of access time, and more specialized data bases cost significantly more ($50–$60 per hour). These costs are coming down, but they are still prohibitive for most students and institutions. (It should be noted that many commercial data bases and information retrieval services have "off-hours" rates that are considerably lower than their weekly rates.)

Difficulty of use is another problem. Use of many data bases requires learning a complicated structure of commands, a particular nuisance because mistakes waste time on line and thus waste money. Data bases are likely to become easier to use in the future, but at present, preparatory coaching is essential for students who are expected to make their own searches.

Problems related to cost and difficulty of use may have technical solutions. However, one additional problem with using on-line data bases that is of concern to many academicians may not. They fear the loss of social contact among students who never browse through libraries or engage in informal inquiries with other students who are involved in similar investigative projects.

*Accessing People.* If the use of computers as a resource threatens to cause problems through social isolation, it can also offer at least a partial solution to those problems. In addition to accessing data, students can use computers to access people, including experts in many fields, faculty, and other students. They can send and receive messages related to investigative projects or other endeavors. They can also discuss themes assigned by a course instructor or other leader or chosen by the students themselves. Like in-person discussions, discussions mediated by computer are often lively and incisive, breaking new ground in students' understanding of a discipline and enriching their preparation of theses, essays, and reports.

Communication by computer can be particularly helpful in making a college education accessible to off-campus students, such as working students and some disabled students. It can also allow students to take remote courses from the most talented professors, even if those professors live in a distant state. (Tele-learning's Electronic University Network, described in Chapter One, provides an example of a network devoted to computer-delivered remote courses.)

Communications networks exist in different forms and can be used in different ways. Computer conferences are usually organized around a particular topic. They may be set up by private institutions or by commercial information services, including some of the same ones that offer access to data bases (CompuServe, for example). Often individual conferences are grouped together in a conference system. People interested in a conference topic can post public messages, leave private "electronic mail" messages for each other, or even (if both are using their computers at the same time) "chat" directly.

Bulletin boards are similar to conference systems but tend to have more general announcements and also frequently offer public domain software for downloading. Bulletin boards are usually run by private individuals or businesses and are small and local, while conference systems often cover a much wider area. Messages in both conferences and bulletin boards are relayed through a central computer. Except for those run by commercial services, most conferences and bulletin boards are inexpensive to use. Available topics are extremely diverse (Davis and Marlowe, 1986).

Another form of communication network is the distributed network. BITNET, ARPANET, and USENET are examples. These differ from conferences and bulletin boards in that they do not involve a central computer; rather, messages are relayed in batches from one computer "node" to another. Direct chatting is not possible on a distributed network, and a message left on such a network may take anywhere from a few hours to a week to reach its destination. However, such networks are useful in that they allow a user to send a message across the country or even abroad for the cost of a local phone call. Many scientists and other professionals use these networks. (For more about communication networks, see Quarterman and Hoskins, 1986.)

An example of use of the computer as a resource to access people is provided by St. Louis Community College, where an electronic bulletin board is sponsored by the English department. Students in the department's courses create drafts of their compositions using word processing software and then "post" the drafts on the bulletin board. Students are required to access one another's drafts, read them, and add evaluative comments via the bulletin board. These comments are used both by the students who composed the drafts and by the faculty members teaching the courses. The use of the bulletin board is intended to help students improve both their writing skills and their computer literacy (Divine, 1986–87).

One advantage of computer conferences, bulletin boards, or distributed networks is that a student (if his or her computer is connected to a printer) can easily obtain a printed transcript of messages or entries already made in a conference. This can be quite useful if information in the entries is needed for a project. Electronic mail messages may be sent or received at any time; the parties involved do not have to be connected to the system at the same time, as is necessary with telephone or face-to-face conversations. This is often convenient for "resource people" as well as students; indeed, experts in many fields are accessible to students only through computer conferencing.

The expansion of the student's world view and network of interactions with professionals made possible by computer communications can greatly enhance student effectiveness in carrying out research projects. Computer conferencing also encourages more thoughtful and reasoned responses to complex issues than might occur in direct spoken conversation. Computer conferencing tends to promote a broader range of ideas than class discussion sometimes does, and it diminishes the possibility of one or a few students dominating a discussion. Furthermore, because of the constraints of using the system, students are encouraged to make their points concisely. Highly cogent and focused writing can result.

In spite of these advantages, accessing people by computer, like other uses of the new technology, has its problems. Just as computer simulations can never completely reproduce the complexities of the reality they represent, so contact by computer can never capture all the nuances of face-to-face or even voice-to-voice contact. Users of a computer conference cannot perceive subtle but important interpersonal cues such as facial expressions, gestures, and verbal intonations. Mary Washington College's William Kemp observes that "sustaining engagement in [computer] conversations can be quite difficult" and that they lack "the immediacy which being in a live classroom provides" (Meeks, 1987, p. 186). Students who depend on this form of communication too exclusively may find themselves more socially isolated than they would otherwise be, not less. Teaching and learning have always gained from being at least partly social experiences, and the advent of the computer does not change this.

Instructors, too, may find themselves confronted, as one

faculty member was, with "a different challenge, the need to develop a valid teaching personality suitable for use in the computer conference medium. How to express approval? Disapproval? How to pull out responses from students who would prefer to observe silently and noncommittally?" (Richards, 1986, p. 7). Meeting this challenge can require a major rethinking of one's teaching style.

Other problems are more technical in nature. First, like on-line data bases, computer conferences and bulletin boards are often difficult to use. Students who have never mastered typing may have trouble communicating fluently through a keyboard. Similarly, students who are not good writers may be unnerved by the need for cogent and clear writing. At present, computer conferencing is definitely not for everyone.

### Commercially Available Networks: Some Examples

DIALOG (data base system available directly and through CompuServe. One-time subscription fee $39.95; on-line use charges $0.40 per minute). Dialog, accessible through the IQuest "gateway" on CompuServe, carries 260 smaller data bases. One of these is ERIC, the Educational Resources Information Center data base, which is one of the best known in the educational field. ERIC consists of over half a million citations of educational sources. (As an alternative to direct access, ERIC now makes its citations available to libraries on a laser disk that is issued periodically, like a magazine.) Dialog also provides an index for the contents of about 400 magazines, in some cases extending back to 1959.

Knowledge Index is an "after hours" version of Dialog, available only on evenings and weekends. Like Dialog, it is available directly or through CompuServe. It costs less than the main service (one-time subscription fee, $35.00; use charges $0.21 or $0.25 per minute). Knowledge Index offers sixty of Dialog's most popular data bases, including Psychinfo (literature on psychology), Art Literature Bibliographies, Mathsci (literature on math and science topics), and American History and Life (Baskin, 1985).

NEXIS (data base system available through the Mead Corporation. Subscription fee $50.00 per month; on-line use charges $32.00 per hour, plus a search charge of $3.00 to $30.00 depending on file size). This data base system provides, among other things, an extensive bibliographic service that covers 120 popular publications, including *Newsweek, Time,* and *Fortune.* It carries the full text of the *New York Times* back to June 1980; each new edition is added within forty-eight hours of publication (Baskin, 1985).

INFOMASTER (data base system available from Western Union Telegraph Co. One-time subscription fee $25.00; on-line use charges of $0.60 or $0.80 per minute for prime time). Infomaster offers a great breadth of information, retrieving information from Dialog, NewsNet, BRS (Bibliographic Retrieval Service), and many other services. In all, it offers approximately 700 data bases (Badgett, 1987).

NEWSNET (data base system available from NewsNet. Subscription fee $150.00 per year; on-line use charges $0.60 or $0.80 per minute for prime time). NewsNet reads over 300 wire service reports, publications, and newsletters, including United Press International and Associated Press. Students indicate the topics they are interested in. NewsNet searches for information on those topics, notifies students of material found, and "clips" articles on request. Students are charged $0.37 for each "find" (Badgett, 1987).

BITNET (distributed communication network available through the Bitnet Corporation; sliding-scale subscription fee depending on institutional operating budget; no on-line use charges). This interinstitutional distributed network connects about 250 academic sites, as well as about 50 research institutes and nonprofit organizations, in the United States. Faculty and others at member institutions use it to exchange messages, documents, programs, and data relevant to their scholarly or administrative interests and needs. Today, BITNET is the largest communication network in higher education. Evolving from a small volunteer effort to a larger, funded project, BITNET incorporated as a separate entity with its own board of trustees in July 1987 (Mace, 1987).

EIES (Electronic Information Exchange System communication network. Subscription fee $60.00 per month; on-line use charges $3.00 or $9.50 per hour during prime time). Developed by the New Jersey Institute of Technology with support from the National Science Foundation, EIES is the oldest and one of the best known computer conferencing systems. Conferences available through EIES include The EIES Poetry Corner, Information Science, Emerging Trends: Food and Population, Computers in Education, Religion and Technology, Essays and Letters, Science/Math/Technology Info System, French, and Politics. EIES can also customize communication services so that groups of scholars can focus their collective inquiries on particular issues or problems (telephone interview, August 1987).

USENET (distributed communication network available to anyone using the UNIX operating system and possessing suitable communication software. No subscription fee or on-line use charges). This network has over 5,000 sites worldwide and over 200,000 users. It is something like an electronic magazine, or rather a group of different magazines (called newsgroups) that are devoted to different topics. Users type in informal articles on topics of interest and, in turn, read what other users have written. Topics range from space technology and artificial intelligence to philosophy and religion. In addition to articles, USENET includes announcements, classified advertisements, and reviews of new hardware and software (Henderson, 1987).

ARPANET (distributed communications network sponsored by the Department of Defense. Access limited to organizations doing research funded by federal money). ARPANET was originally part of a military network but currently has a strong research orientation. Many higher education institutions have access to it (Quarterman and Hoskins, 1986).

## Evaluating Networks for the Computer as a Resource

The first step in determining which part of a course, if any, might be enhanced by the use of the computer as a resource is to analyze the course, as described in Chapter Two. Once an instructor has determined that this form of computer use is appropriate to a course, he or she most likely will want to analyze existing on-line data bases or communications networks to determine whether any of these meet the course's needs.

It is most practical to begin analysis with intrainstitutional networks and data bases, if any exist. If these do not exist or are not suitable, the instructor can go on to consider extrainstitutional networks that can be accessed from the institution at an acceptable cost.

The following checklist is intended to help instructors evaluate existing on-line data bases and communications networks. The first items on the checklist apply to both on-line data bases and communications networks; some questions specific to one or the other of these forms of computer resource follow. In addition to consulting these guidelines, the instructor might want to review the general criteria for evaluating software that are presented in Chapter Seven.

- What information needed for the project or course can students obtain through this network that they could not obtain, or could not obtain as easily, in other ways? What learning objectives of the course or project would gaining this information help students achieve?
- What area does this network cover—department? campus? other campuses? region? nation? Is this range appropriate for the course or project?
- How will students access this network—by modem? through a workstation connected to another computer by cable? Will students have access to needed communication devices and software?
- What is the cost per unit of time for use of this network (including subscription fee, on-line use charge, and telephone charge)?
- About how much time will be spent on each data search or communications session? How many searches or sessions per student are likely to occur during the project or course? What is the total on-line time (time per session x number of sessions) per student?
- What is the probable total cost per student for on-line time

(total on-line time x cost per unit of time) during this project or course? Who will pay it? Will the payer be able to afford it? Will the usefulness of the search or communication justify the expense?

- How easy is this network to use? Is on-line help available? What training will students need to use the network effectively? How will they get that training? Is the network's ease of use appropriate to students' level of ability and independence?

(for on-line data bases and information retrieval services)

- What data base(s) can be accessed through this network? What subjects are covered by the data base(s)? Which data base(s), if any, contain information relevant to this project or course?
- Who will conduct data searches—students? reference librarians? other staff? If searches are done for students, what scheduling factors must be considered? How long after students request searches will they receive results?
- What information will students need in order to conduct or request searches?

(for communication networks)

- What form(s) of telecommunications does this network support—on-line "chatting"? electronic mail? public announcements? Which of these forms of communication, if any, is appropriate for this project or course?
- With whom can students communicate through this network—other students? course instructor? other faculty? off-campus experts? With which of these do they need to communicate in order to complete the project or course? How will this communication help students fulfill the learning objectives of the project or course?

# 6

⊡⊡⊡⊡⊡⊡⊡⊡⊡⊡⊡⊡⊡⊡⊡⊡⊡

# The Computer as Tool:
# Improving Analytical Skills

Used as a resource, the computer can help students gather data. Used as a tool, it can aid them in classifying and analyzing data, tasks that are even more important to their academic development. Chet Meyers observes, "Today both teachers and students have at their hands an overwhelming abundance of information. Teachers sometimes despair of knowing how all these new developments in their disciplines can be sorted through to determine what students need to know. Students feel the onslaught of the information age even more acutely than their teachers and are less capable of coping with its demands and of making sense of the complex world it presents. College teachers can help their students cope with this complexity by suggesting analytical frameworks and perspectives for sorting things out" (1986, p. 113).

This chapter explores possibilities for using computers to enhance development of the analytical skills necessary to fulfill the learning objectives of "knowing what" (classificatory knowing, or the ability to categorize and come to new understandings about sets of information based upon the discovery of common patterns) and "knowing why" (conceptual and theoretical knowing). Used as a tool, the computer does not directly teach facts, theories, or even skills. Rather, it provides ways for students to use their own skills more effectively in whatever projects they wish to apply them to, much as a lever or pulley can help someone move almost any kind of heavy object.

Because of this broadness of application, the computer as tool gives great flexibility to the instructor as well as the student. Unlike some other kinds of software, "tool" programs such as word processors and spreadsheets can be incorporated into courses with little or no modification of existing teaching structure. An additional advantage of such programs is that most of them exist as widely available, relatively inexpensive software that requires little or no modification for educational use.

### The Importance of Classificatory and Analytical Skills

Soltis (1968) suggests that analysis allows us to "force abstract and vague ideas into concrete and more meaningful contexts" (p. 73). He likens analysis to a microscope or telescope. As a result of analytical probing we discover "what and why," arriving at new classifications of information and new conceptual and theoretical understandings.

Dressel and Marcus (1982) describe the outcomes of analysis in terms of particular classification systems ("knowing what") in a variety of disciplines. For example, the biological sciences use taxonomies to characterize plants and animals through the hierarchy of phylum, class, order, family, genus, and species. Chemistry has its periodic table of elements. In mathematics there are classes, sets, groups, and fields. Languages use classifications for such things as parts of speech, verb tenses, and sentence types.

John Wilson, in his book *Thinking with Concepts* (1969), explores analytical techniques that result in conceptual understanding. He points out the close relationship between questions of fact ("knowing that") and questions of concept ("knowing why"). Understanding concepts begins with mastering facts and goes on to analyzing the relationships among those facts. Ultimately, concepts help us grasp meanings that underlie and link arrays of facts. Dressel and Marcus (1982) list a number of types or subsets of concepts, including theories, ideas, rules, generalizations, principles or laws, problems, and aspects of life processes.

Students naturally engage in analysis when it bears on their future careers or personal lives or when it helps them ease some disequilibrium or dissonance they are experiencing. Jean Piaget (1947) described the dissonances that result when young children discover that some aspect of reality does not fit their existing mental patterns. Creative instructors sometimes take advantage of or even foster dissonance in order to encourage their students to employ analysis in an academic context.

Analysis involves the separation of a phenomenon into its constituent parts in order to determine the relationship of each part to the whole. Academic forms of analytical problems often involve computation, writing, or both. Students use these skills as they structure, interpret, clarify, and make sense out of information or realities. Through the application of analytical skills students learn to generalize and categorize, distinguish similarities and differences between phenomena, infer theoretical implications from concrete experience, draw conclusions, make judgments, and engage in abstract thinking. The results of analysis and judgment help to shape the conceptual frameworks through which students come to perceive the world.

## The Computer as Tool

The "information explosion," caused in part by computers, underscores the need for new tools to help in analyzing information. Computer application programs such as "idea generators" and statistical analysis software can provide such tools. Students can use these tools to apply and manipulate the raw data gained from observation or experimentation with realities in ways that aid development of classificatory and analytical understanding.

*Spreadsheet Programs.* A computer spreadsheet automatically changes all related numbers on a matrix of rows and columns when one number is changed. Spreadsheets can be used with text, formulas, instructions, and other nonnumerical data as well as with numbers. A spreadsheet can help students analyze data by creating "what if" scenarios. In effect, spreadsheets let students create their own simulations. Stephen Manes asserts that the computer's ability "to carry out quick-and-dirty simulations is the real revelation of the personal computer revolution" (1987, p. 93).

Lowman (1984) observes, "College teachers . . . prompt students to think like literary critics, biologists, political scientists, or mathematicians. Practice in 'as if' thinking can lead to better and better intellectual discourse" (p. 122). "As if" thinking and "what if" thinking are closely related, and spreadsheets can help students practice both.

Colorado State University's Economics Department has found spreadsheets to be very useful in its instructional program. The challenge of instruction, according to Colorado economics professor Harold Cochrane, is to link theoretical understanding with the practical, and he has found the personal computer equipped with a spreadsheet program to be an effective vehicle for doing that (Balestri, Cochrane, and Thursh, 1984).

Cochrane uses spreadsheets to enhance the role-playing activities he employs in his economics courses. Students set up problems derived from role-playing situations and then solve them with the spreadsheets' help. Cochrane says, "The spreadsheets I use are familiar commercial programs. They resemble a blank tablet that can reflect any set of relationships the user desires. Columns of numbers can be added, subtracted [and so on]. Formulas can be stored, replicated, and edited. The results can be printed or graphed. . . . The key advantage is that students become active problem solvers" (p. 12).

Cochrane illustrates his point with an example from consumer theory: "Individuals will attempt to plan purchases in a way that balances the current year's standard of living with that anticipated during retirement. . . . With electronic spreadsheets, my students build life-cycle models. This does not require sophisticated training in mathematics; instead, students must think about the subject matter logically" (p. 12).

Cochrane continues, "Students are not simply recording data for the computer to manipulate; they are building their own models that the spreadsheet helps them develop and manipulate. . . . They begin to understand and use complex theoretical principles by generating manageable models of real experience on the computer" (p. 13). Thus the computer as tool shades into the computer as simulator.

Not surprisingly, since they were developed for business, spreadsheets are used widely in business school curricula. They are useful in many other kinds of courses as well, however. For example, Drexel University psychology professor Thomas Hewett uses spreadsheets to simulate neural circuits and networks that may be responsible for a variety of visual phenomena. Students have the chance to explore neural networks and experiment with the simulation. Here the spreadsheet provides the basis for a simulation created by the instructor and manipulated by the students (Hewett, 1986).

In another nonbusiness example, the University of Maryland employs spreadsheets in the instruction of physics. Spreadsheets allow students to focus on the underlying concepts of physics rather than becoming bogged down in mathematical processes, which makes the course accessible to a far larger audience of students than it would otherwise be. Spreadsheets also allow the introduction of advanced concepts much earlier in the physics curriculum than would be possible with traditional instruction. Finally, spreadsheets provide graphics displays that allow abstractions to be made concrete in a way not possible before (*Agenda, Academic Information Systems*, 1985).

As the preceding examples show, advantages of spreadsheets as analytical tools include the linking of theoretical understanding with practical applications; the discovery of new relationships among pieces of information; the building of student-controlled simulations that employ theoretical constructs taught in the course; and the development of computer skills that are likely to be applicable in many careers.

One disadvantage of this form of "tool" software is the risk that students will miss the concepts underlying the mathematical operations performed by the program. Another is that students (or instructors) may become preoccupied with the computer to the detriment of the subject being analyzed or the theoretical underpinnings of a course.

*Statistical and Graphics Programs.* Like the spreadsheet, statistical packages heighten the ease and effectiveness with which students perform analytical and computational manipulations. These programs calculate measures of central tendency, standard deviation, correlation, and other statistical measures useful to analysis in numerous curricular areas. Obviously it is easier to learn the commands necessary to use the software than to learn how to perform manually all the kinds of analysis that such packages include.

Graphics software can help students visually enhance reports and projects and instructors enrich or extend presented material. Graphics programs offer an array of design elements and color combinations to create charts, graphs, and pictures or even reproduce overhead transparencies and 35 mm slides. Such programs include map drawers for geography and history courses, drawing tablets and painting packages for architectural design and art courses, pie and bar graph makers for economics courses, graph creators for mathematics and science courses, and computer-assisted drafting (CAD) programs for engineering drafting courses (McGrath, 1986). Often graphics programs create visual material from data generated in other computer "tools," such as data base or spreadsheet programs. Most graphics programs require special features in the computer or certain peripherals, such as a color graphics card and a printer with color capability.

The Colorado School of Mines Department of Mathematics uses a graphing program in calculus instruction, to give one example. Students use the program to graph various mathematical functions. For example, they graph a given derivative of a function with the program and then are asked to determine certain properties of the derivative by studying the graph. After seeing students use this technique, mathematics professor R. S. Fisk concluded, "The ability to show calculus students . . . dynamic (as well as static) graphing of certain types of functions can lead to a greater depth of understanding of certain mathematical concepts" (1984, p. 235).

An interesting example of the use of several computer "tools" in combination with a simulation is demonstrated by the California Polytechnic State University Biological Sciences Department in their general ecology laboratory. Each part of this course was restructured to take advantage of computers. A central focus of the laboratory experience was an analysis of the impact of a sewage treatment plant on the water quality and biology of San Luis Creek and on vegetation and the living patterns of small mammals in the adjacent chaparral community. To this end, instructors in the course wrote three specialized programs on vegetation sampling; created a data base to help students compare seasonal and long-term changes in the areas studied; and chose a statistical package for students to use in examining and analyzing data.

Students were first taught to use the statistical package. They learned how to perform statistical tests on data related to the two areas of investigation, calculate indices, transfer data, print annotated data tables, produce histograms and data plots, and store and retrieve data in permanent files, all with the help of the computer. "Students do need an appreciation of why particular information is collected. . . . However, repeated labor-intensive hand calculations with large data sets are not necessary to achieve such understanding," noted one of the instructors who taught the course (Bowker and Bowker, 1986, p. 4).

After students were familiar with the software they were going to use, they were assigned to teams that played the role of "environmental consultants" to state agencies. They had to decide how to deal with hypothetical emergencies resulting from the spill of toxic chemicals into the creek. The teams were permitted to use whatever features of the statistical package they felt were appropriate to the problem. At the conclusion of the activity, they prepared a written report for submission to a "review board."

*Data Base Programs.* Data base programs such as Ashton-Tate's dBASE III Plus provide students with a powerful tool for storing, organizing, and analyzing data. These programs are quite different from the on-line data bases described in Chapter Five. On-line data bases are created by research or other organizations and are stored in a large computer that is accessed by personal computers at remote locations. With a data base program, however, the individual student or instructor creates his or her own data base for a specific project or purpose. Students develop classificatory and analytical skills as they set up and use data bases, since they must decide which kinds of information are important and how these kinds of information will be accessed and sorted.

For example, an instructor might assign geology students to create a data base of minerals. The students would first have to think about the qualities, such as luster and hardness, that distinguish one mineral from another. They would probably establish one field for each of these qualities. They would then enter data about the particular luster, hardness, and so on of each mineral, determined either by direct testing or by literature search, into a separate record of the data base. Finally, using appropriate commands and keywords, they would call up particular kinds of data or instruct the program to sort the data in various ways—arrange the minerals in order of hardness, say, or list all minerals that have purple crystals. Analyzing the sorted data, they could arrive at conclusions about ways in which various minerals are similar to or different from each other. Use of the data base program allows such students to compare more minerals in more ways than would be possible without the program and greatly increases their chances of discovering unsuspected and interesting relationships.

Data base programs can be useful in any area of the curriculum. For example, a data base created by students in a history course might contain geographic, political, social, economic, and demographic information about different countries. Students might use this data base in attempting to answer research questions by, say, comparing the number of physicians per hundred people with the death rate in different countries. Similarly, marine biology students might use this kind of computer "tool" to classify and analyze data collected from sea water samples or from observations of mammal, bird, or fish populations (Watt, 1984).

Like other computer "tools," data base programs have some disadvantages as well as advantages. The primary one is that the more complex and powerful programs are often hard to use. They may require more training than an instructor has time to deliver or students have the ability to master. Some of these programs are also quite expensive.

*Word Processing Programs.* Turner (1987a) found that word processing is currently the most common use of the computer in education. Flexible and powerful word processing programs are increasingly available and easy for students to use. These programs often include or can be supplemented by such ancillary writing aids as spelling checkers, thesaurus programs, grammar and usage checkers, and style checkers.

Word processors make the physical process of writing and revising drafts much easier. Students can select paragraphs from one part of a report and move them to a different place in the report, for example. They can add material at any place or delete whole paragraphs with a few keystrokes. Such changes would have required complete retyping in the past. The labor involved tended to discourage students from making needed revisions of their work. By taking the mechanical fuss out of composition and revision, word processors give students more time to spend on the thoughts behind their words and more incentive to revise their work until it is truly as good as they can make it.

The ease of revision provided by word processors can encourage students to reconceptualize the writing process in a beneficial way. Dougherty (1985) observes that most inexperienced writers conceive a finished piece of writing as the result of three discrete phases, performed one after the other: planning, writing, and revising. However, she suggests, good writing often is not crafted in such a linear fashion. For example, even the planning phase can include writing and revising. Dougherty recalls her own days as a new writer: "I felt that my first drafts should be fairly polished and that all I had to do to revise was to find better words, rephrase awkward sentences, or reduce wordiness. . . . What I believed I ought to be doing and what in fact I did were frequently at odds. When I wrote on things I was familiar with, I would write and revise rather quickly because I was merely reporting what I already knew, but when I was exploring a new topic, I found my outlines difficult to use because I kept discovering ideas and relationships I hadn't accounted for. I also found my writing took much longer than I expected" (pp. 9–10).

In contrast to inexperienced writers, Dougherty suggests, experienced writers use a "recursive model of composing" that takes into account the fact that "meaning is not something fully formed in your head waiting to be released. Rather, it is the process of using language to construct meaning. . . . Your initial drafts are discovery drafts where you more fully discover what you mean, while in subsequent drafts you focus more on your readers' needs" (p. 10).

By making revision an integral part of the writing process, word processors can encourage students to discover ideas as they write. University of Delaware English faculty member Deborah Andrews comments, "Revision on paper creates messes. You scratch lines between lines, erase, write sideways in margins. When the mess makes the text incomprehensible, then you retype for successive drafts and more messes. Revision on a computer is clean and instantaneous. The new simply replaces the old. Insertions move directly onto the line. You don't need to wait and retype between versions to see how a new idea looks. . . . Because it's easy to move whole sections around, revision on a computer encourages the writer to rethink more than just where commas go. You can restructure whole documents retrospectively in minutes" (1985, p. 315).

At times, use of word processors can also modify the relationship between students and instructors. For example, at Villanova University in Pennsylvania, students participating in an experimental writing class in which they used word processing software met with their instructor for individual conferences in the computer laboratory. During each conference the faculty member examined printouts of the student's work. Then, working with the student, the instructor inserted suggestions and revisions. A new file was created to hold the revised draft, while the original draft remained in another file; this allowed the two to be compared easily (Martinez, 1985). The conference process made possible much more personal collaboration between instructor and student than would have been possible with the traditional red-pencil method of correcting papers.

Experience with word processors can cause students to reconceptualize the learning process in ways that reach far beyond the mechanics of writing. After his students began using word processors, Lawrence Schwartz of Montclair State College noted in amazement, "Something quite startling and unexpected has happened! Slowly, our students have begun to approach error in a new way. Their stifling and inhibiting search for correctness, which in reality is the vain struggle to avoid error, was transcended" (1985, p. 190). Students became willing to experiment with thought and language, even permitting mistakes, because the mistakes could so easily be corrected or modified in the revision process. This new approach could well lead to less inhibited and more creative thinking in all areas of the academic curriculum, including those that do not involve writing.

Despite the many advantages of using word processors as tools, students and instructors alike must remember that the contribution of these tools to the development of analytical and writing skills is, at best, indirect. Word processors will not in themselves make students good writers, or even necessarily better writers than they had been before or would be without computers. Students may gain the time to spend on more careful thought and still not use the time in that way. They may be able to make revisions easily and still not make those revisions, or not make them effectively (they may even revise too much). A word processing program, even with added spelling checkers or other aids, will not substitute for a student's own knowledge of grammar, vocabulary, and style. Writing and the thoughts behind it, after all, are and must always be produced by the mind of the writer, not by a computer.

In evaluating the effectiveness of word processors as aids to student writing and learning, one study (Teichman, 1984) noted "favorable performance . . . in the areas of writing quality and apprehension" (p. 226) of an experimental group of students who used word processors, as compared to a control group who did not. However, experienced teacher Kenneth Eble

admonishes, "I have seen little evidence that it [word process-
ing] will make either [writing or publishing] better" (1986,
p. 41).

Other problems may exist as well. Some students, especially those who are not good typists, may find word processors
daunting and difficult to use. Collier (1983) observes that less
able students tend not to benefit from using word processors in
doing revisions as much as better students do. Computer monitor screens usually hold only a limited amount of text (twenty
lines or so), so students may have trouble getting a perspective
on a piece of writing as a whole unless they can look at printouts of their drafts. Some students, too, may fear—sometimes
rightly—that work done at the computer may be lost because of
disk failures or other malfunctions. (Making a second, "backup"
copy of one's work on a disk different from the one holding the
original work can eliminate most of this risk, however.)

Finally, some of the writing aids often connected with
word processors, such as spelling and grammar checkers, have
raised the same kinds of objections as calculators and spreadsheets. Many instructors feel that students gain from being to-
tally responsible for error detection and correction at some
stage in the writing process.

*Other Tools for Building Analytical Skills.* Several other
kinds of software can help students develop classificatory and
analytical skills. "Idea generator" programs let students brainstorm ideas and consider various approaches to a topic before
composition. By asking questions about the specified topic,
these programs encourage the students to think about the topic
systematically and remind them of things they might otherwise
overlook. Outlining programs help students organize their
thoughts through creation and revision of outlines, including
the ability to "zoom in" on particular levels of an outline. If the
outliner is part of a word processor, students can use the outline as a framework around which to compose writing.

As noted in earlier chapters, new hypertext software allows students to trace a web of cross-references among articles
or other information that instructors or even the students them-

selves have assembled. Advanced students may also classify and demonstrate their knowledge of subjects with clearly formulatable rules by using generation or "shell" software to create a so-called expert system that answers questions about a subject.

Perhaps the most useful tools of all are the so-called integrated software packages, such as "Symphony" (Lotus) and "Framework" (Ashton-Tate). These programs combine word processing, spreadsheet, data base, graphing, and often telecommunications in a single system. Students need to learn only one set of commands to use all the system's components, and data can be easily transferred from one part of the system to another (numbers from the spreadsheet can be incorporated into the text of a report created on the word processor, for example). It should be noted, however, that these combined programs are often expensive and require a considerable amount of memory and other computer resources. They also may not be as good for any single function as a program devoted to that function. The word processor in an integrated software package may lack some of the formatting or other features found in a program devoted entirely to word processing, for example.

### Commercially Available Programs: Some Examples

LOTUS 1-2-3, Version 2.01 (Lotus Development Corp., $495.00). The Lotus package is the top-selling spreadsheet software nationally, and it is widely used in colleges and universities. It features a large worksheet (256 columns by 8,192 rows) of cells into which data can be entered. The format is flexible; rows can be reoriented to columns and vice versa, for example. The program includes graphics and data base functions as well as the spreadsheet. This means that, for instance, a user can call up information, apply calculations to it on the spreadsheet, and then draw a graph of the results without entering the data more than once. Graphs that can be produced with the program include bar charts, stacked bar charts, line graphs, x-y graphs, and pie charts. The user can streamline many activities by grouping program commands together in macros. Lotus 1-2-3 combines considerable power with ease of use, and the company offers its own courseware for teaching the program (*A Pocket Guide* . . . , n.d.).

SYSTAT (Systat, $595.00). "Systat" and other statistical packages help students perform statistical analyses on data by doing calculations on batches of data and by performing statistical tests, such as standard deviation. Spreadsheet software can do some of the same things statistical packages do, but statistical programs are not limited to two dimensions and usually can perform much more complex analyses than spreadsheets can. Systat has both data base and graphics capability and can present information in a variety of chart formats, including histogram, scatter, bar, contour, and probability charts (but not line or pie charts). Functions it can perform include correlations, T-tests, regression, analysis of variance, and many others. Like most other major statistical packages, it assumes that users already know basic descriptive statistics, the rules of statistical inference, and the major types of statistical procedures (Fridlund, 1986).

CHART-MASTER (Decision Resources, $375.00). "Chart-Master" produces eight kinds of charts: clustered and stacked bar charts, high/low charts, scatter charts, line charts, pie charts, and area and mixed charts. The program allows students to generate several different styles of charts from the same data without reentering the information. It can be set up to read data directly from ASCII text or "Lotus 1-2-3" files. Its charts can be made much more elaborate than those created with spreadsheets or statistical packages; for example, "Chart-Master" offers eight different character fonts and sixteen sizes of type. Text can be underlined, italicized, or justified, and charts can be dressed up with images from the program's ninety-symbol library. Charts can be made any size and moved to various positions on a page. In spite of its sophistication, "Chart-Master" is simple to use, thanks to its built-in prompts (Needle, 1986).

DBASE III PLUS (Ashton-Tate, $695.00). Ashton-Tate's dBASE series has been popular in the data base program market for years. Software in this series, of which "III Plus" is the most recent, is programmable, which means that users can design their own data bases. It is also relational, which makes it much more sophisticated than a simple data base program such as an address list maker. It allows different categories of data to be called up and different sorts of data to be performed. Users can apply "dBASE III Plus" to such tasks as filtering records, setting up relationships between records, and grouping files. A single data base record can have as many as 128 different fields, which means it can hold up to 128 different kinds of information about its subject.

Serious users of "dBASE III Plus" will need to learn its programming language. However, the program also offers an extensive system of pull-down menus for its major functions, which makes those functions accessible to beginners. (When a menu is used, the program also displays the equivalent dBASE command, so a user can become somewhat familiar with the programming language even while using the menus.) Report and label generating can be done without programming, for example. Both disk and manual tutorials are provided with the program (Miller, 1986).

MICROSOFT WORD (Microsoft, $450.00). "Microsoft Word" is a good example of a sophisticated word processing program. It includes an outliner, a glossary, and a thesaurus. It also offers windowing, so a user can, for example, look at the outline of an essay in one window while editing the text of the essay itself in another window. The screen display is the "what you see is what you get" type; that is, the text appears on the screen exactly as it will be printed. Underlines appear as underlines, for example, not as, say, numeric codes before and after the words to be underlined. The program is well suited to desktop publishing activities. It is compatible with laser printers and allows special formatting, such as newspaper-style columns. It can store special formats for letters or reports. "Microsoft Word" includes a self-paced tutorial that a new user of the program can run on the computer ("Microsoft Word," 1986).

THINKTANK (Living Videotext, Inc., $195.00). "Think-Tank" is designed to categorize notes or brainstormed ideas and build them into an outline. Students type their ideas into the computer as they think of them and then use the program to arrange and rearrange them (including cutting and pasting) until a coherent outline emerges. The outline can be produced in both extended and collapsed versions. The program includes a search feature, which allows students to search a long outline for a key word and then, if they desire, combine all entries containing that word into one section of the outline. It also has a sort function, which can reorganize items alphabetically or chronologically. "ThinkTank" is adaptable to outlining problems and solutions, analyzing alternatives, and creating lists as well as outlining articles or letters. Its editing commands are easy to use, and it includes a tutorial (Johnson, n.d.).

FRAMEWORK II (Ashton-Tate, $725.00). "Framework II" is an integrated software package that matches the performance of some of the best programs devoted to its individual functions. These functions include telecommunications, word processing, spreadsheet, data management, outlining, and graphics. Many of these functions can be active and visible on the screen simultaneously. This kind of software is particularly valuable to students working on lengthy papers that combine text, graphics, and numeric information. "Framework II" is compatible with many other programs and often can read data directly from them. It features pull-down menus for easy learning and selection of commands, and command structure is consistent and logical. However, because the program has so many functions, there are an exceptionally large number of commands to learn, and this may frustrate students who are interested in only a few of the functions ("Ashton-Tate Framework II . . . ," 1985).

### Evaluating Software for the Computer as Tool

The first step in determining which part of a course, if any, might be enhanced by the use of the computer as a tool is to analyze the course, as described in Chapter Two. Once an instructor has determined that this form of computer use is appropriate to a course, he or she most likely will want to analyze existing commercial programs to determine whether any of these meet the course's needs.

It is most practical to begin analysis with programs already available in the institution or likely to be owned by students. Instructors might also check computer bulletin boards and other sources for public domain "tool" software (though software from this source is likely to be less sophisticated than commercial programs). If none of these programs is suitable and acquiring new software is financially possible, the instructor can go on to consider other available programs. (Chapter Two suggested some ways to find out what is available.)

The following checklist is intended to help instructors evaluate existing software designed for use in the computer as tool. In addition to consulting these guidelines, the instructor should consider the general criteria for evaluating software that are presented in Chapter Seven.

- What task(s) will this software allow students to do more efficiently? What objectives of the course are students more likely to achieve if they can do the task(s) more efficiently?
- To what information will students apply this tool? In what way will students analyze the information? What objectives of the course will this analysis help students achieve?
- What features of this program (tasks it performs or helps students perform) will students use in this project or course? Can most or all of these features be found in other software that is cheaper and/or easier to use?
- Can this program easily use text or data generated by other programs? Can the output of this program be used with other programs?
- Is this program widely used in general society or the business world? Is learning how to use this program (or kind of program) likely to help students later in their careers?
- How easy is the program to use? Is its level of difficulty appropriate for students' level of ability and independence?
- What training will students need to use the program effectively? How will they get that training?
- What, if anything, that is important to course objectives are students NOT likely to learn if they use this tool? Do potential gains from using the tool offset this loss?
- If graphics are appropriate for this program, are the graphics offered by the program adequate?
- If this program integrates several "tool" functions, are the

advantages of such integration (ease and consistency of use, ability to transfer data from one program to another) great enough to outweigh any lack of sophistication in particular functions? Are the institution's computers powerful enough to run the software effectively?

# 7

Acquiring and Implementing
Educational Software

This chapter is intended to help instructors make decisions about acquiring educational software (choosing existing software or developing their own software) and about integrating that software into their courses. It will give general guidelines to keep in mind when evaluating existing software or buying commercial software, and it will also provide a brief discussion of the promises and pitfalls of authoring systems for creating custom software. It will then offer some tips for implementing software (putting it into actual use) in a course, focusing on training, student use, and evaluation.

### Evaluating and Acquiring Educational Software

As noted in Chapter Two, an instructor's search for appropriate software should begin at home—that is, in the institution where he or she works. The institution may already own software that can be used "as is" or modified to meet course needs. Software exchanges and electronic bulletin boards should also be searched for low-cost or free "public domain" software that can be used in a course.

If none of these sources produces software suited to the instructor's course, and resources are available for acquiring new software, the next question becomes, "Should the new software be bought or made?" The best answer to this question in a given instance will depend on a number of factors. Buying software, obviously, requires money, so budgetary constraints become important. Making software, too, requires money, but in a less obvious way: it requires faculty time, often a good deal of faculty time, and instructors often should be compensated in some way for that time.

Creating educational programs also usually requires faculty access to some kind of authoring system and the ability to use this kind of software effectively. One need not be a computer programmer to use today's authoring systems, but skill in organization and ability to learn and use a fairly complex command structure is still required. Faculty members also need to be familiar with at least the basic elements of instructional design. Even talented and experienced faculty members may not have all the skills needed to create effective educational software.

Educational considerations are at least as important as practical ones in deciding whether software for a particular course should be bought or made. On the one hand, commercial software often does not meet pedagogical needs very well. There are obvious advantages in being able to tailor a program precisely to a course's needs. On the other hand, software created by instructors for their own courses does not always meet pedagogical needs very well, either. It is difficult, if not impossible, for one or a few faculty members to create software with anything like the complexity, graphics, and other features found in most of today's commercial software. There is no easy answer to the "Buy or make?" question.

*Evaluating Existing Software.* An instructor locked in earnest conversation with a computer science department colleague, leafing through pages of reviews in computer magazines, or surrounded by brightly colored software packages in a computer store may feel faced with a bewildering embarrassment of riches. How is one to choose the program or programs that will be of the greatest help to students in a certain course?

Guidelines to be kept in mind when choosing software for particular uses of the computer were provided at the ends of Chapters Three through Six. Certain basic criteria, however, are important to consider when evaluating software for any educational purpose. The following checklist should help instructors focus on some of these criteria. Members of the academic computing staff or other faculty experienced in software selection and use may be able to suggest others. These criteria can guide the instructor in questioning colleagues or salespeople, looking for salient facts in reviews, or requesting information from companies that make particular software packages. Except for items related to cost, the criteria should be equally useful in evaluating software already owned by the institution (or available free) or software being considered for purchase.

- Does the software run on the type of computer that students will have access to?
- What peripheral devices (color monitors, printers, plotters, modems, or the like), if any, will students need to use this software? Can the institution make these devices available in appropriate numbers?
- What special features of the computer (graphics card, math coprocessor chip, or the like), if any, does the program require? Do the institution's computers have these features?
- If the software must be purchased, what does it cost? Is its price appropriate for its potential usefulness in the course (that is, is it cost effective)?
- Where will students use this software—in the classroom? the library? the computer science department? their own rooms? What scheduling considerations, if any, are likely to be involved?
- Does the software have any copyright or licensing restrictions that would make it difficult to use with a class? (Copy protected software cannot be copied for backups or for use with multiple students.)
- Are reviews or accounts of other instructors' experience with the software available? If so, what do they say?
- What learning objective(s) does the software claim to achieve or could it be used to achieve? Are these objectives clearly stated? How close is/are these objective(s) to the objective(s) of the course?

- Is the program instructionally sound? Are the facts and concepts in it accurate and up to date?
- Are program materials free from racial, gender, and other stereotypes?
- What instructional strategies does the program employ? Does it employ a variety of strategies? Are the strategies appropriate to the kind of material presented in the program and in the course as a whole?
- Does the program have graphics? color? video? If so, do these visual features make the program more interesting to students and/or more effective pedagogically? Does the program use sound effectively?
- What, if anything, can this program do for students and/or the instructor that existing instructional methods cannot do or cannot do as well?
- Can the program be easily integrated with other materials and activities in the course? What modifications, if any, will need to be made in existing course components to use this program effectively?
- How easy to use is the software? How much and what kind of training will students need before they can use it effectively? Can this training be given during the course? If not, where will students get it—preceding or concurrent course? weekend workshop? CAI module?
- How clear is the software's documentation (manual or other printed matter that comes with it)?
- Are there any "help" functions built into the program itself? If so, how helpful and how easy to use are they?
- What other training or background instruction (for example, in problem solving, group processes, or categorization) will students need to use the software effectively?
- How much time will students spend in using the program? Is the program's usefulness great enough to justify the amount of time spent on it rather than on other course activities? Does the program save time for students or instructor in any way?
- What does the program ask students to do? How appropriate are these activities for students' level of ability and independence and the learning objectives of the course?

- What aspects of the program can students control or change? How do they do this?
- Does the program offer sufficient chances for students to practice skills?
- Does the program provide for or encourage any interaction between the using student and other students or the instructor?
- Does the program score or evaluate student performance in any way? What feedback, if any, does it provide after students make responses to it? How helpful is this feedback? Does the program provide scoring or diagnostic information to the instructor?
- In what ways can students apply knowledge and skills gained through this program to other parts of the course? to work or life outside of the course?

*Creating Software.* Some institutions have authoring systems that let instructors create their own courseware (educational software designed for a particular course) without needing to have computer programming experience or master complex programming languages. Such systems include Comware's "KSS: Author," "The McGraw-Hill Authoring System," and "Camelot" (created by Miami-Dade Community College, under the leadership of Kamala Anandam and with the help of the League for Innovations in the Community College and Exxon support, and now available for purchase by other colleges and universities [Anandam, 1985]).

To give one example of an authoring system in use, a faculty member using "KSS: Author" to construct a "learning episode" would begin by setting course design specifications, including standard correct-answer and feedback routines, keystrokes that students will use to obtain on-line help, background and foreground color settings, and border colors. The instructor would then build text and graphics for instruction windows, using word processing, color selection, highlighting, and graphics characters. The material could be "dressed up" with lines, boxes, circles, ellipses, and any of seven type fonts. Material from other programs might also be captured for inclusion in the developing module. The instructor would specify the way windows are read to the screen, including branching where appropriate. Help and wrong-answer feedback windows would also be designed.

As noted earlier, instructors can use an authoring system effectively only if they become proficient both in operating the system and in applying principles of instructional design. They must be able to determine appropriate learning outcomes, activities that will help students achieve those outcomes, and assessment processes that will diagnose student mastery and prescribe remediation when appropriate. They must also be able to take advantage of the computer's special educational potential. For example, they could apply its potential for interactivity by creating problems or situations for which students select solutions or responses from a menu of possibilities. They could apply its potential for individualization by creating courseware that "branches" to different new problems depending on the solution a student chooses for an initial problem.

An important limiting factor to keep in mind when considering the possibility of creating software with an authoring system is time. A hundred or more hours of development time may be required to produce even a simple one-hour CAI or "teaching machine" module (Neff, 1986b). With educational software, as with any other creative computer project, programming and pilot testing frequently take longer than planned. Institutions may not be willing or able to compensate faculty members for this much time, nor may the faculty themselves be able to spare it from other tasks.

The time requirement can be eased somewhat if the work of development is spread out among a number of people, even though a single faculty developer may provide most of the creative effort. A study coordinated by the Higher Education Management Institute ("Colleges and Universities Experimenting . . . ,") indicated that the greatest factor in determining the success of an authoring project was the quality of the support network provided to the faculty developer. Such support included access to a computer, along with necessary software and peripherals; released time; and support from a task force of graphics, instructional design, programming, and other professionals at the university.

Instructors also need to keep in mind that the sort of software that can be produced with authoring systems is, at best, limited. It is most suited for short, highly focused supplements to other instruction, such as testing routines, drill and practice, or modest simulations. Instructional design is often limited by the more or less rigid templates that the systems provide. The systems' ability to add graphics and other electronic "bells and whistles" is very slight compared to what is available in the best commercial software.

Indeed, some academicians believe that authoring systems have limited value. In 1984 Alfred Bork of the University of California, Irvine stated, "The development of authoring languages . . . has been an enormous waste of large sums—perhaps billions of dollars, by now—that could have been paid instead for the development of useful learning modules. Virtually no software of educational consequence has been developed with the use of any of the authoring systems or languages" (1984a, p. 241). Bork maintained that the level of interactivity and sophistication that he saw as a minimum requirement for educationally valuable software "is one that *cannot* be undertaken by two or three faculty members, or even by a single university. Such a development is expensive, and so probably needs national support, perhaps with a consortium of universities" (1984b, p. 14).

Many educators feel that Bork's criticism is still valid, although others disagree. The latter point out that even a relatively small courseware module, such as a simple problem-solving activity or an hour-long CAI tutorial, can be educationally valuable within the context of a course—and creation of such a module need not involve a massive development effort.

Unquestionably, creation of courseware is still a task suited to only a bold and skillful few among any faculty. Such creation, however, is likely to become more common in the future as authoring systems and other software creation tools become both more sophisticated and easier to use. More integrated institutionwide planning for computer use in education (see Part Two of this book) can also encourage local creation of software by making it possible for larger intrainstitutional or even interinstitutional faculty groups to work together on development projects.

## Implementing Computer-Enriched Instruction

The job of integrating software into a course is by no means over when the software is finally chosen. It must still be implemented or put into use in a way that provides maximum educational benefits and a minimum of disruption for both instructors and students. Students, many of whom may not be experienced with computers, must be trained to use the software and helped to find the most effective ways to apply it to their work. After the work has been completed, the instructor must evaluate that work and, finally, evaluate the contribution of the computerized instruction itself. Preparation, implementation, and evaluation all raise challenging questions that require an instructor's most thoughtful attention to answer.

*Training and Preparing Students.* Training becomes a matter of primary importance whenever an instructor plans to integrate computer work into a course. Computers are becoming more common in the life of today's college students, but there are still many undergraduates who have never used a computer. To determine what training is necessary before students use a particular piece of software, an instructor must first know the students' current level of "computer literacy." How many students have or are likely to have used computers before? If they have used computers before, what kind of experience are they likely to have had? (Is an introductory course in computers or in the use of particular software required or recommended for majors in the instructor's discipline, for example?) How many are likely to own their own computers?

The complexity of the software will also affect the amount of training that is necessary. Some programs are not very "user friendly" and take quite a bit of practice to master. Complex data base programs are an example. Consultation with members of the computer science or academic computing department or with colleagues who have used particular programs or types of programs before can give an instructor an idea of the kind and degree of training that might be necessary and also, perhaps, what forms of training are available.

For many CAI programs and simple simulations, training can be accomplished in class (or wherever the computers are to be used) in a single session. Normally, such training should include both a demonstration of the software by the instructor and a chance for students to ask questions and practice using the software. Some programs come equipped with a CAI-type "tutorial" module that students can take by themselves. Complex programs may require a special weekend workshop or even a whole course, which could be made prerequisite to or be required to be taken concurrently with the course(s) in which the software will be used.

Instructors planning training sessions should keep in mind that in order to use any software effectively for learning, students must know more than which keys to press and which commands to type in. They must know *why* they are using the software—what learning objectives they are expected to accomplish with it and how its use fits in with the objectives and the content of the rest of the course. This information is unlikely to come with the software; the instructor must provide it. The instructor should also plan to point out the software's limitations, such as the oversimplification of reality inherent in a simulation. In addition, the instructor might want to suggest readings or other materials to supplement the computer activity and make up for its deficiencies.

Students may need training or review in background skills as well. For example, if they will be working in groups, their preparation might include communication exercises and discussion of group processes. If they will be using a simulation, they might need a review of problem-solving skills. If they will be using on-line data bases for information searches or "tool" software to prepare their own data bases, they might need practice in organizing information in the logical, hierarchical way that is necessary for using these kinds of software. (For example, if using on-line data bases, they might need to know the series of commands necessary to find information about a particular topic within a particular data base available through a group of data bases like Dialog or a general-purpose information retrieval service like CompuServe. If creating their own data base, they might need to discuss what kinds of data are necessary to have in each record of the data base and in what ways they might want the records sorted.)

*Integrating Computer and Noncomputer Materials.* The precise way in which computer and noncomputer materials are integrated in a course also takes careful thought. For example, after twenty years of research, Glen Fisher (1983) concluded that when CAI programs are used in class, learning is most likely to be maximal when students work at the computer for sessions of only fifteen to twenty minutes each and these sessions are interspersed with team inquiry or discussion sessions away from the computer. This breaks the monotony of working with the machine as well as providing for interpersonal exchange. Mixing computer and noncomputer materials also provides variety in instructional approaches, which increases the chance of reaching students with a variety of learning styles and backgrounds.

Whenever possible, computer and noncomputer materials should be arranged so that they support and enhance each other, each making up for the other's defects. Assignments of textbook chapters or other outside readings might be complemented by short CAI tutorial or drill-and-practice sessions, for example. Students might be given background information in a lecture and then apply that information by working with a computer simulation.

*Using Learning Teams.* John Naisbitt, author of *Megatrends* (1982), argues that in order to enhance organizational and personal effectiveness in a rapidly changing world, each technological enhancement needs to be balanced with more personal processes—what he calls "high tech, high touch" (p. 1). In the sphere of higher education, this idea is reflected in the need to balance solitary aspects of computer activity with interpersonal processes. One of the best ways to accomplish this is to have students work together on computer-related projects.

A United States Army experiment found "significantly better performance" on CAI programs for pairs of learners who used the programs together and evaluated each other, as opposed to students who used the programs alone ("Learning How to Learn...," 1984). Many higher education institutions have also found the value of larger support structures, sometimes called "learning communities," that consist of half a dozen to a dozen students. Learning communities can help students even when the students are not actually working on the same project (students working on different projects can still report to and encourage each other), but they are most effective when the projects themselves are shared. Some simulations are designed for group use, for example, as noted in Chapter Four. Groups can also work together on data base studies or projects involving telecommunications.

An instructor planning to have teams of students use the computer in a group project or support each other during individual projects should initiate new teams with a communication exercise to help them become acquainted and also to express concerns about using the computer (if they are unfamiliar with the particular computer application) before they begin working together. (For example, in a "dyadic encounter" exercise, students are divided into pairs. The members of each pair take turns completing orally such sentences as "My greatest concern about using the computer for purpose X is..." After completing a dozen or more statements of this type, students in the pair have become much more aware of each other's concerns.) Students should be brought to realize that team members will be expected to take a degree of responsibility for each other during the course. Some instructors go so far as to give each team a group grade.

Students should be encouraged to share ideas about solutions to problems or strategies for completing projects. If desired, the instructor can provide particular questions or topics for student discussion. Student pairs or teams might be told to communicate about projects by telephone or electronic mail once a week (or at some other suitable time interval) and to keep a log or journal recording any insights that occur during these communications. Team members also could periodically evaluate each other's work, perhaps in sessions where individual members present portions of projects or are given oral examinations by the rest of the team. These presentations or examinations would be followed by feedback and coaching by the other team members.

*Using Learning Agreements.* Some computer assignments benefit greatly from group interaction, while others are best done alone. "Computer learning agreements" worked out between instructor and student can provide a particularly meaningful way to enhance and evaluate learning in individual projects, though they can be used for group projects as well. The collaboration involved in drawing up such an agreement strengthens the interpersonal relationship between student and instructor and also gives the student a chance to at least partly direct, take responsibility for, and "own" his or her learning. These agreements are more appropriate for fairly long, complex, independent-study-type projects than for short assignments such as writing a simple essay or completing a CAI module.

At the heart of the computer learning agreement is a definition of the intentions or objectives of the project (see Exhibit 2). These objectives may be worked out by discussion between student and instructor, prescribed by the instructor, or a combination of both. Specifying objectives increases the chances of learning success by focusing student work, both at the computer and away from it, on a particular task or tasks. Specifying objectives also helps in writing the remaining parts of the agreement, which state how the student is expected to demonstrate accomplishment of the learning objectives (for example, by producing a written report or graphs analyzing data) and how the instructor will evaluate the accomplishment of the objectives. Particular resources and learning experiences to be involved in the project, including specific uses of the computer, may also be spelled out in the agreement. The agreement may cover an entire course, or different agreements may be used for different course assignments. A meeting to review the agreement and the success of its accomplishment at the end of the project is essential.

## Exhibit 2. Computer Learning Agreement.

Course title: _____

Title of this learning project: _____

Student's name: _____

Faculty's name: _____

Learning peers: _____

Today's date: _____ Date of completion: _____

---

LEARNING OBJECTIVES:

---

LEARNING EXPERIENCE: [clarify the learning experience with particular attention to uses of the computer and software]

---

DOCUMENTATION: [specify evidence of accomplishment of the learning outcomes for this learning agreement to be submitted]

---

EVALUATION: [clarify means by which the faculty member agrees to assess student achievement ot the learning outcomes]

---

SIGNATURES:

_____ student's name

_____ faculty member's name

*Encouraging Student Feedback.* Students should be encouraged to ask questions and offer feedback at every stage of the introduction and use of computers in a course. During training sessions they should have a chance to discuss their previous computer experience and any fears they have about using the machines or particular kinds of software. If possible, they should be allowed to sample and explore different kinds of relevant software and discuss ways in which these might be applied to their work in the course. As course work proceeds, instructors should encourage students whenever appropriate to develop independent projects and use software in original ways, and students should be rewarded for successfully doing so. At the end of the course, students might be given a questionnaire asking their opinion of particular software or computer-related assignments (did they enjoy the assignments? what, if anything, did they feel they learned from them? were the assignments too hard, too easy, or about right?). Students might also be given an opportunity to offer suggestions about possible changes to make in computer-related material when the course is given again.

Encouraging student feedback regarding computer-related activities in a course serves a number of useful purposes. It helps to relieve the tensions that are likely to arise when students deal with a technology that, to many, is quite new and perhaps threatening. Encouraging student feedback also helps students feel a part of the course, owning their participation in the teaching and learning process (see Ericksen, 1984). Finally, student feedback can help an instructor evaluate the effectiveness of computer instruction and perhaps modify it for future courses.

*Evaluating Student Work.* In many respects, evaluation of student work at the computer is no different from evaluation of student work in any other part of a course. Accurate evaluation requires specification of clear and measurable learning outcomes and precise ways in which those outcomes will be demonstrated (test scores, papers, accounts or other artifacts demonstrating completed group projects, and so on). Evaluation may consist of testing on or off the computer, critiquing of papers or other academic artifacts, and similar techniques. It must include not only measurement but also judgment about what the measurement (such as a test score) is worth in academic "currency."

Particular forms of evaluation will depend on the mode in which the computer is used and the purpose for which it is used. Many CAI programs contain, or even consist primarily of, built-in tests designed to measure mastery of factual information. If testing is not included in a CAI presentation, paper-and-pencil testing could reveal whether students remembered and understood the material presented by the program.

Simulations often include either explicit or implicit tests of problem-solving. If groups of specific problems are not presented to students by a simulation, the instructor might judge students by their success in and strategies for achieving the overall aim of the simulation (preserving wild habitat while allowing economic development, achieving maximum profit in a business, or whatever). Depending on the simulation, the instructor may need to question students to find out what strategies they used.

Investigative skills involved in using the computer as a resource might be demonstrated in the quantity of information retrieved, its relevance to the assigned topic (did the student use a "shotgun" search strategy that gathered a great deal of irrelevant information, or did the student efficiently "zero in" on the target topic?), and perhaps in the search times involved (a relatively short search time coupled with an adequate quantity of relevant information suggests an efficient search strategy). If students used computer conferencing in a project, transcripts of the conference might prove useful in evaluating the contributions of particular students. (Students should be told ahead of time if transcripts will be used in this way.)

Evaluation of use of the computer as a tool might focus on mastery of the skills necessary to use the software effectively (entering data into a spreadsheet and using the software to perform calculations, for example), the product of that use, or, preferably, both. An essay created on a word processor would probably be judged by the same criteria of coherence, logic, accurate grammar, and so on that would be used for an essay created in any other way.

Naturally, these forms of evaluation may be combined when appropriate. For example, a term paper based on gathering of data through an on-line data base and analysis of the data with a spreadsheet might be judged on the completeness and relevance of the data, the accuracy of the formulas used for the spreadsheet calculations, the logic of the analytical conclusions reached in the paper, the coherence of the paper's writing, and so on.

Bloom's taxonomy of educational objectives (1956) provides a useful way of thinking through evaluation approaches. The main categories in the taxonomy are knowledge, comprehension, application, analysis, synthesis, and evaluation. As an example, consider how the objectives of knowledge and application might be evaluated in a unit on paragraph writing in a writing course in which the computer has been used as a "teaching machine" to instruct students in principles of writing. Knowledge might be evaluated by a written test in which students are asked to identify and describe concepts such as paragraph unity and coherence. Application might be evaluated by having students use the computer as a resource to search a data base (perhaps a simple one prepared by the instructor rather than an on-line one) for pertinent data about which paragraphs might be written and then use the computer as a word processing tool to write and revise their paragraphs. Evaluation would hinge on whether students are able to find appropriate information and incorporate it into a unified, coherent paragraph.

*Evaluating and Modifying Computer-Based Instruction.* Evaluation of student achievement of learning outcomes, combined with evaluative feedback both from students and from an instructor's own observation, leads to evaluation and possible modification of computer-based instruction after it has been used in a course. This evaluation will probably have both subjective and objective elements. Particularly when using a computer application for the first time, instructors may find it helpful to keep a journal of thoughts, observations, and insights related to the application (including notes on, for example, the pace of the instruction, students' perceptions of the technology, unexpected equipment breakdowns or student confusion, and student follow-through in doing independent assignments). Information gathered for evaluative purposes should include facts and thoughts about both the course's social context and the learning context (particularly the relationships between assignments or activities that involve the computer and those that do not). At a more objective level, instructors should remember that the machines themselves often accumulate information that is useful in evaluation, such as how long each session at the machine lasted, what functions each student called up, and what sequences were followed.

Johnston (1984) suggests focusing on the following three variables when attempting to evaluate computer-based instruction: (1) The function the computer performs in taking the place of some previously used delivery mode (for example, use of the computer as a teaching machine to substitute for certain class lectures), (2) the extent to which the computer substitutes for the previously used mode (was the computer used too extensively? not extensively enough?), and (3) the relationship between the technology and other learning modes (for example, if the course seemed to lack a strong enough group process element, might this element be augmented by substitution of a group competitive simulation for a CAI module?).

The following questions may help instructors consider particular aspects of computer-based instruction that they might wish to evaluate.

- What did the students like about computer-based instruction in the course? What did they dislike? How did their feelings about the computer-based instruction compare with their feelings about other aspects of the course?
- What did I (the instructor) like about the course's computer-based instruction? What did I dislike?
- What aspects of the computer-based instruction, if any, did students have difficulty in understanding or using? Were there any assignments they seemed to find too easy?
- What difficulties, if any, did I encounter in implementing the instruction or helping students use it?

- What technological breakdowns (equipment or software failure), if any, were encountered?
- Did students master learning outcomes more effectively using computer-based instruction than previous students had done with whatever technique or medium (lecture, textbook, or the like) that the computer-based instruction replaced (did they achieve higher scores on a final test or produce more coherent term papers, for example)?
- Did students master learning outcomes more easily using computer-based instruction than previous students had done without it?
- Did students master learning outcomes more quickly using computer-based instruction than previous students had done without it?
- To what extent was computer-based instruction useful in saving my teaching time?
- Was computer-based instruction particularly effective or ineffective in helping students develop certain skills? If so, which ones?
- Was computer-based instruction particularly effective or ineffective in presenting certain kinds of material or concepts? If so, which ones?
- Was computer-based instruction particularly effective or ineffective for certain kinds of students? If so, which ones?
- Did the balance of learning modalities (computer-based work, lectures, in-class group work, independent projects, and so on) seem right? If not, what was wrong with it? What modalities should be emphasized more? less?

All these questions boil down to the crucial ones behind evaluation of any form of instruction or, for that matter, any activity with a purpose: "What worked? What didn't work? Why? And what should I do differently in the future?"

### Acquiring and Implementing Educational Software: Three Examples

*Feature Writing.* Feature Writing was a course taught in a small liberal arts college by the editor of a nearby small city newspaper. The editor noted that all writers at the newspaper worked at computer terminals, whereas most students in the course produced their required eight articles (three to seven pages each) by the traditional means of handwriting and typewriter. He wondered whether word processing software might help the students produce more carefully edited work, containing fewer typographical and grammatical errors, and also whether such software could help them produce their work faster. In addition, he thought that being able to correct papers on a computer terminal rather than by hand might save him time.

Unfortunately, there was no computer writing lab on campus large enough to accommodate the editor's whole class. He thus decided to encourage computer use by class members as an option rather than a requirement. If computer use made enough difference to the students who tried it, he would lobby for a computerized writing lab that could be available for all his students.

A brief class discussion revealed that about two-thirds of the course's students had access to a computer in some way. Some owned a computer; others lived with parents or someone else who owned one; still others had access to a computer somewhere on campus or at their workplace. It was not necessary that all students use the same word processing package, so they were able to use whatever they had access to.

All students completed the same assignments, whether they chose to use a computer or not. The editor asked all students to keep track of the amount of time they spent doing their assignments. This information, recorded on a tally sheet, was turned in at the end of the course, after grades were assigned.

The editor had a Macintosh, so he asked those students who also used Macintoshes to turn in their assignments on disk. These assignments he marked with the help of an inexpensive editing package, "Prose Instructor," which allowed him to enter remarks and suggestions for revision in pop-up windows. Students using other computers, as well as students using traditional techniques, turned in print copies of their work. As a comparison test, the editor marked the traditional papers by hand and edited the computer-generated ones by writing his comments on the computer. Based on timing for one week's assignment, he determined how many minutes per page he spent in editing with each of these three techniques. He also checked the difference in number of misspellings and grammatical errors between the computer and traditional student groups.

The results of his study convinced the editor of the value of word processing for his students. As a result, he met with the dean of the college to discuss the possibility of a larger computer writing lab.

*Political Science.* This was a freshman-level course taught by a graduate student at a large state university. The course included weekly quizzes and two major tests, all of which checked primarily for mastery of factual information. In addition, students had to prepare a research paper three to five pages long.

The university was uniformly computerized, so all students had access to computers and knew how to use them for word processing. Most, however, were less familiar with use of the computer as a resource. The instructor thought that having the students use computer-accessed data bases in preparing their research papers might help to fill this gap. Because computing was managed centrally on this campus, the instructor consulted with the academic computing office to schedule the necessary use of the computer lab.

To prepare the students for the research process, the instructor devoted a class meeting to the writing of term papers about issues and problems in political science. The meeting concluded with a talk by the Learning Resources Center director, describing how the center's staff would help the students use on-line data bases. Cost of the on-line research was paid by the center. The center used the data base system Knowledge Index to give students access to two government publication data bases, GPO Publication Reference and NTIS.

The instructor evaluated the course's new computer-based component by monitoring the extent of use of the on-line data bases and by comparing the amount of documentation in student papers to the amount in those typically produced by previous students in the course.

*Human Service Technician Case Studies.* This was an advanced course offered by a community college. The course was taught by a full-time faculty member who had been teaching it for seven years in standard lecture format. He felt that this format already presented information quite successfully, so he had little interest in the computer as teaching machine. However, he did want to find ways to increase the degree to which students related the principles they were learning to the kind of decisions they would make as human service workers. He also wanted to make sure that all students graduating from the department had some familiarity with computers. At that time, he estimated that 20 percent of the students used computers regularly, an additional 60 percent were computer literate, and the remaining 20 percent were not familiar with computers.

After reading about various kinds of software, the instructor became interested in decision-making programs. He looked at reviews of several decision support programs in computer magazines and, on the basis of these reviews, chose a software package called "Lightyear." He contacted the company that made this program and was sent a sample disk. He found the program easy to learn and applicable to the skills he wanted his students to develop. He also learned that, thanks to a special price offered to educational users, he would be able to obtain enough copies for his students to use in the college's computer laboratory.

The instructor introduced the software in the course's first meeting. He also gave students an information sheet that listed the computer lab's hours, instructions for booting up and using the program, and a dozen hints for "trouble shooting" if problems arose. During the class session the instructor demonstrated the program, working through a model case so the students could see how "decision modeling" applied to work in human services, both in making decisions and in improving ability to document and justify those decisions. To minimize the frustration of students who were not familiar with computers, the instructor assigned students to work in pairs and made sure that at least one student in each pair was computer literate.

All students were able to load and run the program on

their own by the end of the course. In both oral and written case reports, students proved more facile at developing coherent and effective rationales for their solution of case problems than previous students had been. Some students supported their decisions in written reports with graphs generated by the decision-making program.

Instructor and students are, of course, at the heart of the teaching and learning process, whether computers are involved or not. It is the decisions of instructors and the reactions of students that ultimately determine the success or failure of computerized learning. Nonetheless, these decisions and reactions take place in a larger context—that of the higher education institution as a whole—and that context also has important effects.

The second part of this book will concern itself with the institutional context in which computers are introduced and used in teaching and learning. Chapter Eight describes how higher education institutions can go from a vision to an organized action plan for the introduction of academic computing. Chapter Nine deals with creation of an appropriate support environment, and Chapter Ten describes organizational patterns that aid development of institutionwide academic computer use.

# 8

⊡⊡⊡⊡⊡⊡⊡⊡⊡⊡⊡⊡⊡⊡⊡⊡

# Planning an Institutionwide Computer Environment

All meaningful action begins in vision. Before an institution of higher education can organize an effective program for introducing and using computers in teaching and learning, it must formulate a coherent vision of the way computers will fit into the educational scheme of the institution as a whole. This chapter will suggest some ways in which an institution's leaders can clarify this institutional vision, gain support for the vision, and then turn the vision into a concrete plan of action.

### Clarifying the Vision: Use and Needs Assessments

In the area of academic computing, as in other areas, most institutions of higher education have many "visionaries." One may be a creative department chair who is committed to enhancing teaching with computers. One may be a farsighted faculty member who wants to see students use the computer to advance learning goals. One may be an administrative leader who articulates a vision for a whole campus or multicampus system.

All these visions are important, and all should be taken into account in the formulation of the vision for the institution as a whole. The more sources are consulted, the wider the range of creative ideas that will be available for consideration in preparing the final plan. Furthermore, the involvement and commitment of all of an institution's constituencies is essential if any institutionwide plan is to succeed.

Institutionwide use and needs assessments are often the best way to reveal and grasp the implications of these many visions. These questionnaires might be administered to faculty members by the instructional computing center, the staff development office, or the institution's various academic departments and divisions. Ultimately a unified report should be prepared from the resulting tabulated data.

The use assessment is designed to reveal what instructors are currently doing with computers. It presents a picture of the institution's present state of development in the area of academic computing. A sample use assessment is shown in Exhibit 3.

## Exhibit 3. Use Assessment for Computers in Instruction.

Dear Faculty Member:

Please complete one form for each course in which you use the computer in some way in instruction. The results will help in understanding the current state of academic computer use institutionwide and in planning for future development.

Your name:_____

Course title: _____

Date course initiated: _____    Today's date: _____

Did you develop the computer application? _____ yes _____ no

      (If no, who was the developer, or what are the name and manufacturer of the commercial product? _____ )

This is a _____ credit or a _____ noncredit course (check one).

Credit hours:_____ Lab hours (if any): _____

No. sections you instruct per term (fall, winter, spring, summer)

      _____ F, _____ W, _____ S, _____ S

Number of students enrolled per term: _____F, _____W, _____ S, _____ S

How many hours during the week, on average, do students use the computer in this course:  _____ average number of hours

      during the term: _____

**Exhibit 3. Use Assessment for Computers in Instruction, Cont'd.**

PLEASE RESPOND TO EACH OF THE FOLLOWING QUESTIONS BY
PLACING AN *X* IN THE APPROPRIATE SPACE OR SPACES NEXT TO
THE STATEMENT THAT BEST DESCRIBES THE USE(S) OF THE
COMPUTER IN YOUR COURSE.

1.  Which of the following best describes the design of this course?
    a.  _____   The course helps students learn *about* computers. (If
        you checked *a,* check the following as appropriate.)
                _____   computer languages
                _____   computer hardware
                    _____   mainframes, minicomputers
                    _____   personal computers
                _____   software
    b.  _____   The course helps students learn *with* computers
        (that is, students use computers as aids in learning about aca-
        demic subjects not related to computers).
2.  Which of the following best describe(s) the way(s) in which you ask
    students to use computers in the course (check more than one if ap-
    appropriate)?
            _____   I require or recommend that homework assignments be
                completed on the computer.
                estimated time spent at computer per week: _____
            _____   I require or recommend that selected out-of-class proj-
                ects be completed on computer.
                estimated time spent at computer per week: _____
            _____   I assign computer lab time or use computers in class as
                part of instruction, over and above scheduled contact
                hours for this course.
                estimated time spent at computer per week: _____
            _____   I assign computer lab time or use computers in class as
                part of instruction, as a part of scheduled contact hours
                for this course.
                estimated time spent at computer per week: _____
            _____   I require or recommend use of the computer as part of
                negotiated assignments in an independent study course.
                estimated time spent at computer per week: _____
            _____   I use the computer as the sole means of delivery of this
                course to students on campus.
                estimated time spent at computer per week: _____
            _____   I use the computer as the sole means of delivery of this
                course to students who receive it via communications de-
                vice.
                    _____   at home or _____ at work
                estimated time spent at computer per week: _____

*(continued on next page)*

## Exhibit 3. Use Assessment for Computers in Instruction, Cont'd.

3.  Which of the following describe(s) the purpose(s) for which you use
    the computer in this course (check more than one if appropriate)?

    _____  as a teaching machine (some form of computer-aided in-
             struction, such as tutorials or drill and practice)

    _____  as a simulator (a model or game that allows students to
             make decisions that affect the model and observe result-
             ing changes)

    _____  as a resource (an entrance to a communication network
             that connects students with other students, faculty, or
             data bases)

    _____  as a tool (word processing, spreadsheet, data base, or
             other software that helps students do particular tasks
             such as writing or calculation)

    _____  other (please describe briefly): _____

4.  a.  If you use commercial software, indicate the nature of agree-
        ment with producer:

        _____  site license              _____  lease

        _____  networking provi-         _____  multiple copies
                 sion                               provided

        _____  have right to repro-      _____  copy protection
                 duce

    b.  If you use noncommercial software produced by others, please
        briefly describe use arrangement: _____

5.  Which of the following best describes the hardware used by students
    enrolling in this course?

    _____  Students use their own computers or computers avail-
             able to them from noninstitutional sources.

    _____  Students use institution's computers.

             _____  personal computers
                      number available to students: _____
                      make[s] of computer: _____
                      operating system or "family" (IBM, Macin-
                         tosh, or the like): _____
                      ____ departmentally or ____ centrally
                                                  controlled
                      used in a ____ computer lab, ____ library,
                         ____ classroom, ____ learning resources
                         center, ____ other (please specify):
                         _____

             _____  terminals connected to large (host) comput-
                      ers

             _____  workstations (personal computers connected
                      to host computers)

             _____  local area network _____ institutional net-
                                                  work

## Exhibit 3. Use Assessment for Computers in Instruction, Cont'd.

6.  What sources of funds covered software and hardware costs of modifying your course?
    _____  institutional funds
    _____  departmental funds
    _____  grants
    _____  other (please specify): _____

7.  What procedure(s) is/are used to prepare and train students to use the computer in this course?
    _____  none
    _____  prerequisite course required
    _____  self-study materials for students
    _____  in-class instruction
    _____  a technician trains students
    _____  other (please specify): _____

8.  What resources or assistance helped you develop or implement computer applications in your course?
    _____  released time for development
             credit hours released: _____ no. of terms: _____
    _____  extra payment for development
             overload pay: $ _____ no. of terms: _____
             stipend: $ _____
    _____  computer technician support
    _____  recognition for tenure or promotion
    _____  departmental or institutional funds for hardware or software purchases (please specify): _____
    _____

             other (please specify): _____
    _____

9.  What problems (if any) have you had in using computers as part of course instruction? What concerns do you have about academic computer use?

10. Do you feel that computers have been effective in helping to achieve the learning objectives of this course? Please explain.

Thank you for your time. We will share the results of this survey with you.

The needs assessment, in contrast to the use assessment, is aimed at the future. It is designed to unearth faculty visions for the use of computers in instruction and also to determine what kinds of help they would like to have in carrying out their visions. It also allows instructors to describe the approach they think the institution as a whole should take toward the development of academic computing. A sample needs assessment is shown in Exhibit 4.

**Exhibit 4. Needs Assessment for Computers in Instruction.**

Dear Faculty Member:

Please complete this form to describe your interests and needs related to the use of computers in instruction. The results will help in preparing an institutionwide plan for development of academic computing.

Your name: _____
Titles of courses you teach: _____
_____
_____

1.  Please check one choice for each item.
    a.  I ____ do ____ do not use computers in my courses at present.
    b.  I ____ would ____ would not like to use computers in instruction more than I do now.
2.  In the first column, please check those learning activities in which you do not presently use computers but might do so in the future. In the second column, indicate those activities about which you would like information concerning possible computer enhancement.

|  | might use computers to enhance | like info. about how computer can enhance |
|---|---|---|
| lectures | ____ | ____ |
| demonstrations | ____ | ____ |
| reading assignments | ____ | ____ |
| drill and practice, testing | ____ | ____ |
| laboratory experiments and analysis | ____ | ____ |
| simulations, role playing | ____ | ____ |
| out-of-class group projects | ____ | ____ |
| essays, term papers, reports | ____ | ____ |
| independent study projects | ____ | ____ |

Exhibit 4. Needs Assessment for Computers in Instruction,
Cont'd.

|  | might use computers to enhance | like info. about how computer can enhance |
|---|---|---|
| other (please specify) | _____ | _____ |

_____
_____
_____

3. Please check each of the following types of software (computer programs) about which you would like more information.
  _____ computer-assisted instruction (CAI) tutorial programs to teach facts and simple concepts
  _____ CAI programs to provide drill and practice
  _____ simulations and role-playing exercises
  _____ data bases accessed by computer
  _____ communications networks accessed by computer
  _____ spreadsheets, statistical packages, and other programs for computational analysis
  _____ programs that help students prepare graphs, charts, or drawings
  _____ word processing programs
  _____ programs that help students prepare their own data bases
  _____ programs that help students organize ideas for analysis or writing
  _____ other (please specify) _____

4. Please check each of the following forms of assistance in developing uses of computers in teaching and learning that you would like to receive.
  _____ follow-up visit from a resource person from the Computer Center, Learning Resource Center, or library
  _____ training in use of hardware or software
  _____ demonstration of software
  _____ demonstration of hardware
  _____ talk with other faculty members who have used computers in instruction
  _____ seminar or workshop on uses of computers in instruction
  _____ ongoing group devoted to discussion of uses of computers in instruction
  _____ other (please specify) _____

*(continued on next page)*

**Exhibit 4. Needs Assessment for Computers in Instruction, Cont'd.**

5. Please check each of the following that you would like to see this institution do as part of developing an institutionwide program of academic computing.

_____ purchase more hardware (computers and related devices)

_____ purchase more software (programs)

_____ provide financial support for increased access to commercial data bases

_____ give faculty more training in use of computers and software

_____ offer more advice and technical support to faculty who use computers in teaching and learning

_____ give faculty more training in development of custom software and time to develop such software

_____ offer more courses in which students are trained in the use of computers and software

_____ offer more courses in which students use computers to learn about noncomputer subject matter

_____ increase participation in intrainstitutional or interinstitutional communications networks

_____ set up a department to organize and direct uses of computers in instruction

_____ other (please specify) _____

6. Please describe briefly your personal vision of the role and uses of computers in teaching and learning.



7. Please describe briefly what you think should be this institution's overall vision of computers in teaching and learning.



    The results of the use and needs assessments can be used in many ways. For example, the results of the use assessment can be used to improve academic advising, helping counselors to direct students to appropriate instructional opportunities incorporating the computer. Marketing and recruitment programs can more effectively attract potential students by informing them of the diversity of opportunities for using the computer in the institution's curriculum.

The needs assessment can be used to plan faculty development programs centered on the uses of computers in teaching. Ongoing faculty experiments with computers could be featured during such forums. Questionnaire results could also be used as springboards for discussion in meetings of faculty within departments, divisions, disciplines, or colleges of a university. Discussion of the survey results by committees whose membership is designed to cut across departmental "turfs" could be fruitful as well, working toward some systematic application of the computer across the institutional curriculum. Finally, results of the needs assessment could be used in planning development or improvement of support staff and systems (see Chapter Nine) for faculty using computers.

Most importantly, as previously noted, the results of the use and needs assessments can be used in preparing a unified picture of where an institution is and where its members would like to see it go in the area of academic computing. The vision should describe the basic educational goals that the institution would like to see computers help to achieve and some of the specific ways in which computers could be used to achieve those goals.

Unfortunately, many institutions do not make use and needs assessments or prepare unified visions before setting sail on the uncharted seas of academic computing. One report (Bender and Conrad, 1984) noted that many small community colleges "are introducing microcomputing to their campus[es] without any systematic development plan and frequently without any meaningful needs assessment to support planning or decision making. Many of the colleges in this group seem to be following a laissez-faire approach whereby an individual administrator or faculty member will translate his or her interest and enthusiasm in microcomputing into a new voluntary undertaking with the college" (p. 32). Larger institutions, too, often follow this uncoordinated, "patchwork" pattern. The results all too frequently include waste of money and other resources, confusion and dissension within or between departments or between faculty and administration, unnecessary duplication, incompatibility of hardware and software, and a host of other problems.

## Spreading the Vision: The "Star Wars" Lessons

Carnegie-Mellon, Brown University, and M.I.T. have been called the "Star Wars" institutions because of their heavy emphasis on the use of computers in instruction and research. Unquestionably these large institutions have more resources to devote to the development of academic computing than do most other colleges and universities. (For example, Turner (1986c) reported that Eastern Oregon State College, with 1,700 students, had a computing budget of $100,000 in 1986, while Carnegie-Mellon, with 6,000 students, had a computing budget of over $31 million.) Nonetheless, smaller institutions can learn valuable lessons from the ways in which these "superpowers" developed and committed themselves to a unified vision of computer use in teaching and learning and then spread their vision to the surrounding community in order to gain outside support.

As an example, the story at Carnegie-Mellon began with President Richard Cyert, who asserted in 1981, "I have personally committed myself to a major expansion of the role of computing at CMU" (*Preliminary Report...*, 1982, p. 15). Acting on this assertion, Cyert appointed a task force to study the future of computing at the university. The task force was made responsible to Richard L. Van Horn, then Carnegie-Mellon's provost. (Van Horn later became chancellor of the University of Houston, where he achieved national prominence for his institution and took his place alongside Cyert as a leading advocate of academic computing.)

In its preliminary report, delivered in 1982, the task force stated, "Computing will continue to increase substantially, with or without comprehensive planning. Both growth of computation in the external world and the already deep involvement of the university drive CMU along this path. The important issues are then how to seize the moment to make a dramatic move to accelerate the increase in computational facility to attain some worthwhile goals. . . . We take the position that a substantial increase in computing at CMU is fundamentally good" (p. 7).

Richard Van Horn later told how CMU then shared its vision, which depended on both hardware and software expansion, with major figures in the computer industry in the hope of finding a "partner" that would help the university realize that vision. "Armed with a written proposal, a small group consisting of President Cyert, who is an enthusiastic advocate, myself, and, later, newly hired vice provost for computing, Douglas van Houweling, personally presented the ideas to the top management of the companies. We asked for (a) funding for a software development center, (b) equipment and/or financial support to implement an advanced prototype environment at CMU, and (c) a commitment for a complementary development effort inside the company. Our proposal argued that the system and environment we described [networked personal computing] was the dominant model for the future of computing, not only for universities, but for most organizations. . . . Our proposals were received with great interest and strong reservations. Companies clearly were fascinated by the idea but expressed the obvious concerns" (Tucker, 1983–84, p. 9).

The concerns expressed by the companies related to CMU's vision of networked personal computing as the "dominant model for the future." The CMU committee was able to convince them of the validity of this vision, however. The committee also showed the companies how useful CMU's outstanding computer science department and computerized environment could be to them in joint development efforts. CMU's attempts to enroll outside support for its computerization program ultimately paid off in a lucrative contract with IBM.

Most private liberal arts colleges, public community colleges, and state universities will not be as well funded as CMU— nor do they need to be in order to develop a significant academic program, thanks to falling prices for both hardware and software. Nonetheless, Van Horn emphasizes, seeking outside funding or other aid for computer-related projects is worth a try for an institution of any size. For example, a public community college in a small urban area might seek collaboration with local computer manufacturing firms (who might support hardware acquisitions because of the training needs of their employees) or local computer store chains (who would benefit by equipment purchase and might therefore cooperate with the college to provide instruction and technical support for faculty members). Grants from foundations and other funding sources should also be considered.

One small college that has carried out these ideas is Clark Technical College, a small public two-year college in Springfield, Ohio. Its fund-seeking efforts resulted in gifts of hardware and software from several companies. NCR Corporation provided five days of training and four personal computers to four faculty members who agreed to integrate computers into the curriculum at Clark. In addition, the career-oriented programs of this college provided an inducement for software manufacturers to provide their products in exchange for the college's serving as a demonstration site for the software. Software obtained in this way included Auto CAD software for Clark's automotive program, software from the Society for Manufacturing Engineers, and software for use in Clark's agricultural program.

Richard Van Horn suggests that institutions do the following when sharing their vision with potential community partners:

1.  *Build on strength.* Express clearly the strengths of the institution, whether they be programs, faculty, or unique contributions that the institution can make or has made in particular sectors.
2.  *Offer a fair exchange.* Point out reasons why support of the institution's programs will further the interests of the potential partner.
3.  *Have a small, clearly defined set of goals.* Determine specifically what the institution wants and what it is prepared to do for the partner to achieve those goals (Tucker, 1983-84, p. 10).

## Actualizing the Vision: The Action Plan

A clear, unified, exciting vision of an institution's future computer use can capture the imagination of constituencies both inside and outside the institution. Nonetheless, vision is only the beginning. In order to become a reality, the vision must be translated into a concrete, specific action plan.

Since many institutions fail to develop a coherent vision of their future approach to academic computing, it is not surprising that many also fail to develop a coherent institutionwide action plan before they begin purchasing computer hardware and software. Ernest Boyer noted in 1984 that "purchases frequently have preceded planning" (p. 82). Similarly, James C. Emery asserted, "it is better to plan for change than to simply muddle through. . . . [Yet] relatively few institutions have made a serious effort to develop a strategic plan for dealing with problems and opportunities presented by new technology" (1984, p. 4). As noted earlier, failure to develop such a plan usually results in expensive and frustrating chaos.

In moving from vision to action plan, academic leaders should come to grips with each of the following issues:

- the relationship of the institution's vision for the use of computers in instruction to the institution's underlying educational mission and goals
- the environment surrounding the institution (political, economic, social, cultural, educational, competitive) and ways in which that environment is likely to affect the institution's plans for computer use
- the constituencies who will be served by the institution's academic computer use and how computer use can help each of them
- the percentage of students and faculty who are expected to use computers
- the ratio of available computers (including both those owned by the institution and those owned by students and faculty members) to the number of students and faculty members

- the extent of computer integration into the curriculum (in which courses, to what extent, and for what purposes)
- the mode(s) of computer delivery, the intellectual skills, and the teaching styles (see Chapter Two) that the institution and its individual departments wish to emphasize
- the location(s) in which computer use will take place, such as classroom, computer lab, library, or in students' rooms
- possible sources of funding, both within and outside the institution, that can be drawn on to help the institution carry out its plan
- constraints that may retard the institution's development of computer use (limits of time, money, attitude, and so on)
- time lines that should be adhered to in following the action plan (Emery, 1984, notes that such a plan usually takes several years to carry out)
- administrators and faculty leaders who should participate in development and execution of the action plan
- long-term future plans for computer use: five years, ten years, twenty years away.

*Goals.* A plan for using computers in instruction should set forth clear, concise goals in such areas as educational leadership, program development, campus outreach, service, research, and student benefits (Hofstetter, 1980 and 1981). For example, the Rochester Institute of Technology in New York established the following goals for integrating computers into its instructional program in 1982. Rochester's goals, with their precise time lines and specifications, present a model that other institutions might do well to emulate.

1.  Within three years all students receiving an R.I.T. degree will demonstrate fundamental computer literacy.
2.  Within five years every graduating student will demonstrate a level of computer skills appropriate to the current state of computing in his or her field.
3.  Within two years a substantial majority of the full-time faculty in each program will possess a level of basic computer literacy at least equivalent to that specified for students.

4. Within three years every program will have a necessary number of faculty with sufficient expertise to offer instruction in computer applications appropriate to that field.
5. Within five years every program will have courses or segments of instruction that specifically represent computer applications appropriate for that field.
6. Within two years computer systems will be used to support instructional processes such as testing, grading, and word processing.
7. Within five years R.I.T. will achieve recognition as a national center for the use of computer graphics in instruction, consulting, and research [Plummer and others, 1985, p. 242].

*Budgets, Purchase Considerations, and Intellectual Property Rights.* As the administration of any higher education institution knows, institutionwide computerization is anything but cheap. Just before his retirement, Notre Dame President Theodore M. Hesburgh noted, "Now on my desk is a task force report calling for an upgrading of computer services on campus. It will cost $26.6 million up front, with a $9.7 million additional outlay. When I took over the presidency thirty-five years ago, the whole annual operating budget was $9.7 million" (Hesburgh, 1987, p. V-3). Raymond Neff (1986b) has estimated that the University of California, Berkeley, will spend $300 million on computing between 1985 and 1995.

Furthermore, as Diether H. Haenicke, president of Western Michigan University, has commented, "Computerization came at the worst possible time for universities" ("In Brief: Computers," 1986, p. 28). The need for new expenditures to update academic technology, he points out, exacerbated financial stresses caused by reduced federal support and declining student enrollments. As a result, Haenicke suggests, "The investment in computer technology is overwhelming the financial capability of many an institution" (p. 28).

The pressure to spend large amounts of money on computer technology is often increased by unrealistic hopes and expectations. J. A. Turner notes, "Many small and medium-sized

colleges and universities are scrambling to find money to provide computing resources on their campuses, while casting envious eyes at institutions that have received massive cash grants
and donations of sophisticated equipment. Some observers suggest that publicity about the advances by a few well-known
institutions—Brown University, Carnegie-Mellon University, and
the Massachusetts Institute of Technology, for example—has led
some colleges to aim for levels of computing that are out of line
with both their missions and their budgets" (1986c, p. 1).

Rather than getting stars in their eyes because of the
"Star Wars" campuses' success, smaller institutions would do
better to determine their niche—their unique contribution and
historical mission in serving students—and evolve a computer
strategy that is appropriate to that niche. Even institutions with
a relatively small computer budget can mount a program that is
beneficial financially as well as educationally, as was shown by
Southwestern College, a community college in California. Sher-
rill Amador, a dean at Southwestern, stated that her institution's intention was to provide "viable computer-related instruction" that would result in enough new student enrollments and
tuition income to offset the initial purchase costs for computer
resources (1984). In its first year of using computers in instruction, the college spent $150,000 for hardware, and in the sec-
ond year it spent $250,000. But Amador reports, "The entire
$150,000 spent on the configuration was recovered at the end
of the first year by a 46 percent increase in weekly student contact hours [a measure of student enrollment at the college] in
that particular discipline [business/data processing, in which
most of the computers were used]" (p. 20). In the second year,
too, new revenues completely offset the year's capital expenditures for computer equipment. To be sure, expenditure on computer equipment is by no means guaranteed to increase enrollment—let alone increase it enough to completely offset the
computer investment—but Southwestern's experience shows
that such an approach *can* work.

In 1986 the average computing budget for all colleges and
universities was 3 percent of total operating expenses (Turner,
1986f). James Emery (1984) suggested that the computing bud-

get be divided roughly as follows (with hardware shown as a capital expenditure, its total cost being spread over the useful life of the equipment):

| hardware | 20 percent |
|---|---|
| software | 20 percent |
| communications | 10 percent |
| technical support | 40 percent |
| maintenance/supplies | 10 percent |
| | 100 percent |

The high proportion of the computing budget earmarked for support is particularly worth noting. Emery pointed out that many institutions budget too little for this aspect of their computing needs, focusing excessively instead on hardware costs. As he noted, once an academic computing program begins, "demand for a wide variety of software and support services will grow explosively; like a newborn babe, it is not the initial cost but the upkeep that counts" (p. 11).

Decisions about purchasing particular types of hardware and software should be based on local circumstances and the teaching and learning outcomes that the computers and software are intended to achieve. Ideally, purchase decisions, particularly those involving software, should be made in consultation with the faculty members in whose courses the software will be used, or at least after considering faculty input as expressed in the needs assessment.

Bender and Conrad (1984) offered some good general advice about making hardware and software purchases: "Don't purchase unless you know what's needed. Seek technical assistance but avoid depending too much upon vendor sales staff, for they naturally have a self-interest involved. Have a competent head of computing and a computer-advising committee. . . . Plan ahead and establish policies" (p. 33). Vendors should be evaluated in terms of both price and support. Discount houses or mail order vendors often sell hardware and software for considerably less than the list price. However, they may not be very willing to offer advice about the comparative merits of different products or to answer questions about the use of products after the products are purchased. Software manufacturers usually will answer questions about their products, but sometimes they charge a fee for this "technical support."

Administrators may find the general evaluation criteria presented in Chapter Seven (and perhaps the more specific criteria for different types of software presented in Chapters Three through Six) useful when purchasing software. The following checklist suggests some relevant questions to ask about potential hardware purchases:

- Will the product work with a wide range of software, including the software needed for particular courses or educational aims?
- Is the product's performance good? (Performance criteria may include the following:
  computer—speed, memory size
  printer—speed, type [dot matrix, laser, daisy wheel], quality of output
  monitor—resolution, color capability
  modems—speed of transmission)
- What is the reputation of the product's manufacturer?
- What is the reputation of the local distributor (store from which purchase might be made) for service and follow-up support?
- Is the product easy for novices to learn to use?
- Is the product's documentation (instructions and other accompanying written material) clear and adequate in detail?
- Is the product sturdy and difficult to break?
- If a computer, can the product be expanded or added to? Is it likely to be able to run software of interest to the institution that will be developed in the next five years?
- Is the brand of the product widely accepted in business or other parts of the general society?

Unfortunately, a solution to limited budgets for purchase of software that is practiced by faculty members at some institutions is piracy. Victor Rosenberg, president of a software publishing business, complains, "It's incredible. These are people who are full professors and wouldn't think of shoplifting a pair of socks, and they are stealing tens of thousands of dollars worth of software" (DeLoughry, 1987, p. 31).

Kenneth A. Wasch, executive director of the Software Publishers Association, says piracy is a bigger problem in higher education than in, say, the business community because copyright laws often are not enforced on campus. "It's almost as if they were looking the other way. . . . University administrators do not want to look at this problem" (DeLoughry, 1987, pp. 31-32).

This situation may be changing, however. In the spring of 1987, EDUCOM and ADAPSO released a statement that opposed software piracy as a violation of both legal and intellectual property rights. The organizations urged colleges and universities to adopt the statement as a component of their rules for students and faculty. The statement reads, in part:

1. Unauthorized copying of software is illegal. Copyright law protects software authors and publishers, just as patent law protects inventors.
2. Unauthorized copying of software by individuals can harm the entire academic community. If unauthorized copying proliferates on campus, the institution may incur a legal liability. . . .
3. Unauthorized copying of software can deprive developers of a fair return for their work, increase prices, reduce the level of future support, and inhibit the development of new software products.

Respect for the intellectual work and property of others has traditionally been essential to the mission of colleges and universities. As members of the academic community, we value the free exchange of ideas. Just as we do not tolerate plagiarism, we do not condone the unauthorized copying of software, including programs, applications, data bases, and codes [Turner, 1987b, p. 18].

*Action Planning Guidelines.* The following outline is intended to guide educational administrators in preparing an action plan for development of an institutionwide program for teaching and learning with computers. Many points referred to in this outline are discussed further in Chapters Nine and Ten.

I.  Physical facilities
    A.  Determine appropriate location of computer facilities (central computer laboratory; decentralized laboratories in departments, divisions, or colleges of universities; facilities shared through a network; library or learning resource center; combined decentralized facilities).
    B.  If computers will be used in more than one place, establish appropriate physical and administrative relationships among locations.
    C.  If facilities will be joined by a network, determine how the network will be coordinated.
    D.  Determine approximate quantities and types of hardware (computers and peripheral devices, including hardware for a network if one is planned) and software that will be needed.
II. Organizational factors (see Chapter Ten)
    A.  Specify administrative personnel responsible for decisions about computer use in instruction.
    B.  Clarify offices, positions, and reporting relationships of persons responsible for decisions about computer use in instruction.
    C.  Clarify organizational relationships between these people and other relevant parts of the institution's administration (computer center, library or learning resource center, computer science department, deans, chief academic affairs officer).
    D.  Distinguish between staff and line authority in relationships among administrators responsible for computer use in instruction.

E.  Specify degree of centralization appropriate for decision making regarding computer use in instruction.

F.  Specify locus of control for academic computing program (computer center or computer science department, academic computing department, library or learning center, individual departments, or other).

G.  Specify who will be responsible for overseeing provision of technical support.

H.  Clarify organizational authority for hardware and software purchases.

I.  Specify level at which actual decisions about hardware and software purchases will be made (central staff office, college or division level, department level).

J.  Specify level at which academic policies regarding computer use in instruction will be set.

K.  Specify structure of interinstitutional committee(s), if any, to advise the institution on the development of plans for computers in instruction.

III.  Support network (see Chapter Nine)

A.  Choose faculty members (perhaps one from each department) to serve as liaison or representatives to institutionwide planning and review committees.

B.  Prepare staff development or training programs focused on teaching and learning with computers (courses, workshops, lectures, travel stipends to view programs at other institutions, and so on).

C.  Establish a clearinghouse or resource center for the demonstration of software and hardware, display of model faculty applications, and collection of literature on teaching and learning with computers and related technology.

D.  Specify types and sources of technical support (full-time professionals, part-time student assistants, outside consultants, and so on).

E.  Specify sources of support staff to assist departments in developing plans and budgets for employing the computer in their instructional offerings.

F. Specify procedures by which faculty may apply for minigrants for development of educational software or pilot projects involving the computer (release time, compensation, and so on).

G. Clarify faculty rewards for development of excellent teaching and learning activities involving computers.

H. Work out a process for formation of a users' group in which faculty, staff, and students can share and extend their knowledge of hardware, software, and pedagogical approaches that use computers.

IV. Budgetary factors

A. Clarify mechanisms for funding computer facilities and hardware and software purchases (tuition income, grants from private and public sources, gifts and donations, other sources).

B. Decide who (institution as a whole, departments, students) will pay for various aspects of academic computer use (hardware, software, searches of commercial data bases, use of communication networks, and so on).

C. Specify the process of internal accounting for computer-related purchases (charges levied against departmental budgets, charges levied against central accounts, special grants or funded projects, and so on).

D. Specify mechanism for determining percentage of institutional or individual budgets (college, departmental, and so on) that should be devoted to computer-related purchases and how those funds should be allocated.

E. Adopt EDUCOM's statement about software piracy and intellectual rights and disseminate it widely among staff and students.

The major consideration to be kept in mind during the formation and carrying out of an action plan for development of academic computing is flexibility. Flexibility is essential, first, for helping an institution adapt to rapid changes in hardware and software technology. Flexibility is also essential for allowing computers to be used in all the different ways required to meet the educational needs of diverse departments, faculty members, and courses. An institutionwide plan for academic computing is necessary in order to avoid "patchwork" chaos, yet within that plan there must be room for considerable school, division, department, and faculty autonomy, particularly in choice of software. Individual faculty members remain the best judges of the needs of their students and subject matter, and they must be allowed to express that judgment as fully as possible within the framework of institutional goals.

# 9

◨◨◨◨◨◨◨◨◨◨◨◨◨◨◨◨◨

# Overcoming Resistance
and Building Support
for Computer Use
in Instruction

Turning vision into reality is hard work. Those who are trying to turn the institutionwide vision of academic computing into reality need to fashion a structure of support that motivates their peers. Indeed, the need for support begins even before the institution's vision is fully formulated, when a few creative faculty members or administrators begin trying to make others aware of the possibilities for computer use in education. The need continues, too, after the vision is finally actualized, for the reality must then be maintained—and ultimately helped to grow beyond the bounds of the original dream.

This chapter will begin by discussing the constituencies that need support and explaining how a support system can help them. It will then describe the four parts of the support system necessary for a healthy academic computing environment: education, incentives, technical support, and group support. Finally, it will give examples of support systems in large and small institutions and provide a checklist for creating an institutionwide structure of support for academic computing.

## Who Needs Support and Why

A structure of support should be as inclusive as possible. It should aid not only students, faculty, and staff, but also administrative personnel and the trustees and board members to whom those personnel are ultimately accountable. It should be sensitive to an institution's environment, traditions, and mission as well as to the positive potential of the changes it is working to introduce and maintain.

When the process of introducing computers into teaching and learning activities is just beginning, people trying to carry out the process need support to help them overcome the resistance they are almost sure to face. Resistance to change is a normal human tendency, and it is certainly not lacking in higher education institutions. As Kenneth King has observed, "Curricular changes tend to move at the rate of a pig through a python" (1985, p. 20). Resistance to computer introduction may be expressed as suspicion, overly scrupulous review processes, anxiety about job security, dislike or distrust of computers and technology, passive resistance, unnecessary restrictions on use of resources, fears about possible depersonalization of instruction, or in many other forms. A good support system can speed up movement from vision to action by giving heart to those trying to achieve change in the face of opposition.

Kurt Lewin (1935) suggested that in institutions an equilibrium is created between driving forces (in this case, desire to see computers used in instruction) and restraining forces. The forces restraining the development of academic computing include not only practical factors such as shortages of funds or technical difficulties with implementation but also the negative attitudes just described. Achievement of change requires decreasing the restraining forces, adding to the driving forces, or both. It has been observed that intensifying the driving forces often simply results in a comparable strengthening of the restraining forces, so diminishing resistance may better serve to hasten change.

An effective support system can diminish attitudinal restraining forces as well as strengthening driving forces. Education can substitute understanding for groundless suspicions and fears. Incentives can increase willingness to try something new. Technical support can ease anxieties about having to cope with unfamiliar technology. Group support can diminish feelings of isolation and help people share insights and work out solutions to problems. Indeed, it could be said that the opponents of computer introduction need a support system even more than the proponents do.

A support system takes on somewhat different but equally important roles once computer technology is in place on a campus. Education becomes "continuing education," helping faculty members discover new applications of computers in instruction. Incentives encourage creation of new educational software or pilot programs involving computer use. The focus of technical support shifts from problems of installation (compatibility and so on) to problems of maintenance, repair, and upgrading to incorporate new technological advances and needs. Members of users' groups or other support groups spend less time sharing fears and problems or reassuring each other and more time sharing new ideas.

## Education

As part of a support system for an institutionwide computer environment, education about computers and their use in teaching and learning can be aimed at students, faculty, staff, administration, or any combination of these. It may be applied actively in courses, workshops, seminars, lectures, or demonstrations, or it may be made available for learners to draw on at need through resource centers (featuring demonstrations and samples of hardware and software and a collection of current literature about computers in instruction), newsletters, or consultants "on call." It can range from basic computer literacy instruction for people who have never touched a computer before to exchanges of ideas on the latest and most innovative advances among professionals who are highly skilled in the use of computers in teaching and learning.

According to Steven Gilbert (1984), individuals pass through the following four stages of growth as they learn new knowledge or skills:

1. *Prebeginner:* a learner who has no knowledge of the skill or subject and little awareness of its possible applications (for example, someone who has never used a computer and has heard only general remarks about computer use in instruction)

2. *Beginner:* a learner who has had a general introduction to the skill or subject but has not had much practice with it (someone who has used a computer for some purpose, even possibly for some educational purpose, but has not had extensive experience with such uses)

3. *Active learner-user:* a learner who has mastered the basic aspects of the skill or subject and is actively and independently seeking out new applications (someone who has made several uses of the computer in instruction and is actively looking for more ways to do this)

4. *Productive user:* a learner who has mastered the subject or skill sufficiently to create new applications for it and coach learners at earlier stages of development (someone who can create new software or new applications of computers in instruction and who can advise others who are learning how to use computers in instruction).

As Gilbert points out, institutions as well as individuals go through these growth stages when coming to grips with something new. His institutional stages of awareness, introduction, exploration, and productivity correspond approximately to what we have called awareness, vision, planning, and implementation (see Chapter Eight). Obviously it makes sense for the bulk of an institutional support system's educational efforts to be aimed at learners in the stage of growth through which the institution as a whole is passing. However, the directors of educational programs should keep in mind that individuals in all four stages of growth will exist in the institution and will need support during any of the institutional growth stages.

*Computer Literacy Courses: Two Examples.* The Rochester Institute of Technology developed a good example of a computer literacy education and training system for 250 of its faculty and staff and about 100 teachers from a nearby school district. The program began with an assessment of faculty needs and went on to feature a training sequence that included computer workshops for faculty, special topical seminars, hands-on demonstrations of hardware and software, discussion of classroom applications of computers and software, and in-service training sessions. The computer workshop was available either as an eighty-hour intensive taken over a two-week period or as a regular four-credit-hour course. A mobile computer laboratory and follow-up support were also provided to faculty (Plummer and others, 1985). Later R.I.T. presented an additional workshop that focused on instructional applications of off-the-shelf software ("Development of Instructional Applications," 1985).

Memphis State University helped its faculty and staff learn about computers by providing a course called "Personal Computing for University Faculty and Staff." The course was organized into twenty-one two-hour sessions, each session being divided between one hour of lecture and one hour of work in the personal computer laboratory. Classroom sessions used a projection monitor to display key characteristics of selected software. Of the forty-two hours of instruction, twenty hours were spent on the personal computer and programming, including interfacing devices and selecting a personal computer; twenty hours were spent on software that allowed use of the computer as a tool, including data base managers, spreadsheets, and word processing programs; and two hours were spent on using the computer in the classroom (McHenry and Franklin, 1986).

A survey questionnaire was given to 180 participants who enrolled in this course over several semesters. Of these, 109 (57 percent) completed the questionnaire. Over three fourths of those responding believed the course was of considerable value; indeed, 10 percent of the participants wrote letters of thanks to the course instructors or to the vice president for academic affairs. For example, one English department instructor commented, "I have just completed one of the most traumatic yet exhilarating experiences of my life . . . and I want to thank you sincerely for managing it in such a way that you inspired hope and motivation even among the most inept" (p. 177).

The most attractive aspects of the course, as judged by participants, were that it allowed hands-on experience with the computer (29 percent of survey respondents), provided familiarity with and understanding of computers (28 percent), and provided instruction in word processing (27 percent). A quarter of the respondents said they had applied what they learned in the course to selection of computer equipment. Only 5 percent, however, said they had applied their knowledge in the classroom.

*Teaching and Learning with Computers: A Different Approach.* The Memphis State computer literacy course design was typical of such offerings. It focused on demonstrations of off-the-shelf software, introductions to programming languages, and instructions for the operation of the personal computer. The course provided an excellent balance between theory and practice. It was a good beginning—but was it enough?

A literacy program focused on "teaching and learning with computers" would differ in several significant ways from a program like Memphis State's. It would position teaching and learning centrally, treating the computer merely as the (still very important) delivery medium for instruction. Like the Memphis State program, it would provide direct experience with the computer, but its primary objectives would be to create awareness of and develop action plans for using the computer in teaching and learning. The basics of personal computer use would remain an essential part of the program, but their importance would become secondary.

The following list shows some possible specific learning objectives for a faculty development course on teaching and learning with computers. The list uses terminology and concepts developed in the early part of this book. Others drawing up a similar list of objectives might phrase them somewhat differently, but the basic ideas most likely would be the same.

*Teaching and Learning*

1. Participants will be able to identify the four primary modes of computer delivery of instruction (teaching machine, simulator, resource, and tool) and will become thoroughly familiar with one piece of software that uses the computer in each of these four ways and is applicable to the participants' field of study.

2. Participants will be able to distinguish four basic teaching styles (teacher, facilitator, mentor, broker) and related learning styles and will be able to identify their preferred teaching style and one piece of software that uses the computer in a mode of delivery that reinforces or extends that teaching style and the learning outcomes of the participants' field of study.

3. Participants will be able to state whether the chosen mode of computer delivery primarily facilitates theoretical or applied learning and whether it primarily facilitates self-directed or other-directed learning.

4. Participants will be able to distinguish four basic categories of intellectual skills (informational, integrative and problem-solving, investigative, and analytical) and identify the mode of computer delivery that best facilitates each.

5. Participants will be able to list the primary learning outcomes and intellectual skills involved in one course they teach and identify the outcomes and skills that can best be enhanced by the computer.

6. Participants will be able to create an action plan for the implementation of a computer enhancement for one course or part of a course they teach, including selection and/or creation of necessary software, modification of learning outcomes, reconceptualization of assignments or meeting structure, training of students, and so on.

*The Personal Computer*

7. Participants will be able to identify the primary components of a personal computer.

8. Participants will demonstrate the ability to perform basic operations on the personal computer (loading software, saving data, and so on).
9. Participants will be able to identify the computer and other devices needed for the proposed computer enhancement of a course.

### Authoring Systems

10. Participants will become familiar with the basic operation of the primary authoring systems used in their institution.
11. Participants will be able to identify the primary capabilities of these authoring systems.

### Software

12. Participants will be able to identify four pieces of software for each of the primary modes of computer delivery that are appropriate to their field of study.
13. Participants will be able to evaluate one piece of software using each of the four modes of computer delivery to determine the software's effectiveness.

### Impact

14. Participants will be able to explain the impact that the computer, used to enhance a course or part of a course in the proposed way, is expected to have on students and the teaching and learning process.
15. Participants will develop processes and structures appropriate for the intended use of the computer that will minimize potential negative impact of the computer use.

As noted earlier, there are many forms of supportive education in addition to computer literacy and staff development programs. These include the use of outside consultants and trainers, arrangements for faculty travel to institutions pioneering uses of computers in teaching and learning, and provision of resource areas that students, staff, and faculty can visit to engage in self-directed learning about particular computer applications and programs. Newsletters that feature educational perspectives on computing, the latest advances in hardware and software, and model programs developed by teaching faculty are also a useful form of educational support. It should be noted that many of these forms of support stress "continuing education," the idea that exploration of new approaches to the use of computers in teaching and learning is desirable not only for computer novices but also for those with considerable experience in the field.

## Incentives

A structure of support for faculty and staff requires more than just education about the possibilities for computers in instruction. It also requires mechanisms for rewarding faculty for academic computer use and development of software and pilot programs. As Michael Carter, Director of Instruction and Research Information Systems (IRIS) at Stanford University, comments, "With so many really smart faculty members out there, I want to give them enough devices so they know exactly what they want to do, and then follow them, rather than to control the way they use computers. The trick really is to remove the obstacles so that those people can lead the way" (Osgood, 1987, p. 168).

One novel incentive for exploring the use of computers in teaching and learning was used at Dickinson College in Pennsylvania. Dickinson offered 125 full-time and 20 part-time faculty members the chance to borrow one of forty personal computers that the institution owned. In order to get a computer, a faculty member had to write a short proposal describing how he or she planned to use the computer in courses. Over 60 percent of the chosen faculty submitted proposals for the first round, and 33 percent received a computer to use in their offices. In addition, an open access area equipped with thirty personal computers was made available to faculty and students, and an introductory course and specialized minicourses were offered to all faculty members ("Highlights: Dickinson College," 1985).

Mills College in California took a different approach, devoting a small but growing budget to provision of release time to faculty who were developing teaching and learning programs that incorporated the computer. The college's appointment, promotion, and tenure committee also added development of educational software to the list of activities used during the tenure process to determine professional contribution. As a result, a number of untenured faculty members were encouraged to develop interesting applications of the computer in their instructional programs (Lennox, 1985).

Other possible incentives include minisabbaticals and cash awards for conducting projects to enhance instruction with computers. These awards may come at the beginning of the development process, based on a proposal that indicates intended approaches and outcomes (including descriptions of supporting activities and a budget), or they may come after the development and implementation of the application in recognition of the contribution it provided.

## Technical Support

Technical support can take several forms. It may mean help with instructional design and programming during faculty development of new software or new computer applications. It may mean answers to technical questions and problems. It may mean maintenance and repair of hardware.

Drexel University shows how elaborate a technical support system can be. Its instructional support group, made up of approximately twenty-five programmers and educational consultants, provides information to faculty regarding the latest developments in the use of computers in instruction. This group also gives ongoing training and helps departments and individual faculty members create educational applications for the computer. A second group, the equipment support group, services and repairs the over 6,000 computers used by students and staff at Drexel and handles the logistics of distributing new equipment. This component of the technical support system consists of four trained repair technicians. Finally, a users' support group maintains walk-in consulting sites in convenient places around campus and a "hot line" staffed sixteen hours a day to answer questions about software or hardware (*The Microcomputing Program at Drexel University: Organizing the Program,* n.d.).

As another example, the Office of Computer-Based Instruction at the University of Delaware provides support and advice to faculty through 34 full-time professionals and 53 part-time staff members. Over 100 faculty members have developed materials in 30 subject areas with the assistance of this office, using the PLATO authoring system (Hofstetter, 1980).

## Group Support

Group support, in which faculty members or others using computers in instruction help and encourage each other, can occur within an institution or reach beyond institutional boundaries. Groups may be general users' groups, special-focus groups that explore uses of computers in instruction in a particular discipline, or regional or national organizations like EDUCOM. The groups may meet in person, by computer (through computer conferences or bulletin boards), or both.

A users' group serves as a forum for faculty, staff, and others on the subject of computers in learning. It allows members to give and receive support in overcoming technical obstacles, share excitement and frustration as they develop particular projects, and discuss the latest breakthroughs in software and hardware technology. For example, at California State University, Long Beach, the Learning Assistance Center created OPEN, a user support group intended to "increase computer literacy, help members discover and use various software applications, develop new computer-assisted instruction methods, and share ideas" ("Highlights: OPEN at California State . . . ," 1985, p. 2). OPEN's membership numbers about 280, and meetings attract 100 to 125 members each month. OPEN also publishes an eight-page monthly newsletter, provides a large library of literature and public-domain software for copying, sponsors an electronic bulletin board system, supports prospective and new owners of personal computers, and encourages special-interest groups who want to focus on particular software applications.

Of particular significance is the way OPEN has taken on the role of missionary and consultant, providing ongoing training to faculty, staff, and students. Tutorial sessions to run newly released software are an important part of most OPEN meetings. Sessions are provided concurrently for three levels of users: first-time, intermediate, and advanced. The sessions are led by members, vendors, and software authors. Meetings conclude with a "random access" period, during which members can address the group to ask for help with particular hardware or software problems, announce hardware or software for sale, offer uncopyrighted or public-domain software, or share experiences with vendors or equipment.

Similarly, La Salle University spawned the Philadelphia Area Computing Society (PACS), which serves the entire Philadelphia area. This group broadened its scope from an initial engineering and computer science thrust to a general emphasis on the computer as a tool. La Salle provides facilities free of charge to the group, which has over 1,000 participants.

PACS monthly meetings attract approximately 600 people. The main part of each meeting features presentations by vendors, followed by panel discussions on topics of interest to the whole group. The meeting then breaks up into subgroups that meet further to discuss hardware, education, programming languages, data bases, telecommunications, or other special-interest subjects. A monthly publication called *Data Bus* reports on the activities of the subgroups. In addition, a free annual computer festival held on the La Salle campus features various hardware and software products. La Salle's academic computing director, Stephen Longo, states that PACS "acts as a real force not only in educating faculty, college administrators, and other professionals in both instructional and administrative uses of the computer, but also in making computer education easily accessible to the entire community" ("Highlights: Philadelphia Area Computing Society . . . ," 1985, p. 3).

A users' group can provide vital support in helping faculty and staff enrich their knowledge of computers. However, one problem with many such groups, even those based in academic institutions, is that they tend to concentrate on technological rather than educational issues. This problem may be offset by forming a special-interest subgroup that focuses on the use of computers in teaching and learning.

## Examples of Practice

The following section describes two model support systems for an institutionwide computer teaching and learning environment. One is a large program at Drexel University, while the other is a modest program at a small branch campus of the University of Wisconsin. Both programs exemplify a system of support that encompasses interconnected services, technical support, communications, education, and rewards.

*Drexel University.* One of the most remarkable institutional commitments to the use of the personal computer in instruction is demonstrated at Drexel University. Beginning in the 1983–84 academic year, all entering freshmen at Drexel were required to have a personal computer. (Drexel arranged for students to purchase computers at highly discounted prices and, when appropriate, provided for computer purchase as part of the basic student financial aid package.) The computer would be used in all of their studies.

Naturally, such an extensive commitment to computer use required an equally extensive support system. The system's first task was preparing the university faculty to handle the increased emphasis on computers. As a report on the Drexel program noted, "At the time of the microcomputer decision, Drexel had a teaching staff whose computer knowledge and skills varied greatly. Some faculty knew little or nothing about computers and had no idea how the computer could be used in the classroom. Others were seasoned computer users who had long relied on computers for research and teaching. Most lay somewhere in between. . . . Enabling a large faculty (350 full-time and over 200 part-time) to use computers across the curriculum posed some obvious problems. The training format had to be flexible enough to fit a wide variety of skill levels and individual teaching and research schedules" (*The Microcomputing Program at Drexel University: Preparing the Faculty*, n.d., p. 1).

Seasoned computer users at Drexel formed a core group that helped to construct a faculty development program for their peers. A twenty-hour introductory course, which faculty were given release time to attend, treated elementary programming, various computer tools, and the computer as a teaching machine. Special seminars were also given, including "Searching a Bibliographic Data Base," "What Computers Do," "Beyond Proofing and Editing," "Statistical Analysis Using a Microcomputer," and "Workshop on Developing Instructional Software."

During the first year of the program almost one third of the full-time faculty members participated in the introductory course. Release time for attendance was ultimately phased out, but "this didn't seem to discourage participation," the report notes. "Others [who had not had the training] were eager to 'catch up.' Moreover, the arrival of the computers was imminent, and faculty now experienced a genuine 'need to know' " (p. 4).

In addition to release time for the faculty development program, Drexel offered other incentives to faculty members to encourage them to participate fully in computerization. Release time for development of new software or adaptation of off-the-shelf software was provided to about 10 percent of the faculty, amounting to about a 25 percent load reduction. Faculty were also given technical assistance on campus and travel funds for visiting model programs at other institutions.

The Drexel support system had other components as well. A newsletter called *Boot* was published weekly to "seed" interest in computers throughout the university. It featured faculty innovations and applications of the computer in instruction as well as general information on personal computer developments. A software review center was established in the library to hold a sorted collection of commercial software and related publications and manuals. A "developer's session" was presented in the center each week, with each session featuring a different

computer "work in progress" and a discussion of particular development problems and applications encountered in connection with that project. Faculty receiving release time for software development were encouraged to attend and present their
work at these sessions, which were open to the entire university
community.

Faculty were given a major role in choosing the hardware
and software that the university purchased. For example, administrative decisions to buy computers were based on recommendations by a faculty selection committee. Each college set
up its own proposal evaluation committees to review proposals
for release time, support staff, and other forms of assistance,
judging them in terms of its own priorities for curriculum development.

Drexel's extensive support system reflected the university
administration's awareness of the importance of faculty participation in the institutionwide computerization project. "For the
microcomputer project to succeed, it had to have the full back-
ing and cooperation of all faculty members," the program report notes. "It required their creative input—ideas for software
and for new computer applications in the classroom" (p. 2).

The Drexel education and support system had the desired
effect: the ranks of faculty competent to use computers in
some aspect of their teaching and learning program swelled rapidly. "Today, every department in the university, from the sciences to the humanities, has its own core of experts who are
actively engaged in training their colleagues. As a result, training
is now more specifically tailored to individual disciplines and
needs," the Drexel report claims (p. 3).

*University of Wisconsin.* Effective support systems for
academic computing programs need not be limited to large universities like Drexel. The University of Wisconsin Center in
Marinette County has a teaching staff of only fourteen people
and a student population of 450, but it, too, has developed an
institutionwide computing program with a support network.
The coordinators of the project noted, "The larger campuses
that have decided to attempt this have had major corporate in-

volvement to subsidize their projects. We took a different approach and were able to fund our project with small grants" (Wresch and Hieser, 1985, p. 254). Indeed, the entire budget for the Marinette Center's support network was only $25,000.

The primary thrust of Marinette's faculty education program was the teaching of programming skills in conjunction with instructional design principles. For one semester, faculty members met each Friday afternoon for an hour and a half. They learned how to write simple programs in the BASIC computer language and how to evaluate off-the-shelf software. Faculty then met daily for five-hour sessions led by consultants for six consecutive weeks during the summer. According to a report on the program,

> A typical day would often begin with one of the consultants demonstrating a piece of commercial software, and then leading a critique of it. He would often follow with a lecture on a specific programming technique which might be useful for CAI programs. . . . Essentially locked in a room together for six weeks, faculty helped each other with their programs and with materials design. . . . We got to see firsthand what the major goals of each of our colleagues are, and to hear what they normally do to overcome [their] problems. What we found was that while we may be in separate disciplines, most of us have the same general problem—how to communicate the basic vocabulary and intellectual tenets of our discipline to lower division students. The similarities were sufficient for us to be able to help each other devise teaching approaches for our common problem—and at the same time to fully appreciate that our problem was in fact a *common* problem [Wresch and Hieser, 1985, p. 255].

The Marinette program shows how a support system for academic computing can produce the serendipitous result of "a renewed sense of collegiality": "turf" barriers were broken down as faculty explored together how best to design and deliver instruction. The education program had a good many other positive results as well. The coordinators of the project reported, "Of the twelve faculty who began the program, eleven completed and used a CAI program in one of their classes. Student attitudes toward these programs were generally very positive. . . . The only two faculty members who missed the CAI training [due to previous commitments] asked for and received computer training; purchases of commercial programs are up on our campus, with faculty routinely using such packages in business, math, art, English, and psychology classes; two of our faculty have signed contracts to have their software published by a major software house; two others are nearing such an agreement (p. 255).

## Creating a Support System

The following checklist should prove helpful to administrators or others trying to create a support system for an institutionwide computer environment. It summarizes many of the points made in this chapter.

### General

- Ensure administrative and trustee approval of the support system.
- Clearly establish the rationale and objectives of the system.
- Work initially with a small group of faculty and staff opinion leaders who are already exploring teaching and learning with computers.
- Ensure the active involvement of all institutional constituencies (as much as possible) in development of the system.
- Create an organizational unit (either short term or permanent) to be responsible for the system.
- Choose someone to coordinate and guide the system who is respected and liked by a broad section of the institution's personnel.
- Plan the actions necessary to create the support system.

- Develop structures for education, incentive, technical support, and group support components.

*Education*

- Communicate face to face with key institutional constituencies regarding possibilities for teaching and learning with computers.
- Encourage faculty and staff to express their concerns and reservations about academic computing at all junctures.
- Establish objectives for all education and training programs.
- Tailor educational efforts to the stage of institutional development: focus on attitudes initially, then shift to knowledge and skills after a sufficiently favorable climate for computer use has been created.
- Clarify intended learning objectives for faculty development and computer literacy efforts (that is, minimum computer literacy competencies) and establish the responsibility of all key constituents for achieving those objectives.
- Establish a faculty development program that provides for both basic computer literacy and instruction about using computers in teaching and learning.
- Provide a library of materials related to the use of computers in instruction.
- Create a resource area that encompasses such a library as well as demonstration copies of commercial software, locally developed software, and hardware that the institution owns or is planning to buy.
- Provide lectures, demonstrations, seminars, and/or workshops in special topics related to the use of computers in instruction.
- Provide a continuous flow of information (via memos or a newsletter) regarding new uses of computers in instruction.
- Identify consultants and trainers who might be available to conduct training sessions or help faculty members develop applications of computers in instruction.
- Arrange for faculty or others to visit institutions with model programs that use the computer in teaching and learning.

## Incentives

- Arrive at a fair and equitable means of reimbursing staff for time spent developing educational software or computer applications for their instructional programs (release time, special pay).
- Establish a minisabbatical or development fund for making awards to faculty who present promising proposals for uses of computers in instruction.
- Modify promotion, tenure, and merit pay review processes to include recognition for development of educational software or applications of computers to instruction.
- Loan computers to faculty or staff as an inducement or award for experimentation with applications of the computer to instruction.
- Pay travel costs for faculty visiting other institutions with model programs that use the computer in instruction.

## Technical Support

- Provide assistance in programming, use of authoring systems, and instructional design to faculty who are developing educational software.
- Provide a means of answering technical questions and solving problems related to use of software, computers, and peripherals. (This might be done through a "hot line," a conference or bulletin board set up on an intrainstitutional communication network, or an "expert system" developed by the computer center or computer science department.)
- Provide for necessary service and maintenance of hardware.

## Group Support

- Create users' groups and/or an intrainstitutional communication network for faculty, staff, and students using computers in instruction.
- Provide membership in organizations and professional associations committed to the effective use of computers in instruction.
- Encourage faculty to participate in special-interest groups fo-

cusing on the use of computers in the instruction of a particular discipline.

- Investigate the possibility of joining or establishing interinstitutional groups that share software, development projects, resource people, and/or information about the use of computers in instruction.

A support system can minimize strain and maximize benefits at all stages in the development of an institutionwide computing environment. In the beginning of the process, such a system can increase understanding of and enthusiasm for the use of computers in instruction and can help to allay both groundless and justifiable fears. As institutional computer use grows, it can encourage the discovery or creation of new, more effective ways of teaching and learning with computers. At all stages it can help faculty, staff, and students discover new ways to communicate with, relate to, and support each other, turning the challenges of new technology into new opportunities for collegiality.

# 10

░░ ░░ ░░ ░░ ░░ ░░ ░░ ░░ ░░ ░░ ░░ ░░ ░░ ░░

# Organizing and Managing
# Academic Computing Programs

Like other parts of a higher education institution, the realm of academic computing must have a system of organization or governance. This chapter describes some aspects of that organizational structure and some forms it may take. The chapter distinguishes between formal and informal organization, between line and staff positions, and between centralized and decentralized authority. It also considers different loci of control for academic computing programs, describes the organization of such programs at several example institutions, and offers advice on choosing an organizational structure for managing computers in instruction.

### Formal and Informal Organizational Structures

The formal organizational structure of an institution (or any part of an institution) is manifested in fixed roles and patterns of accountability and responsibility. By contrast, informal organization, in the form of committees and task forces, is usually temporary, created to handle a particular task and dissolved when that work is completed. Both formal and informal organization are important to the establishment and maintenance of a healthy environment for academic computing.

*Formal Organizational Structure.* The formal organizational structure involved in academic computing, like the formal

168

organizational structure of other parts of a higher education institution, involves both individuals and groups (academic departments, for example). The official posts occupied by the individuals remain in a fixed relationship to each other, even though the individuals who occupy those posts may change.

Formal organization provides for formal authority, the official (as opposed to personal) power to command the actions of others. Formal organizations provide stability by establishing fixed authority relationships between departments and staffs and by establishing accountability for organizationwide results. However, formal organizations can also promote rigidity and narrow-mindedness. They often facilitate communication within departments but diminish communication between departments.

Drexel University, whose academic computing program and support structure were described in the last chapter, demonstrates the complex set of interrelationships necessary to support an ambitious program for teaching and learning with computers. The organizational structure for academic computing at Drexel is described in Figure 5. In this organization, the managers of the academic computing program collaborate with the managers of the computer center. At this time these two groups are organizationally separate, but ultimately Drexel plans to integrate them in a single management structure (*The Microcomputing Program at Drexel University: Organizing the Program*, n.d.).

*Informal Organizational Structure.* Informal organizational structure, in the form of committees and task forces, allows for short-term, broad-based staff participation in decision making. Committees may serve in an advisory capacity to a dean, department chairperson, or other administrator. For example, a committee might advise administration on ways to support faculty in the development of applications of the computer in teaching. Committees may also directly assist administrators in carrying out some action, such as purchasing hardware and software for the institution. These informal groups can give significant guidance to officials who have formal authority over an instructional program.

Figure 5. Organizational Chart for the
Drexel Microcomputing Program.

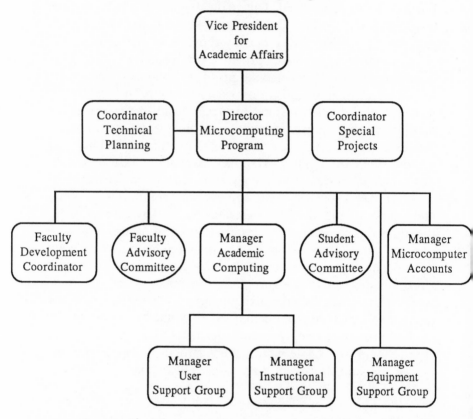

*Source: The Microcomputing Program at Drexel University: Organizing the Program,* n.d.

Standing committees have continuity in time, though the membership of the committees may change periodically. Committees may also be created for a particular function or for a fixed period of time, dissolving at the completion of that project or period. This form of committee is called a task force. For example, a task force that includes a faculty member from each department in a College of Arts and Sciences might meet for a four-week period to work out the design of a faculty development program that explores uses of the computer as a resource.

Committees and task forces can be a useful means of permitting faculty and staff contributions to decision making and for making faculty and staff feel that they have a personal stake in an academic computing program. They can bring together a cross section of viewpoints, creating a sense of community that cuts across discipline and "turf" lines.

In spite of these advantages, certain problems can arise from the informal nature of these groups. Membership in the groups is more or less voluntary, and participants may not take their responsibilities seriously enough. Members may fail to attend meetings, causing the committee as a whole to be slow to act. Indeed, members often drop out of participation entirely, causing frequent hunts for replacements. Constantly changing membership can make continuity of action difficult. These problems may be made worse when officials with formal authority do not pay sufficient attention to a committee's recommendations. Committee members, feeling powerless and discouraged, conclude that they are wasting their time. Reliable membership and concerted committee action then become more difficult to achieve than ever.

Drexel University's academic computing program involved considerable input from committees who reported to the officials formally in charge of the program. To ensure the institutionwide participation and cooperation necessary for the university's extensive program, three committees were created: the Selection Committee, the Users' Committee, and the Faculty Advisory Committee (*The Microcomputing Program at Drexel University: Organizing the Program*, n.d.).

The Selection Committee reviewed the computing needs of students and faculty and the qualities of various hardware products with the aim of recommending what equipment the institution should purchase. (Drexel ultimately made large purchases of the chosen computers for resale to incoming freshmen at highly discounted prices.)

The Users' Committee consisted of about fifteen persons, all experienced computer users, who served as representatives of their particular colleges in the university. The committee assisted in program planning and policy formulation regarding copyright and computer allocations by department. It also provided for a range of logistical and academic support and service needs.

The Faculty Advisory Committee was established to facilitate communication about the development program. The deans of Drexel's six colleges each appointed a liaison person to represent that college on the committee. These liaison people served as "prime sources of information about the program and as conduits for faculty input as the program further decentralize[d] and bec[a]me more directly controlled at the departmental and college levels" (p. 2). Liaison people also offered recommendations of software to be purchased for university-wide use and advice on the development of software, including shared development between colleges and departments.

Committees were also important in the support structure of Drexel's program, as described in the last chapter. The Instructional Support Group, the Equipment Support Group, and the Users' Support Group were all in effect committees that reported to officials in the formal organizational structure of the academic computing program.

Student participation in the design and implementation of Drexel's computing program was secured through the creation of a Student Advisory Committee and a student users' group called DUsers. The Student Advisory Committee offered advice regarding the achievement of overall program goals and the policies that would affect student use of computers. It also created a competition featuring academic computer applications developed by students. The DUsers publicized information about academic computer use that was of interest to students and also provided training for student computer users. For example, they helped plan an orientation to computers for incoming freshmen, and they organized a computer fair.

The administrative affairs component of the university (as distinguished from academic or student affairs) also made an informal contribution to the academic computing program in the form of the Facilities Committee. The introduction of personal computers throughout the curriculum required extensive alterations to the university's physical plant, including a new warehousing unit, a print area, and numerous computer laboratories. The Facilities Committee "was charged with anticipating the need for new and expanded facilities and with evaluating existing facilities" (p. 3). The committee consisted of the director of the microcomputing program, the director of the physical plant, the director of planning and construction, the university architect, the manager of the Equipment Support Group, the director of residential living, the manager of academic computing, the dean of students, the university comptroller, and the director of campus security.

## Authority and Centers of Control

"Who's in charge here?" is a vital question that must be answered in any organization. In a program for using computers in instruction, this question can be broken down into questions of line versus staff authority, the degree of centralization of authority, and the administrative locus of control of the computing program.

*Line and Staff Authority.* Line authority is the power to act and/or to command the action of others. A vice president of academic affairs is a line administrator, for example. A line administrator has authority to decide such matters as the kind of personal computers to be purchased for use on campus, the nature of faculty development activities, and the location of academic computing laboratories.

Staff departments support, advise, or assist the activities of line departments. Staff administrators work with and usually are supervised by deans, department heads, and other line administrators. For example, staff officers might assist line administrators in designing software appropriate for particular course needs or in formulating hardware needs to be met by either centralized purchase through the academic vice president's office or decentralized purchase at the departmental level.

There are two basic kinds of staff departments. One is the advisory department, which provides advice and sometimes other forms of support to line departments. An example might be a central academic computing department that helps faculty members design computer applications in their courses. The other kind of staff department is the service department, which provides services for other parts of the institution or for external constituencies. A department that assists in the preparation and analysis of reports that evaluate the effectiveness of particular applications of computers in instruction would be a service department, for example.

Both line and staff authority are delegated within the formal organizational structure of an institution. For example, the vice president of academic affairs might create an office of academic computing (a staff advisory office) and delegate formal authority to the director of that office. That director would then have line authority in supervising the staff employees of the office.

An important distinction between line and staff is fiscal accountability. A line administrator is fully accountable for the implementation of a budget (including the part earmarked for computers and computer-related purchases), while the staff administrator usually just coordinates with and advises departments regarding the development of a budget.

Staff departments can greatly enhance the effectiveness of line departments through provision of expert advice and services. However, tensions can arise between line and staff departments or managers if they disagree about the best uses of computers in teaching and learning. (For example, line managers may be older, more conservative in their views, and less experienced with computers than staff managers.) Such tensions create morale problems and inhibit the aims of both kinds of departments. Establishment of open lines of communication between line and staff administrators is essential for resolving differences and clarifying possibilities.

*Centralization of Authority and Locus of Control.* Centralized authority is authority held by administrators at high organizational levels. Decentralized authority is authority held at departmental levels. Designers of an organizational structure for an academic computing program need to determine whether the program will be controlled by centralized authority, decentralized authority, or a combination of both. They then need to decide precisely what the administrative (and sometimes physical) locus of control of the program will be. This section will consider several loci of control commonly used for such programs and the advantages and disadvantages of each.

Administrators with limited experience with computers in instruction have often given authority for academic computing programs to existing sources of technological know-how within their institution, specifically the computer science department and/or the administrative computing center (the latter a centralized staff department). These departments can bring immense technical experience to the management of such a program. However, because they tend to treat computing as a technological rather than an educational matter, allowing them to control an academic computing program may limit the impact of computers on teaching and learning.

As an alternative locus of control, an increasing number of institutions have created an academic computing department headed by a dean or director or, occasionally, a vice president. The head of this department may report to the president or the chief academic officer. The post may be defined as either a staff or a line position, although most often it is considered a centralized staff position. At institutions that prefer a more decentralized approach, each college or division within the institution may have its own academic computing center.

The advantage of creating a new department specifically devoted to academic computing is that such a department may discover instructional applications of the computer that academic departments would not have the resources or the time to find for themselves. However, conflict may arise between academic computing centers and academic departments if the departments feel (rightly or wrongly) that the center's centralized authority is limiting their autonomy in making hardware and software purchase decisions.

A few institutions have given the responsibility for computers in instruction to the director of the learning resource center or library. Raymond Neff, assistant vice chancellor of information systems at the University of California, Berkeley, advocates the library as a prime source for facilitating computer use in teaching and learning (Neff, 1985). He notes that at many institutions, the librarian and the computer center director are at the same organizational level and report to the same person. U. C. Berkeley, indeed, is one of those institutions: the director of the library and the director of information systems are both considered vice chancellors and report to the chancellor. "I don't control the library; it doesn't report to me. But we work very closely together, and I think synergistically; certainly not competitively," Neff comments (1986b, p. 2).

Neff points to many similarities between a library and a computer center: "The library is a repository of packaged information and the computer center stores and retrieves information; the library lends information and the center displays it; the library acquires and borrows information and the center inputs information. In one form of service or another, storage, retrieval, input, and output of information are common to both" (1985, p. 8).

Neff sees a series of trends leading toward the merging of computer center and library: libraries are increasingly using computers, including computerized data bases, to provide a higher level of information service; computer centers and libraries will in the near future provide information services (using the computer as a resource) at no charge to the users; scholars and students will have greater and greater access to information sources as institutional networks develop; information sharing among institutions will increase with the growth of interinstitutional networks; and libraries and computer centers will have the same type of devices for archival storage, so it will not matter who actually controls the devices.

A merger of library and computer center has already taken place at Columbia University, where Patricia Battin, vice president and head librarian of the university, is also now in charge of academic computing. Battin emphasizes use of the computer as a resource for scholars. She believes it is inappropriate for scholars to have to go to a library for information stored in books and journals, then to a computer center for information stored electronically, then to another computer to organize the data that have been collected. Instead, they should be able to find everything in a single "scholarly information center"—a new kind of library that is more a concept than a place (Turner, 1986b).

Battin claims, "Librarians don't organize books, they organize knowledge and ways to gain access to that knowledge. It so happens that knowledge has been in books for a long time, so we equate librarians and books" (p. 39). In fact, however, she observes that many librarians have also become expert at organizing and gaining access to information electronically.

The focus of a university information center ought not to be on either computers or the management of collections, Battin states. Rather, it should be on what the scholar needs. Accordingly, computer center staff should become increasingly sensitive to the information needs of persons in particular disciplines, and librarians should become increasingly adept at using computers to access data electronically. Battin has helped to create an amalgamation of computer and library sensitivities and functions at Columbia.

The advantage of consolidating library and academic computing functions is the synergy it produces: the library as the primary repository of recorded information can heighten its effectiveness for students as a result of computerized information storage and retrieval. Disadvantages can arise from managerial problems and authority conflicts created by the merger and from the difficulty of assembling a staff that is competent to deal with the unique challenges associated with both organizations. Another problem with letting the library control the entire academic computing program is a possible overemphasis on the computer as a resource at the expense of other modes of computer use that might be more directly involved in instruction.

There has been either a deliberate or a *de facto* decentralization of authority at some institutions, allowing particular departments, divisions, or colleges within a university to establish their own facilities and processes for using computers in teaching, learning, and research. This has been particularly likely to happen with certain science, math, engineering, and sometimes business components of colleges and universities.

The advantage of decentralizing authority is that it places decisions directly in the hands of those who use computers in teaching. A difficulty with this approach is that powerful departments or units may secure computers and development resources that less powerful departments are forced to do without. Decentralization may also cause an institution to wastefully duplicate effort in training programs, for example, or find itself with a potpourri of incompatible computers and peripheral equipment that have been acquired wastefully and cannot be maintained efficiently.

Responding to problems presented by strongly centralized or strongly decentralized authority, a growing number of institutions have established an authority structure that has both centralized and decentralized elements. Such a structure allows departments autonomy in designing and implementing their computing programs while at the same time realizing the efficiencies that come from centralized purchasing and institutionwide coordination of plans.

As an example, an institution using a combination of centralized and decentralized authority might have decisions about hardware and software costing over $1,000 made by a central authority, while decisions about lesser purchases would be made by the departments. Ideally, the centralized decisions about major purchases would be made on the basis of input from all the departments that would use the equipment or programs.

Another pattern of shared centralization and decentralization might leave budget authority entirely within the departments, who would manage and control their own computer facilities. On the other hand, authority over staff development, use of computer-related resources in instruction, design and development of computer networks, and purchases of large systems might be vested in a central department. Many other permutations and combinations of centralized and decentralized authority are possible.

## Examples of Practice

The following models illustrate various patterns of authority and organizational structure that have been tried by higher education institutions establishing academic computing programs. Most of these models include both centralized and decentralized elements.

*The University of California, Berkeley.* At the University of California's Berkeley campus, the executive in charge of academic computing is the assistant vice chancellor for information systems. This post is vested with line authority and represents considerable centralization. No computer hardware or software costing more than $200 can be purchased without permission from this central authority.

Raymond Neff, the current occupant of the post, admits that he has applied a "tight rein" in guiding the development of the Berkeley campus's academic computing program. In fact, he attributes at least part of the program's success to this approach. "I'm afraid it takes a computer czar . . . to push this" (1986b, p. 10). Neff says he persuaded faculty to accept this high degree of centralization "by offering them something they can't get anywhere else. By giving them quality service that they cannot get on their own. By giving them the kinds of discounts on microcomputers, workstations, giving them the high-performance networking, giving them the supercomputing, giving them specialized people services, buying software for workstations of a higher quality at a lower price than they can buy on their own" (p. 10). At the same time, Neff notes, the authority structure at Berkeley allows considerable departmental autonomy in designing applications of the computer in teaching, learning, and research (Turner, 1986a).

*The University of Delaware.* The pioneering work of the University of Delaware with the mainframe-based PLATO authoring system for CAI programs was managed by an advisory staff department called the Office of Computer-Based Instruction. This office supported and advised faculty members who were using the PLATO system. The office maintained a combined full-time and part-time staff of over eighty persons. The director of the office reported to the university's provost.

Centralized control over finances, instructional development, hardware, and system operation characterized the Delaware program's organizational pattern. Fred Hofstetter, the architect of the program, warns, "If centralized control is not maintained over system and programming resources, a dangerous fragmentation and alienation within a project can occur" (Hofstetter, 1980, p. 7).

At the same time, Hofstetter is an advocate of independence in project management. For example, recommendations from a faculty advisory committee regarding proposed new projects are received by the Office of Computer-Based Education. Upon consulting with the faculty committee and his own staff, the director of the office forwards recommendations, along with funding requirements, to the university provost for review and action. The director, by virtue of his reporting relationship to the provost, is also in regular communication with major academic directors.

As another example of decentralized authority, each department at Delaware designates a project leader. This faculty representative has final authority over the content of computer-based materials developed by the department and their position in the departmental curriculum. The project leader serves as the spokesperson for the department, meeting with other departmental faculty members to determine computer applications in the curriculum and collaborating with programmers and coordinators from the Office of Computer-Based Instruction to design particular projects.

Delaware used a "team" approach to develop computer resources for teaching and learning. Each project began with an advisory committee that worked with faculty and staff to refine the proposal for the project until it best addressed all the issues involved. After the project was funded, the proposal proceeded to a design stage that involved a team, including a faculty author, designers, and programmers. The completed design was reviewed by a committee that made suggestions for instructional refinements. When the design was finally approved, it was submitted for programming. The faculty author regularly reviewed the project during programming and also during subsequent testing by students. Finally, the author participated in the evaluation of the finished program and gave demonstrations of it as part of the project's dissemination stage (Hofstetter, 1980).

*Brown University.* Brown University's unusual advances in the use of computers in instruction are in part due to its Institute for Research in Information and Scholarship (IRIS). IRIS has a dual mission: to explore and develop experimental computer technologies for scholars and to coordinate the incorporation of new technology into applications on campus. IRIS is an entirely self-supporting applied research and development institute, with an annual operating budget of about $2 million. (For example, IRIS received substantial funding from IBM to develop workstations with graphics capability.) IRIS is also a service staff department of the university.

Development of the Brown sampler program described in earlier chapters of this book was sponsored by IRIS. More recently, IRIS administered the Education Software Project, which is intended to create a model by which instructors can create educational software without having to master programming (O'Brien, 1985).

Another major focus of IRIS has been developing and implementing an institutionwide network of workstations (high-powered personal computers with graphics capability, designed to be connected to a host computer or used as part of a network). IRIS assisted academic departments to assess their needs for computing workstations and network services, then tested prototypes of instructional programs, workstation communications software, and network services. The associate provost for budgets and planning collaborated with IRIS to help academic departments plan, find common problems, and develop centralized solutions for those problems.

Other components of the formal organization and related committee structure at Brown included the following:

- the vice provost for computing, who had responsibility for planning and management of centralized computing services and final authority for making universitywide plans for computers in instruction
- the Faculty Advisory Committee on Computers, which advised about computing services that affected the faculty
- the Office of the Provost, which approved budgets for computing in academic departments through 1985, after which time funds for computing were allocated directly to the departments (decentralization of authority)
- two users' groups involving faculty, staff, and students, which served as liaison between IRIS and the Brown community
- the Undergraduate Council of Students Computer Committee, which provided a mechanism for communicating students' needs
- the Development Office, which was responsible for raising funds for computing.

At Brown, as at many other institutions, authority for management of academic computing takes both centralized and decentralized forms. This is particularly striking in the area of support services. As M. R. Pear, support group manager for the IRIS workstation project, notes, "It is no longer possible for central services alone to provide personal service for the entire user community. With computer-proficient support personnel located in departments, the central services can concentrate on providing expert-level support to a smaller number of computer users. Departmental support personnel can respond effectively to daily problems and provide pertinent advice by being familiar not only with appropriate computing tools but also with the context in which problems arise. In turn, central support services can provide expert-level support for departmental support personnel" (1985, p. 5). The centralized part of Brown's support system also offers "train the trainer" programs and strengthens communication channels that keep departmental support people informed and competent to carry out training (Pear, 1985).

## Choosing an Organizational Structure

As the preceding examples have shown, different organizational structures for management of academic computing programs work well in different institutions. No one combination of formal and informal structures, staff and line authority, centralized and decentralized control will work best for all. The choice of the best structure for a given institution will depend on a number of factors.

One important factor to consider in determining the optimal organizational structure for a particular institution's academic computing program is the mode of computer delivery of instruction that the institution has chosen to stress. An institution committed to the use of the computer as a teaching machine, like the University of Delaware, needs to provide organizational support for faculty who are trying to develop suitable software and/or adapt existing CAI programs to their needs. An advisory staff department with both centralized and decentralized components may serve this purpose best. By contrast, an institution like Brown that focuses on development of an institutionwide network using the computer as a resource might need a centralized staff service department like IRIS to design the network.

The size and overall organizational structure of the institution are also important to consider. An organizational structure for academic computing that is appropriate for a multi-campus community college system or a large university like U. C. Berkeley may not work well for a small liberal arts college or an urban state university, and vice versa. For example, universities have historically decentralized authority to school and department levels, while many community colleges and some smaller private liberal arts colleges usually have had more centralized control. Accordingly, resistance to centralization of authority in an academic computing program is likely to be higher in a large university, where faculty members are used to considerable autonomy, than in a small college. Similarly, choice of the organizational structure for academic computing will depend on whether the institution traditionally relies on committees and task forces or whether decisions are made primarily by administrators.

An institution's budget, the strengths and weaknesses of its staff and leadership, its mission and cultural climate, and many other factors are also important to consider in determining the best organizational structure for an academic computing program. The best structure is the one that most fully meets the institution's computing and support needs.

# 11

New Technology
and the Future
of Teaching and Learning
with Computers

People in general, and educators in particular, have always been dubious about technological change. In Plato's *Phaedrus,* Socrates expressed the following doubts about the effects of introducing writing into education, which until his time had been primarily a matter of oral inquiry: "This invention [the written word] will produce forgetfulness in the souls of those who have learned it. They will not need to exercise their memories, being able to rely on what is written, calling things to mind no longer from within themselves. . . . And as for wisdom, you're equipping your pupils with only a semblance of it, not with truth. Thanks to you and your invention, your pupils will be widely read without benefit of a teacher's instruction; in consequence, they'll entertain the delusion that they have wide knowledge while they are, in fact, for the most part incapable of real judgment. They will also be difficult to get on with, since they will have become wise merely in their own conceit, not genuinely so" (1956, pp. 68-69).

Resistance to change, according to systems theorist George Land, is a property not only of all human beings but of all living things or aggregates of living things (from a bacterium to a city, a nation, or a higher education institution) at a certain stage in their development. In its first or formative phase, Land explains, "The growing thing reaches out and attempts to discover what within the whole environment will work, what can make a pattern. . . . Gradually it starts to find a pattern, and the pattern starts to stabilize. . . . When organisms find a pattern for dealing with the environment, they no longer have to experiment" ("Report from the Leading Edge," 1981, p. 5). Land goes on to describe the second phase of growth, which he calls the normative phase. "Every organism, every organization does something interesting when it finds the pattern and goes into Phase II: it sets up an immune system to *protect it from anything different*" (p. 5). During this phase ("typically a long period in all living things"), the organism becomes more and more proficient in exploiting the resources in its environment.

Ultimately, the organism or organization uses up its resources. It then enters a third phase of growth, the integrative phase, in which it attempts to return to the earlier pattern of exploration and experimentation. During this phase, a "180° shift" from the second phase, material that was considered foreign or unfitting during the normative phase becomes fodder for new growth.

The arrival of new technology catches most people and organizations in the second phase of their development, when their "immune system to protect them from anything different" is strong. Thus it is not surprising that they resist the technology and the changes it implies. The fact that most infant technologies do not work very well makes it easy for critics to "have a field day" with a new system, as Dustin Heuston points out. In the early 1900s, he notes, "a car would race a horse at a race track. Part way through the race the car would break down, and the horse would then tow the car across the finish line, proving once again that cars would never replace horses" (1986, p. 3).

It is little wonder, then, that many educators resist the advent of computer technology in spite of its potential for enhancing teaching and learning. They recognize that computers may cause sweeping changes in their traditional ways of doing things, and they have a vested interest in maintaining the existing system of classrooms, lecture sequences, and fixed class schedules and calendars bounded by registration periods and grade reports.

Some of this vested interest is quite practical. In a public community college or state university subsidized by the state based upon classroom contact hours, for example, funding requires students to be physically present in classrooms for fixed lengths of time. Administrators of such a college or university will naturally try to get as much use out of classrooms and assign as many students to each faculty member as possible in order to get the maximum number of contact hours signed up and thus get the maximum amount of tuition and subsidies. Tuition-driven operating patterns in most private education institutions are similarly tied to classroom credit hours. There is thus a strong disincentive to change existing class arrangements in either public or private institutions.

## Changes in Structure of Education

Major technological changes have always brought about equally major changes in society, in the way people live their lives and view themselves and their world. These changes include changes in people's view of the proper methods and purposes for education. The spread of writing and literacy (which so worried Socrates) and later the invention of the printing press, for example, turned the emphasis of education from oral encounters and practice in tasks important to the culture to the study of written materials.

Computers, which allow more people to gain access to more information and manipulate it with more ease and sophistication than ever before, have the potential for making equally great changes in not only the techniques but the very concept of education. According to the president of Johns Hopkins University, Steven Muller, "We are, whether fully conscious of it or not, already in an environment for higher education that represents the most drastic change since the founding of the University of Paris and Bologna, some eight or nine centuries ago"

(Bok, 1985, p. 3). Dustin Heuston (1986) believes that changes brought about by computers in education will result in a shift like that described by Land as occurring at the beginning of the third phase of an organism's growth. The nature of these changes, and whether their effects will be positive or negative, will depend on the attitudes and actions of the people involved: students, faculty, and administrators.

The introduction of computers into institutions of higher education is likely to be part of a feedback process: widespread use of computers will encourage considerable change in traditional class scheduling and other institutional structures, and willingness to consider such changes will in turn encourage the fullest and most creative use of computers.

A foretaste of some changes that are likely to occur with increased computer use is suggested in the Experience-Based Education (EBE) program of an innovative college, Sinclair Community College in Dayton, Ohio (Heermann, 1977). The EBE program included a flexible degree program in which students made learning plans that involved both considerable independent study and experiential projects outside the classroom (some of these projects got faculty out of the classroom as well). Students worked at their own pace, independent of fixed quarter schedules. If students demonstrated mastery to the satisfaction of their instructors in the seventh week of the quarter, their work was considered complete and evaluated at that point. If they required twenty weeks to complete their work, they took twenty weeks.

This considerable flexibility in student scheduling necessitated a drastic change in the way faculty pay was calculated. Instead of being compensated on the basis of credit hours instructed, Sinclair faculty received one credit of full-time pay or overload pay for every five students they worked with. (The total number of students taught by each faculty member was determined by the department chairperson, so faculty members were not tempted to take on extra students in order to make more money.)

One of the positive economic outcomes of the EBE program was related to adult enrollment patterns. Heretofore adults had usually studied as part-time students, enrolling for three to six credit hours a term. Funding for Ohio community colleges like Sinclair was based on FTE (full-time equivalent) enrollments for the fall quarter, with a greatly reduced rate given for summer enrollment. Adults taking the flexible degree program, however, were permitted to enroll for full course loads (typically fifteen to eighteen credit hours), even if they worked full time. As a result, students enrolled in this program triggered considerably more subsidization than their counterparts in the traditional program had done.

The use of computers in instruction will encourage the sort of flexibility and individualization demonstrated in the Sinclair program. This flexibility and individualization, in turn, can both encourage and benefit by related changes in institutional procedures such as the change in the way students were permitted to spend their time in completing academic assignments and the change in the basis upon which the Sinclair faculty were paid.

The higher education institution of the future that gets the most out of computers in instruction—and provides the best educational climate for its students—will encourage and nurture flexibility. An administrative emphasis on flexibility, aided by increasing ability to create and modify educational software, will allow faculty to experiment constantly in seeking the form of educational delivery that is most effective for students.

## Changes in Technology

Certain predicted improvements in hardware and software during the next decade or so are likely to make computers more able than ever to help students develop critical thinking skills and apply them to actual experience. These changes involve the areas of synergy, publication, portability, transparency, diversity, and performance.

*Synergy.* A major breakthrough will involve a synergy of technologies, a multimedia show orchestrated through the computer using CD-ROM (compact disk—read-only memory) and CD-I (compact disk—interactive) (Seymour, 1986; Needle, 1986). Both use a compact disk, something like the ones used for musical reproduction. Information stored on the disk is read by a laser player driven by computer software. The software cannot change the information. One side of a CD-I disk can store about thirty minutes of moving images or 54,000 still frames, and a CD-ROM disk can hold approximately 600,000,000 characters of information, the equivalent of 1,000 books of 300 pages each. The disks are extremely durable and deteriorate much less quickly than tape, film, or slides. Even at present they are relatively cheap—less than $50 each—and they may well become cheaper as the technology improves. Incompatibility problems limit the current availability of CD-I and CD-ROM, as do the high cost of the players (about $1,000 each), but these problems will probably be solved by technological advances in the next few years.

In the classroom of the future, CD-ROM and related technology will create images on large-screen computer monitors that take the place of chalkboards or on "flip-up" monitors that will be as integral to classroom desks as the inkwells of a former age. They will permit students to view motion pictures with extraordinary sound reproduction, three-dimensional models, and other graphics; have access to hundreds of thousands of pages of text; and have the capability to receive color printouts of graphics, text, or both as needed.

*Publication.* Raymond Neff speculates that future computer printing technology will greatly change the role of the book in higher education (1986a). Neff asserts that most, if not all, information that students need will eventually be stored electronically and will be easily accessible through computer networks. In many cases, students will use this information without ever needing to place it on paper.

Nonetheless, Neff notes, people will still usually prefer to do extensive reading from paper rather than from a computer screen. Instead of borrowing books from a library, though, students will be able to print the portions they need to see, producing even whole books in just a matter of minutes on laser printers attached to their workstations (a 300-page book currently can be printed in a little over half an hour). A fee would go to the publisher each time a book is reprinted.

*Portability.* A decade or two ago, most computers filled a whole room. Today's microcomputers, even with monitors and disk drives, fit easily on a desk. Furthermore, a new generation of lightweight, portable, yet powerful "laptop" computers with built-in LCD (liquid-crystal display) monitors, not much bigger or heavier than a large hardback book, are becoming increasingly popular. In the future, laptops probably will be supplemented by computers that are small enough to hold in a student's hand. Students will be able to take these computers on field trips and enter data into them at the site.

*Transparency.* Computers and software of the future will become much simpler to use, more "transparent" to the user. Keystroke commands will become greatly simplified or replaced by movements of a "mouse" device (used today with many computers), which allows one to make choices by pointing at parts of a monitor screen, or even by voice commands that the computer will be able to recognize. On-line data bases, communication networks, and complex data base or spreadsheet programs will all become more accessible, "friendlier," and easier for students to use.

*Diversity.* A great expansion of computer use in instruction could occur because of increasing diversity and sophistication of educational software. Some new programs will be produced commercially. Others, tailored precisely to specific educational needs, will be created by groups of educational institutions, individual institutions, or even departments or individual faculty members. Local production of software will be greatly aided by new high-level authoring languages, artificial intelligence programs that take an active role in helping faculty members design software, and "shell" or "construction kit" programs that let instructors create their own expert systems or simulations for classroom use.

*Performance.* Increasingly the future of academic computing will center around the workstation. (Raymond Neff has estimated that a third of the $300 million that U. C. Berkeley plans to spend on computing by 1995 will be devoted to workstations [1986b].) This dedicated personal computer will provide a student/scholar with most or all of the computing power needed for any academic task and, in addition, allow him or her to share other intrainstitutional or extrainstitutional computing resources including a wide range of software, peripheral devices such as printers, and access to communication networks and remote "host" supercomputers. The amount of memory and the speed and power of processing in these workstations will far exceed anything available today. In time, workstations will be found in virtually every classroom and laboratory on campus.

## Effects of Technological Change

Computers will continue to be used to deliver instruction in each of the four modes (teaching machine, simulator, resource, and tool) used today. In the future, however, all of these modes will be applied in much more powerful and sophisticated ways than is possible today. The lines of demarcation between the modes also will become less strongly drawn. Simulations will be integrated into CAI programs, for example. Students will be able to call up data from a data base and then sort or analyze it using spreadsheets, hypertext, or other tools available on the same computer.

*Future Computers as Teaching Machines.* Students a decade from now will master factual information using a far more dynamic mode of computer delivery than the computer-aided instruction of the 1980s. Future CAI will be able to be much more complex both pedagogically (thanks to better authoring systems) and graphically (thanks to CD-I and CD-ROM). It will include realistic scenarios and simulations with which students can interact. It will be specifically targeted at popular undergraduate survey courses that lend themselves to the medium. CAI related to these courses will be capable of being used alone, but most often the programs will be used as a supplement to lectures, group meetings, and other instructional activities.

Future "teaching machine" programs will be much more individualized than today's CAI, thanks to artificial intelligence. Their diagnostic abilities will be much more comprehensive and will include learning style as well as mastery of content. Based on this built-in diagnosis, the programs will be able to give each student exactly the amount of instruction and practice that he or she needs. The programs' diagnostic powers will also guide instructors in giving personal help to students, as well as leaving more time free to provide that help. Dustin Heuston predicts, "Just as the computer will offer more individualization for the student, so will the teacher also be freed to give more individual attention to each student" (1986, p. iii).

Expert systems are very likely to be important in the development of these new CAI programs. Expert systems model the structural and procedural knowledge that experts in a particular field possess. An expert system used in educational software would model the procedural and conceptual knowledge of a discipline, along with teaching processes for delivering that knowledge and also learning styles necessary to mastery of that discipline. Such expert systems will be able to produce programs far more interactive than a mere series of screens called up in linear or branching fashion. Their knowledge data bases will be triggered in a variety of ways by student interaction (Merrill, 1987).

*Future Computers as Simulators.* The new CD-I and CD-ROM technologies will be used to their fullest in creating complex, realistic, highly interactive simulations that help individual students or student groups develop problem-solving skills. For example, in a simulation used in a behavioral science class, a student might have to decide how to "handle" a conflict situation involving a group that is portrayed on a video screen. After the student makes a response, the reactions of the simulated group to that response (frustration, anger, pleasure, or whatever) will also appear on the screen.

Simulations will also be combined with expert systems on

occasion. After offering a solution to a problem themselves, students will be able to watch a skillful master solve the same problem and then query the expert about why he or she made certain decisions and why those decisions had certain impacts. Such a simulation could help students understand the rationale, theory, and principles that underlie particular choices or actions.

Finally, simulation construction software will allow students to build their own simple simulations. Such construction will give students an unparalleled chance to apply rules and principles that they have learned in a course by setting up realistic situations in which these rules and principles operate. Groups of students might create simulations and then trade them with other groups so that each group could "play with" and critique another's simulation.

*Future Computers as Resources.* Future students using the computer as a resource will be able to "call up" a visually powerful and highly interactive encyclopedia (either on videodisk or accessed through an institution's communication network) that will present visual, auditory, and verbal information on topics from astronomy to zoology at the request of a few keystrokes. If students want to know more about some aspect of a topic, they will be able to call up additional references through hypertext software, creating a "three-dimensional data base." Such references might appear first as summaries in a "window" of the computer monitor. Then, if the student requests it, the whole reference could be called up. Students will also be able to obtain quick printouts of any text or photographs that they need as "hard copy."

The future computer used as a resource will bring the educational institution's whole library system to a student's fingertips. Students will be able to call up titles, tables of contents, annotated bibliographies, and indexes of all the volumes in the system. They will be able to see and reproduce any book or article instantly; gone will be the frustration of finding that the item one wants has been checked out by someone else. Computers will also give students access to architectural drawings, geological diagrams, theses and dissertations, television broadcasts of live performances, scholarly works, engineering diagrams, pictures (even perhaps three-dimensional laser holograms) of scientific specimens, works of art, musical performances, and much more.

As an example, a student preparing for an American history report on Franklin D. Roosevelt will be able to call from the computer a bibliography of literature about Roosevelt, a record of Roosevelt's major actions and accomplishments, a motion picture and sound reproduction of Roosevelt giving a landmark speech on the economy, and an accompanying analysis of the effects of his ideas and actions. The computer presentation might also include filmed or recreated interviews with farmers, unemployed workers, and investment brokers from the late 1930s, bringing to life the human dimension of Roosevelt and his time.

The computer will become more widely used as a resource in the future as on-line data bases and communication networks become cheaper and easier to use. Both data bases and networks will also come to include video and sound as well as printed text. Teleconferencing will become more like face-to-face encounters because it will feature either "live" or taped video and sound.

*Future Computers as Tools.* Within the next decade the computer "tools" used today, such as spreadsheets and word processors, will become both more powerful and easier to use. More and more different tools will be combined in integrated packages so that students can apply any or all of them to the same data. As with other software, these tools will have enhanced capability to both incorporate and (where appropriate) produce graphics. They will enable students to analyze data in increasingly complex and sophisticated ways.

Entirely new tool software will aid students much more directly in developing analytical skills than does most of the tool software used today. Software that questions students in ways that encourage intuitive or creative as well as logical thinking will become possible. Finally, future tool software will be easily modifiable to meet the special needs of particular students, instructors, or disciplines, making new experiments with computers in instruction not only possible but easy.

### The Future Student: A Vignette

Raymond Neff predicts that in the future, because of the increased efficiency and potential for sophisticated analysis made possible by the computer, "what Ph.D.s did twenty-five years ago will be term projects for [undergraduate] students" (Bok, 1985, p. 3). One can picture an undergraduate in an introductory psychology course a decade from now doing any or all of the following things:

- participating in a discussion with the instructor and other students based on an interactive video presentation of situations from daily life that illustrate approach/avoidance conflict
- self-administering drill-and-practice routines that teach and test the vocabulary and basic concepts of psychology
- working with a small group of fellow students to analyze a simulation that illustrates the parts of the brain and query an "expert" embedded in the program about various brain functions
- participating in a game and receiving points for correctly identifying parts of the brain and fixing accurate definitions to each part in competition with other students doing the same exercise
- preparing a report on the contribution of Freud to psychology by accessing a data base of bibliographic and other information about Freud, including a taped presentation of a simulated psychoanalytic session that demonstrates some of Freud's theories
- joining other students in a computer conference about the application of Freudian theory to real-life experiences
- writing the Freud report on a word processor and preparing a graph resulting from analysis of data on the popularity of Freudian psychoanalysis as compared to Jungian, Rogerian, or other major analytical systems.

Compare the opportunities for depth of content exploration, real-world application, and both critical and creative thinking presented by this range of activities with those available through today's traditional round of lectures, textbooks, and term papers!

Of course, whether these opportunities actually result in deeper or more creative learning will still depend on the student and the instructor. The computer, like all technology, is merely an instrument. Neither it nor any other educational medium can in itself make anyone learn anything. Derek Bok (1986) points out that research over five decades has not resulted in any conclusive evidence that any single medium exerts a unique influence on learning achievement—and computers are not likely to be any different.

Integration of computers into teaching and learning will not and should not change certain basic aspects of the instructional process. Whether they use computers or not, good educational programs facilitate student mastery by providing opportunities for human contact, creative inquiry, use of critical thinking skills, and experience with the realities being studied. The ideal college or university of the future will commit itself to a program of this type, and computers will provide significant help in carrying out that commitment.

As this book has described, computers can greatly aid student efficiency in absorbing routine instruction and carrying out routine learning tasks, and they can greatly increase the independence and sophistication with which students explore a subject in depth. No longer bound by place (classroom) and time (fixed meeting and quarter schedules), students could master some curricular requirements on their own and could devote the rest of their time to independent exploration alternating with group discussions with other students and faculty.

The way to cast out fear of the changes brought about by the introduction of computers into higher education is to make a positive vision of computers part of a renewed commitment to educational excellence in general. Decisions about the educational use of computers, like decisions about the use of any other invention that can be applied to education, should flow from the unique requirements of an instructor's discipline and the instructor's personal vision of excellence.

# Resource A

▓▓▓▓▓▓▓▓▓▓▓▓▓▓▓▓

## Glossary of Common Computer Terms

The following glossary includes computer-related terms used in this book and also a sampling of the most common terms likely to be used in general discussions of computers. Readers wishing a more systematic discussion of the way parts of a computer work or of particular subjects such as communication networks should consult one of the many excellent introductory books on these subjects.

**access:** make contact with (persons, data, other computers) by computer, usually through a communication network or link.

**application program:** see *"tool" program.*

**ASCII:** the system for representing characters used by almost all computers today.

**authoring system:** software that provides a "template" and other facilities for creating software, including courseware, without knowledge of programming. PLATO and KSS: Author are examples.

**baud:** a measure of the speed (number of pieces of data per unit of time) with which a modem transmits data. A 300-baud modem is much slower than a 1200-baud modem. See also *modem.*

**bit:** binary digit, the smallest unit of information a computer can recognize. Bits are also used as a measure of the power of the microprocessor in a computer's central processing unit. Many older microcomputers are eight-bit machines (can handle a stream of information eight bits wide). New sixteen-bit and thirty-two-bit microcomputers are much more powerful (a sixteen-bit machine can handle twice as many pieces of data at once as an eight-bit machine) and can sometimes handle several tasks (including both input and output of data) simultaneously, which eight-bit machines cannot. See also *central processing unit, microprocessor, power.*

**bulletin board:** a communication system that is usually small, local, and run by an individual or small business (or sometimes by a college or university). May be general interest or organized around a particular topic. Members can enter public announcements and comments, leave private "electronic mail" messages for other members, or "chat" with each other on line. Bulletin boards also often make public-domain software available for downloading to members' computers. Usually these networks are inexpensive to use and relay messages through a host computer. See also *"chat" mode, conference system, electronic mail, host computer, public-domain software.*

**byte:** eight bits, sometimes called a "word." Memory in computers is measured in kilobytes or megabytes. See also *bit, kilobyte, megabyte, memory.*

**CAI:** see *computer-assisted instruction.*

**CD-I:** compact disk, interactive. Like CD-ROM, but includes video and graphics that can be called up by the user. See also *CD-ROM.*

**CD-ROM:** compact disk, read-only memory. Data stored on a compact disk, something like those used for musical reproduction, and used in conjunction with computer software. The data on the disk cannot be changed by the user. A CD-ROM disk holds about 6,000,000,000 characters of information, the equivalent of 1,000 books of 300 pages each. See also *CD-I.*

**central processing unit (CPU):** the part of the computer system that manipulates data; in essence, it *is* the computer. It usually consists of one or more microprocessors (micro-chips) encased in a metal or plastic box. It applies instructions provided by software (programs) to data that have been entered or input into the computer's memory. See also *memory, microprocessor.*

"chat" mode: a mode of computer use whereby two people who are on line at the same time in the same conference or bulletin board can communicate directly with each other by computer. This mode is not possible with a distributed network. See also *bulletin board, conference, distributed network, on line.*

communication network: a network of computers connected to each other either physically (local area network) or electronically (distributed network, conference system, bulletin board) for the purpose of sending data back and forth. See also names of particular types of networks.

communication software: software, usually used with a modem, that permits computers to communicate with each other. See also *modem.*

components: individual parts of a computer system, that is, the computer and the peripheral devices used with it. Sometimes called hardware. See also *configuration, hardware.*

computer-assisted instruction (CAI): educational software used primarily to teach facts and simple concepts and to provide drill and practice and/or testing to students. A computer delivering CAI is being used as a teaching machine. See also *teaching machine.*

conference: a part of a communication network (usually a conference system) devoted to a particular topic. People usually enter comments or messages about the topic that may be read by anyone else in the conference, though the comments may be addressed as replies to other particular members of the conference. Conference members can also leave private "electronic mail" messages for each other. If two or more members of a conference are on line at the same time, they may be able to communicate directly in "chat" mode. See also *bulletin board, "chat" mode, conference system, electronic mail.*

conference system: a communication network set up to handle a group of conferences on particular topics. Conference systems usually cover a wide area and relay messages through a central host computer. See also *bulletin board, conference, host computer.*

configuration: the composition of a computer system, that is, the computer and the peripheral devices used with it (hardware). A common configuration consists of the computer (central processing unit) and the box that holds it, a keyboard, a monitor, one or more disk drives, and a printer. Some of the components of the configuration may be built into the computer box. See also *central processing unit, component, peripheral device,* and names of individual peripheral devices.

copy protection: a means (built into the software) of preventing or limiting the copying of a piece of software, designed to prevent software piracy (illegal copying to avoid purchase). Game software is often copy protected; other kinds of software may or may not be. Strict copy protection can limit the usefulness of software by making it hard to make backups or install the software on a hard disk.

courseware: educational software, usually of a fairly simple kind, created for use in a particular course or type of course.

CPU: see *central processing unit.*

cursor: movable, distinctive character on a computer monitor screen that shows the place that is currently "active" (where the next typed character will appear).

daisy wheel printer: a printer that uses a wheel of raised characters to strike a ribbon and paper, producing output that resembles that of an electric typewriter. Daisy wheel printers are more expensive and slower than dot matrix printers, less expensive and very much slower than laser printers. They produce "letter-quality" output but cannot produce graphics. See also *dot matrix printer, laser printer.*

data: information entered or input into a computer.

**data base, on-line**: a source of information (usually journal articles, abstracts, bibliographies, and the like) that is part of a communication network and is reached via modem. Many on-line data bases are commercial and thus expensive (most have flat-rate subscription fees and charge additional fees based on the length of time the service is actually used), and they may also be difficult to use. Some on-line data bases may be part of an intrainstitutional or interinstitutional communication network. See also *data base software.*

**data base software**: a "tool" program that allows a user to organize, classify, and retrieve data entered by the user. See also *data base, on-line; "tool" program.*

**decision-support software**: a kind of "tool" program that allows a user to analyze a series of scenarios and reach an optimal decision. See also *"tool" program.*

**digitizer**: an input device that enters data into a computer by translating visual images, sound, touch, or movement into electronic impulses. Examples include "mouse" devices, graphics tablets, light pens, touch-sensitive screens, bar code readers, text scanners, and audio translators. See also *input, "mouse."*

**disk**: a storage medium that holds electromagnetically encoded data intended for use by a computer. Disks may be either floppy disks or hard disks. See also *floppy disk, hard disk.*

**disk drive**: a peripheral device connected to or built into a computer that holds and "plays" floppy disks containing software. Most floppy disk systems use two disk drives. See also *floppy disks, peripheral device.*

**disk operating system (DOS)**: see *operating system.*

**distributed network**: a communication network in which computers relay messages from one to another. A distributed network does not have a central host computer, and members cannot "chat" with each other directly as they can on conferences and bulletin boards. Distributed networks allow messages to be sent nationwide or even worldwide for the cost of a local phone call. Messages may take anywhere from a few hours to a week to arrive. See also *bulletin board, conference system.*

documentation: the manual or other printed information accompanying a piece of hardware or software that tells how to use it.

DOS: see *operating system.*

dot matrix printer: a printer that shows characters as groups of dots (the dots often are not visible without a magnifying glass). These printers are fast and inexpensive, but their output is not of particularly high quality. They can print graphics. See also *daisy wheel printer, laser printer.*

download: receive data from another computer, often a host computer, into one's own computer. Receiving a public-domain program on request from a bulletin board is an example.

electronic mail: messages sent over a communication network and addressed to another individual who uses the network. Only the individual to whom it is addressed is allowed to read an electronic mail message.

enter: see *input.*

expert system: a program that allows the user to query a data base representing "expert" knowledge of the rules and principles that apply to a certain subject or discipline. See also *expert system shell.*

expert system shell: software that allows the user to enter rules and principles in a way that creates an expert system. See also *expert system.*

field: a portion of a record in a data base that holds a particular kind of information. A data base record defining a mineral might include fields for hardness, color, luster, and so on. See also *data base software, record.*

file: a collection of data that is stored, retrieved, and used by a computer as a discrete unit. The maximum size of a file, methods for loading or saving it, and so on, are determined by the operating system of the computer with which the file is used, the particular software that uses the file, and the size of the computer's memory. See also *load, memory, save.*

fixed disk: see *hard disk.*

floppy disk: a free-standing disk that stores data and programs to be transferred to a computer. A floppy disk must be inserted in a disk drive and activated by software in the computer (the disk operating system, or DOS) before the computer can "read" its contents. Most floppy disks are either five and a quarter inches across or three and a half inches across. The smaller size of disk is used by many newer systems and is more durable (unlike the large size, the smaller disks are physically hard, though they are still considered "floppy" disks) as well as capable of holding more data than the larger size. The amount of data a disk can store depends on whether it is single or double sided and single or double density. Not all disks will work with all operating systems. See also *disk drive, hard disk, operating system.*

function keys: special keys on a computer keyboard with functions determined by the particular software the computer is running. For example, pressing a certain function key might return the user to the main menu of a program, save a file, or load a file. See also *keyboard.*

game: in educational software, usually a simulation that has an element of competition (against another student or group of students, against one's own previous performance, or against the computer) or "winning" (a goal to be achieved, a time limit to be beaten, points to be gained, or the like). See also *simulation.*

graphics: any visual representation handled by a computer other than text. Depending on the software and the quality (color and resolution) of the computer monitor, graphics may vary from simple, single-color graphs and sketches to complex full-color displays and animation. See also *graphics software, monitor, resolution.*

graphics software: general-purpose software that allows a user to create graphics, such as drawings, charts, graphs, and diagrams. These may be displayed on a monitor or printed, if the appropriate peripheral devices are available.

**graphing software:** "tool" programs that allow the user to produce graphs and charts on the basis of input data.

**hard copy:** printed copy, as opposed to text displayed on a computer monitor screen.

**hard disk** (also called fixed disk): a storage device built into many newer computers (it can be added to some older ones). Like floppy disks, a hard disk holds data to be loaded into or that has been saved from a computer's memory. A hard disk holds far more data than a floppy disk, however—usually from ten to sixty megabytes. See also *floppy disk, megabyte.*

**hardware:** the physical parts (components) of a computer system, including the central processing unit, keyboard, and peripheral devices such as monitor, disk drives, and printers. See also *peripheral devices, software.*

**high-level language:** a programming language that is relatively similar to language and concepts and language used by human beings, as opposed to the form in which data can be read by computers. See also *machine language, programming language.*

**hologram:** a three-dimensional image produced by laser; may be reproduced by future computer software.

**host computer:** a central computer, often a minicomputer or a mainframe, through which messages on a communication network are relayed. A distributed network does not have a host computer, but local area networks, conference systems, and bulletin boards usually do. See also *communication network, distributed network.*

**hypertext:** software that allows the user to create or access a network of references, making a sort of "three-dimensional data base." A user reading a general article could use this software to call up more specific references related to any part of the article, then references suggested by those references, and so on.

**icon:** a simple picture on a computer monitor screen that can be "activated" by a mouse or other pointing device. Some kinds of computers and software allow the user to call up parts of the program by activating icons rather than typing in commands. See also *"mouse."*

idea generation software: a type of "tool" program that asks
    questions about a topic selected by the user, helping the
    user produce systematic ideas about and angles of ap-
    proach to the topic. See also *"tool" program.*
information retrieval service: a commercial organization that of-
    fers a wide variety of computer communication services,
    including on-line data bases and conferences. Such a ser-
    vice is usually fairly expensive and may be difficult to
    use. The best known information retrieval services are
    The Source and CompuServe. See also *bulletin board,*
    *conference system, data base, distributed network.*
input: data input or entered into a computer by means of a key-
    board or digitizer. See also *digitizer, keyboard, output.*
integrated circuit: a group of circuits wired together on a modu-
    lar board; allowed the evolution of the much smaller
    minicomputer from early mainframe computers, which
    depended on vacuum tubes or transistors. See also *mini-*
    *computer.*
integrated software: a software package that combines several
    kinds of "tool" programs, such as a spreadsheet, a data
    base program, and a word processor, so that data can be
    moved easily from one part to another. Lotus's Sym-
    phony and Ashton-Tate's Framework are examples. See
    also *data base software, spreadsheet, "tool" program,*
    *word processor.*
interactive: capable of responding to input from the user. An
    interactive simulation, for example, changes in response
    to decisions made by the user and entered into the com-
    puter. See also *simulation.*
keyboard: input device for a computer (built into the computer
    box or attached by a cord). It is similar to a typewriter
    keyboard but usually possesses additional keys (function
    keys or others). See also *function keys.*
kilobyte (K): a measure of the capacity of a computer's mem-
    ory or of a storage device such as a disk. A kilobyte is
    two to the tenth power, or 1,024 bytes. The memory of a
    640K computer can hold 655,360 bytes, or about 350
    double-spaced typewritten pages. See also *byte, memory.*
LAN: see *local area network.*

language: see *programming language*.

laptop: a new form of personal computer that is as powerful as an ordinary (desk-size) microcomputer but is not much bigger or heavier than a large hardback book. It often has built-in disk drives and liquid-crystal display monitor. See also *liquid-crystal display*.

laser printer: a high-speed, high-quality printer that literally burns text onto a page, producing output that looks like typeset copy at a rate of about eight pages per minute. It can also print graphics. Currently these printers are more expensive than other kinds (about $2,000 each). See also *daisy wheel printer, dot matrix printer*.

LCD: see *liquid crystal display*.

liquid crystal display (LCD): a form of monitor often built into new laptop computers that allows monochrome display without a video screen. See also *laptop*.

load: transfer from disk or other storage device into a computer's memory. See also *memory, save*.

local area network (LAN): a communication network of computers directly connected to a host computer (and therefore each other) by cable. It allows the computers to share data, software, and resources such as printers. A LAN can be used over only a limited physical area (a whole campus, at most). See also *communication network*.

machine code, machine language: a programming language that is very close to the form in which a computer actually reads data and thus is very different from the form in which human beings read and understand data. Programs in this kind of language are handled quickly by the computer, but they are hard for anyone except experienced programmers to write. See also *high-level language, programming language*.

macro: a series of commands grouped together by software in a way that allows the whole series to be treated as one command, thus saving typing time for the user.

mainframe: a very large, very expensive computer used today only for tasks too complex to be handled by smaller computers, such as plotting the trajectory of a spacecraft or handling very large data bases. The first computers, built in the 1940s, were mainframes. They used vacuum tubes and, later, transistors. Minicomputers and microcomputers are now powerful enough to do work that used to be done by mainframes (but today's mainframes are, of course, far more powerful than the earlier ones). See also *microcomputer, minicomputer.*

**megabyte:** about a million bytes (actually 1,024 x 1,024 bytes, or 1,048,576 bytes). Used as a measure of the capacity of a computer's memory or a storage device such as a disk. See also *byte.*

**memory:** space available for data in the central processing unit of a computer. It is usually measured in kilobytes (K) or megabytes. Memory includes both read-only memory (ROM) and random access memory (RAM). See also *central processing unit, kilobyte, megabyte, read-only memory, random access memory.*

**menu:** structure used in some software that presents a limited number of clearly displayed choices to a user at a given time, thus making the software easier to use. Menu choices may be made by typing in commands, moving a cursor, or, in many cases, designating appropriate areas of the screen with a "mouse" device. See also *cursor, "mouse."*

**microchip:** see *microprocessor.*

**microcomputer** (also called personal computer): the smallest (in terms of power and price as well as size) and most widespread category of computer in use today, and the only one likely to be used directly in instruction. Microcomputers use microprocessors or microchips. See also *mainframe, microprocessor, minicomputer.*

**microprocessor:** a silicon wafer that permits a microcomputer to manipulate data. A microcomputer's central processing unit contains one or more microprocessors. The power of the microprocessor determines the amount of data and tasks that the computer can handle at once. See also *bit, power.*

**minicomputer:** an intermediate-sized computer that uses integrated circuits. Minicomputers today are used by moderately large corporations and universities, but they are beyond the budget (and often the needs) of smaller businesses and colleges (the cheapest ones cost over $30,000). See also *mainframe, microcomputer.*

**modem**: a communication device that (when used with appropriate communication software) connects a computer to other computers via telephone lines. Stands for MOdulator-DEModulator. The modem on a sending computer electronically translates digital signals from the sending computer into tones that can be sent over telephone lines. The modem on the receiving computer reverses the process. The speed with which a modem transmits data is called its baud rate. A high-speed modem can send about one page of single-spaced text per minute. See also *baud.*

**monitor**: a video screen used to display text or graphic data in a computer. Monitors may be monochrome (usually with amber or green characters on a black background) or color. The resolution of the monitor and the computer's video circuitry determine how much detail the monitor can show. See also *resolution.*

**"mouse"**: an input device (a form of digitizer) that allows the user to "point" at parts of the computer monitor screen and send commands to the computer by moving the device around on a flat surface and clicking a button or buttons on it. Only some kinds of computer and some kinds of software use these devices, but they are becoming more common. See also *digitizer, input.*

**network**: see *communication network, local area network.*

**off-the-shelf software**: commercially available software.

**on line**: using one's computer to communicate with others through a communication network. See also *communication network.*

**on-line data base**: see *data base, on-line.*

**operating system** (also called disk operating system or DOS): a program, often permanently resident in a computer's memory, that controls the actions of the computer and tells it how to run other software. Different "families" of computers have different, usually incompatible, operating systems. IBM PCs and other brands of computer that are compatible with them share an operating system called MS-DOS, for example. Other common operating systems are CP/M and UNIX. Software prepared for one operating system usually will not run on a computer that uses another operating system.

output: data sent out of a computer, either to a display device such as a monitor or to a printer or other printing device such as a plotter. See also *input, monitor, plotter, printer.*

peripheral devices, peripherals: devices used with a computer but not physically part of it, such as disk drives (if not built in), monitor, printer, modem, or graphics plotter. See also names of individual devices.

personal computer: see *microcomputer.*

pixel: a point of light on a monitor screen. The resolution of a monitor is determined by the number of pixels per unit area; the more pixels in each area, the higher the resolution and the greater the level of detail available on the monitor. See also *monitor, resolution.*

plotter: a printing device that produces hard copy of graphs, charts, and other graphics.

power: the amount of data a computer or microprocessor can handle at one time, which determines the speed with which data can be handled. The amount of data is measured in bits. See also *bit.*

printer: a peripheral device that prints the output of a computer. The most common types are dot matrix, daisy wheel, and laser printers. See also names of individual printer types.

program: a series of instructions to a computer. In this book, the terms *program* and *software* are used interchangeably. See also *programming, programming language, software.*

programming: writing a series of instructions to a computer in a form that the computer can use. The instructions are written in a programming language. See also *program, programming language.*

**programming language:** a "language" in which a series of instructions to a computer may be written. COBOL, FORTRAN, and C are examples. High-level languages are relatively easy for human beings to understand, while machine language, at the other extreme, is relatively easy for computers to understand. Most programming languages are somewhere in between. See also *high-level language, machine language, program, programming.*

**public-domain software:** software that can be legally copied as often as one wishes. It is often available through bulletin boards or other communication networks.

**RAM:** see *random access memory.*

**random access memory (RAM):** the part of the computer's memory that stores data that is being input, processed, or output. It is measured in kilobytes (K) or megabytes. Personal computers with 512 or 640 K of RAM are common today, though many older computers have only 64 or 128 K of RAM. The larger the amount of RAM, the more data the computer can store in its memory at one time. Part of the memory space, however, will be taken by whatever software the computer is running, and this amount can be considerable for a complex program. Data in RAM will disappear whenever the machine is turned off or loses power. To be kept permanently, therefore, data must be transferred (saved) onto a disk or other storage device. See also *kilobyte, megabyte, memory, read-only memory.*

**read-only memory (ROM):** the part of a computer's memory that cannot be changed by software or user input. It frequently contains the operating system necessary to run the computer. It does not disappear when the computer is turned off. See also *memory, operating system, random access memory.*

**record:** a single unit in a data base. For example, a data base of minerals would probably have one record for each mineral. The record would contain a number of fields holding different kinds of information about the mineral. See also *data base, field.*

resolution: the fineness of detail visible on a computer monitor. A high-resolution monitor shows more detail than a low-resolution monitor, which means that it can display both more detailed graphics and more readable text. Resolution is determined by the number of pixels per unit area. See also *monitor, pixel.*

resource: a model of computer delivery of instruction in which the computer is used as part of a communication network to access data or people. Use of the computer in this mode helps students develop investigative skills and attain the learning objective of "knowing where." It is often encouraged by an instructor with the preferred teaching style of Mentor. See also *communication network; data base, on-line.*

ROM: see *read-only memory.*

run: operate or function, usually said of a piece of software "running" on a particular computer.

save: transfer data from a computer's random access memory to a storage device such as a disk. See also *disk, random access memory.*

shareware: software that may be legally copied but for which the author requests a voluntary payment (usually $10–$70) from anyone who uses the software regularly. Shareware is often available through bulletin boards and users' groups.

shell: see *expert system shell.*

simulation: a computer program that models a real phenomenon, showing the relationships of parts of the phenomenon to the whole and, frequently, presenting a problem to be solved. Normally the simulation changes to mimic changes in the phenomenon it models. Often it can be changed by the student (is interactive) and responds to changes made by the student by showing the effects of those changes on the whole model. A simulation may have gamelike features. Simulations (or the computer used in the simulator mode of instructional delivery) teach integrative and problem-solving skills and help students achieve the learning objective of "knowing that."

They are often used by instructors with the preferred teaching style of Facilitator. See also *game, interactive.*

**simulator**: see *simulation.*

**smart terminal**: a terminal with its own central processing unit; not as powerful as a workstation. See also *central processing unit, terminal, workstation.*

**software**: programs that allow a computer to do various tasks. Software frequently comes on floppy disks, but the disks are not the software; the software is the information encoded electromagnetically on the disks. This book uses the terms *program* and *software* interchangeably. See also *disk, hardware, program.*

**special-interest group**: a group, often a subgroup in a users' group or computer conference, that focuses on a particular topic related to computers, such as use of computers in instruction. See also *conference, users' group.*

**spreadsheet**: a form of "tool" software that automatically changes all related numbers (or other kinds of data) on a matrix of rows and columns when one number (or piece of data) is changed. It is frequently used for, but is not limited to, analysis related to business and finance. See also *"tool" program.*

**statistical package**: "tool" software that allows the user to perform statistical calculations on input data, such as central tendency, standard deviation, and correlation. See also *"tool" program.*

**system**: see *configuration.*

**system software**: see *operating system.*

**teaching machine**: mode of computer delivery of instruction in which the computer delivers programs that teach students informational skills and help them achieve the learning objective of "knowing that." These programs are usually called computer-assisted instruction (CAI). They are often used by instructors whose preferred teaching style is Teacher. See also *computer-assisted instruction.*

**terminal**: an input/output device with a keyboard and video screen that is connected to a computer, such as a host computer, by a cable or phone line in a communication network. The terminal draws on the remote computer for its software and processing power. A terminal usually has a central processing unit to handle graphics and other simple functions, but it cannot run software. See also *host computer, workstation.*

"tool" program: a program, also known as an application program or utility program, that helps a user do a particular task or tasks. Examples are spreadsheets, data base programs, and word processors. These programs help students develop classificatory and analytical skills and achieve the learning objective of "knowing what and why." They are often used by instructors with the preferred teaching style of Broker. See also names of particular types of tool programs.

transparency: the quality of being easy to use (in computer hardware or software). "Transparent" software lets the user concentrate on the task at hand rather than on complicated commands.

users' group: a group of computer users, often focused on a particular computer topic or type of machine. Group members offer support to each other through meetings or conferences that may involve demonstration of new software, question-and-answer sessions, and so on.

utility program: see *"tool" program.*

word processor: "tool" software that allows a user to manipulate text easily, including adding, deleting, or moving paragraphs at any point in a document, changing the format of the document, and so on. This popular kind of software makes revision far easier than formerly and thus potentially makes students more effective, less inhibited writers. Some kinds of computers in the business world use only word processing software and thus are also called word processors. See also *"tool" program.*

workstation: a personal computer that is connected by cable or electronically to other computers, usually including a host computer, in a communication network. The workstation runs software that is sent through the network and usually stores data in the host computer. Otherwise it usually has all the facilities and power of a regular personal computer, and it often has superior graphics. See also *host computer, terminal.*

# Resource B

▒▒▒▒▒▒▒▒▒▒▒▒▒▒▒▒▒▒▒▒

## Sources of Information
## and Assistance
## for Academic Computing

The following lists of organizations, on-line information sources
and data bases, directories, computer companies, and publications can help colleges and universities find out more about
uses of computers in instruction.

I. Associations, Projects, and Technological Centers

EDUCOM
P.O. Box 364
Princeton, NJ 08540
604-734-1915

Educational Technology Center
University of California, Irvine
Irvine, CA 92717
714-833-7452

PLATO (IV) Project
CERL
252 Engineering Research Lab
S. Mathews Avenue
University of Illinois
Urbana, IL 61801
217-333-6500

Center for Learning and Telecommunications
American Association for Higher Education
One Dupont Circle, Suite 600
Washington, DC 20036
202-293-6440


Association for the Development of Computer-Based Instruc-
tional Systems
Computer Center
Western Washington University
Bellingham, WA 98225
206-676-2860


Project on Information Technology and Education
1001 Connecticut Avenue, NW
Washington, DC 20036
202-463-0747


Society for Applied Learning Technology (SALT)
50 Culpepper Street
Warrenton, VA 22186
703-347-0055


Conduit
University of Iowa
P.O. Box 388
Iowa City, IA 52244
319-353-5789


II. On-line Sources and Data Bases


CompuServe Information Service
5000 Arlington Centre Blvd.
Columbus, OH 43220
800-848-8199

The Source
Source Telecomputing Corp.
1616 Anderson Rd.
Maclean, VA 22102
800-336-3366

Dialog Information Services, Inc.
3460 Hillview Avenue
Palo Alto, CA 94303
800-227-1972

ERIC
Educational Resources Information Center
National Institute of Education
Washington, DC 20208
202-254-7934

III. Indexes and Directories

*The Index*
W. H. Wallace
Missouri Indexing, Inc.
P.O. Box 301
St. Ann, MO 63074
314-997-6470

*Index to Computer Based Learning*
Educational Communications Division
University of Wisconsin, Milwaukee
P.O. Box 413
Milwaukee, WI 53201
414-963-4788

*Software Encyclopedia*
R. R. Bowker
P.O. Box 1385
Ann Arbor, MI 48106
313-761-4700

*COMPendium*
Epicurious
P.O. Box 129
Lincolndale, NY 10540

*Microcomputer Index*
2462 El Camino Real 247
Santa Clara, CA 95051
408-241-8381

*Directory of Online Information Resources*
CSG Press
11301 Rockville Pike
Kensington, MD 20895
301-881-9400

IV. Major Computer Companies

Apple Computer, Inc.
10260 Bandley Drive
Cupertino, CA 95014
800-538-8547

Atari, Inc.
Bid Dept.: P.O. Box 427
1265 Borregas Avenue
Sunnyvale, CA 94086
800-538-8547

Digital Equipment Corporation (DEC)
146 Main Street
Maynard, MA 01754

International Business Machines (IBM) Corporation
P.O. Box 328
Boca Raton, FL 33232
305-998-6007

Tandy Corporation
400 Atrium
1 Tandy Center
Fort Worth, TX 76102
800-433-1679

V. Publications

*Byte*
70 Main Street
Peterborough, NH 03458

*Classroom Computer Learning*
Peter Li, Inc.
2451 East River Road
Dayton, OH 45439

*Collegiate Microcomputer*
Rose-Hulman Institute of Technology
Terre Haute, IN 47803

*The Computer Instructor*
614 Santa Barbara Street
Santa Barbara, CA 93101

*Computing Teacher*
Department of Computer and Information Science
University of Oregon
1787 Agate Street
Eugene, OR 97403

*edu*
Education Computer Systems Group
Digital Equipment Corporation
Media Response Manager
PK3-2/M94
129 Parker Street
Maynard, MA 01754

*Education Computer News*
Capitol Publications
1300 N. 17th Street
Arlington, VA 22209

*Education Technology*
140 Sylvan Avenue
Englewood Cliffs, NJ 07632

*Electronic Education*
Electronic Communications, Inc.
Suite 220
1311 Executive Center Drive
Tallahassee, FL 32301

*InfoWorld*
375 Cochituate Road
Box 880
Framingham, MA 01701

*Journal of Computer-Based Instruction*
ADCIS
Computer Center
Western Washington University
Bellingham, WA 98225

*Personal Computing*
Box 1408
Riverton, NJ 08077

*Popular Computing*
70 Main Street
Peterborough, NH 03458

*T.H.E. Journal*
Box 992
Acton, MA 01720

*Wheels for the Mind*
Apple Computer, Inc.
Box 1834
Escondido, CA 92025

# References

*Agenda, Academic Information Systems, University AEP Conference.* Milford, Conn.: IBM, 1985.

Alverno College. *Competence Assessment Program: Manual for Level 1.* Milwaukee, Wisc.: Alverno College, 1973.

Amador, S. "An Implementation Plan for Instructional Computing." *EDUCOM Bulletin,* Fall 1984, pp. 19–21.

Anandam, K. "Camelot." *Teletrends,* Spring 1985, p. 3.

Andrews, D. C. "Writer's Slump and Revision Schemes: Effects of Computers on the Composing Process." *Collegiate Microcomputer,* Nov. 1985, pp. 313–316.

"Ashton-Tate Framework II Sales Demonstration." Ashton-Tate, n.d.

*The Athena Language Learning Project.* Cambridge: Massachusetts Institute of Technology, n.d.

Badgett, T. "On-Line Databases: Dialing for Data." *PC Magazine,* May 12, 1987, pp. 238–258.

Balestri, D., Cochrane, H., and Thursh, D. "High Tech, Low Tech, No Tech: Three Case Studies of Computers in the Classroom." *AAHE Bulletin,* Dec. 1984, pp. 11–14.

Baskin, C. "On-line Services." *Popular Computing,* March 1985, pp. 74–80.

Bender, L. W., and Conrad, L. P. "Fledgling, Apprentice, or Sophisticate?" *Community and Junior College Journal,* March 1984, pp. 31–33.

Bloom, B. S. (ed.). *Taxonomy of Educational Objectives: Cognitive Domain.* Vol. 1. New York: McKay, 1956.

Bok, D. "Looking into Education's High-Tech Future." *EDUCOM Bulletin,* Fall 1985, pp. 2–10.

Bork, A. "Computers in Education Today—and Some Possible Futures." *Phi Delta Kappan,* Dec. 1984a, pp. 239–243.

Bork, A. "Learning, Computers, and Higher Education." Unpublished paper, AAUP, 1984b.

Bourque, J. H. "Word Processing on a Local Area Network." *Collegiate Microcomputer,* Aug. 1985, pp. 205–211.

Bowen, C. "Gateways, Technology's Librarian." *Online Today,* July 1986, pp. 10–14.

Bowker, L. S., and Bowker, R. C. "Using Computers to Increase Course Efficiency, An Example in a General Ecology Laboratory." *Collegiate Microcomputer,* Feb. 1986, pp. 1–6.

Boyer, E. L. "Education's New Challenge." *Personal Computing,* Sept. 1984, pp. 81–82.

Broudy, H. S. "Mastery." In B. O. Smith and R. H. Ennis (eds.), *Language and Concepts in Education.* Skokie, Ill.: Rand McNally, 1961.

"Colleges and Universities Experimenting with KSS: Author." *The Higher Education Management Institute,* 1986, 4, 6.

Collier, R. M. "The Word Processor and Revision Strategies." *College Composition and Communication,* 1983, *34* (2), 149–155.

Computation Center, University of Texas, Austin. "In Brief: Computers and Technology," *Chronicle of Higher Education,* Sept. 17, 1986, p. 19.

"Computer Software for Higher Education." *Chronicle of Higher Education,* October 2, 1985, p. 32.

"Computer Software for Higher Education." *Chronicle of Higher Education,* June 25, 1986, p. 25.

"Computer Software for Higher Education." *Chronicle of Higher Education,* March 18, 1987a, p. 21.

"Computer Software for Higher Education." *Chronicle of Higher Education,* March 25, 1987b, p. 16.

"Computer Software for Higher Education." *Chronicle of Higher Education,* April 15, 1987c, p. 19.

"Computer Software for Higher Education." *Chronicle of Higher Education*, April 29, 1987d, p. 16.

"Computer Software for Higher Education." *Chronicle of Higher Education*, May 27, 1987e, p. 16.

"Computer Software for Higher Education." *Chronicle of Higher Education*, June 17, 1987f, p. 14.

"Computer Software for Higher Education." *Chronicle of Higher Education*, August 12, 1987g, p. 16.

Davis, B. R. H., and Marlowe, C. "The Computer as a Networking and Information Resource for Adult Learners." In B. Heermann (ed.), *Personal Computers and the Adult Learner*. New Directions for Continuing Education, no. 29. San Francisco: Jossey-Bass, 1986.

DeLoughry, T. "Widespread Piracy by Students Frustrates Developers of Computer Software." *Chronicle of Higher Education*, August 12, 1987, pp. 31–32.

"Development of Instructional Applications." *EDUCOM Computer Literacy Newsletter*, Winter 1985, p. 3.

Diodato, V. "Eliminating Fees for Online Search Services in a University Library." *Online*, Nov. 1986, pp. 44–50.

*Directory of Online Data Bases*. Santa Monica, Calif.: Cuadra Associates. Printed periodically.

Divine, A. R. "An Electronic Bulletin Board for Everyone." *Teletrends—A League for Innovation Cable and Telecommunications Newsletter*, Winter 1986–87, p. 15.

Dodd, J., and Anders, V. "Free Online Searches for Undergraduates: A Research Project on Use, Costs, and Projections." *Library Hi Tech*, Spring 1984, pp. 43–50.

Dougherty, B. N. *Composing Choices for Writers: A Cross-Disciplinary Rhetoric*. New York: McGraw-Hill, 1985.

Dressel, P. L. *College and University Curriculum*. Berkeley, Calif.: McCutchan, 1968.

Dressel, P. L., and Marcus, D. *On Teaching and Learning in College: Reemphasizing the Roles of Learners and the Disciplines in Liberal Education*. San Francisco: Jossey-Bass, 1982.

*Drexel University: The Total Education Plan and Microcomputing*. Philadelphia: Drexel University, n.d.

Eble, K. E. "Word Processors: Zucchini in the Academic Garden." *Chronicle of Higher Education*, July 16, 1986, p. 41.

*The Electronic University Network.* San Francisco: Telelearning, 1986.

Emery, J. C. "Issues in Building an Information Technology Strategy." *EDUCOM Bulletin,* Fall 1984, pp. 4–13.

Ericksen, S. C. *The Essence of Good Teaching: Helping Students Learn and Remember What They Learn.* San Francisco: Jossey-Bass, 1984.

Ewens, T. "Analyzing the Impact of Competence-Based Approaches on Liberal Education." In G. Grant and others, *On Competence: A Critical Analysis of Competence-Based Reforms in Higher Education.* San Francisco: Jossey-Bass, 1979.

Fields, C. M. "Medical Schools Urged to Stress Critical Thinking." *Chronicle of Higher Education,* 1984, *29* (5), 1, 15.

FIPSE Technology Study Group. *Computers in Education: Strategies and Resources.* Washington, D.C.: Fund for the Improvement of Postsecondary Education, n.d.

Fisher, G. "Lemonade (and Other Simulations) For Sale." *Electronic Learning,* Feb. 1983, pp. 78–82.

Fisk, R. S. "Using Apple-Generated Graphics in Calculus Instruction." *Collegiate Microcomputer,* Aug. 1984, pp. 229–235.

Fiske, E. B. "Computers in the Groves of Academe." *The New York Times Magazine,* May 13, 1984, p. 40.

Fridlund, A. J. "Special Report: Statistics Software." *InfoWorld,* Sept. 1, 1986, pp. 31–37.

Gagne, R. M. *The Condition of Learning.* New York: Holt, Rinehart & Winston, 1965.

Gilbert, S. *The EDUCOM Computer Literacy Project: First Year Reflections.* Princeton, N.J.: EDUCOM, 1984.

Grand Valley State College. *College IV Self-Study for North Central Association Accreditation Team.* Allendale, Mich.: Grand Valley State College, 1973.

Green, A. B. "Software Insights: The Unseen Nature of Learning Curves." *InfoWorld,* July 22, 1985, p. 28.

Gueulette, D. G. (ed.). *Microcomputers for Adult Learning.* Chicago: Follett, 1982.

Heermann, B. *Experiential Learning in the Community College.* Topical paper no. 63. Los Angeles: ERIC Clearinghouse for Junior Colleges, 1977.

Henderson, H. "Introduction to USENET." In B. Anderson, B. Costales, H. Henderson, and The Waite Group, *UNIX Communications.* Indianapolis, Ind.: Howard W. Sams, 1987.

Hesburgh, T. M. "Why Higher Education Isn't Making the Grade." *Los Angeles Times,* April 15, 1987, p. V-3.

Heuston, D. *The Future of Education: A Time of Hope and New Delivery Systems.* Orem, Utah: WICAT Systems, 1986.

Hewett, T. T. "Using an Electronic Spreadsheet Simulator to Teach Neural Modeling of Visual Phenomena." *Collegiate Microcomputer,* May 1986, pp. 141–151.

"Highlights: Dickinson College." *EDUCOM Computer Literacy Newsletter,* Winter 1985, p. 4.

"Highlights: OPEN at California State University, Long Beach." *EDUCOM Computer Literacy Newsletter,* Fall 1985, p. 2.

"Highlights: Philadelphia Area Computing Society at La Salle University." *EDUCOM Computer Literacy Newsletter,* Fall 1985, pp. 3–4.

Hofstetter, F. T. "Using the PLATO System: Features, Research, and the Future." Newark: University of Delaware, n.d.

Hofstetter, F. T. "A Model for Administering Computer-Based Education." Newark: University of Delaware, 1980.

Hofstetter, F. T. "Synopsis of the University of Delaware's Office of Computer-based Instruction." Newark: University of Delaware, 1981.

"In Brief: Computers." *Chronicle of Higher Education,* Jan. 8, 1986, p. 28.

Johnson, L. G. "Computer Corner: New Software Helps Organize Thoughts into Outlines." *ABA Journal,* n.d.

Johnston, J. "Research Methods for Evaluating the New Information Technologies." In J. Johnston (ed.), *Evaluating the New Information Technologies.* New Directions for Program Evaluation, no. 23. San Francisco: Jossey-Bass, 1984.

Keeton, M. T., and Associates. *Experiential Learning: Rationale, Characteristics, and Assessment.* San Francisco: Jossey-Bass, 1976.

King, K. M. "Evolution of the Concept of Computer Literacy." *EDUCOM Bulletin,* Fall 1985, pp. 18–21.

Kinsey, T. G., Wiesen, D., and Unertl, A. "Environmental Studies Simulation Modules." In D. T. Bonnette (ed.), *NECC '84: Sixth Annual National Education Computing Conference.* NECC, 1985.

Knowles, M. *Self-Directed Learning.* Chicago: Follett, 1975.

"Learning How to Learn Using Computer-Assisted Cooperative Techniques." *Network Circuit,* Feb. 1984, p. 2.

Lennox, C. *Strategies for Integrating Computing Throughout the Curriculum: Mills College.* EDUCOM Academic Computing Seminar Series. Oakland, Calif.: Mills College, 1985.

Lewin, K. *A Dynamic Theory of Personality.* New York: McGraw-Hill, 1935.

Lowman, J. *Mastering the Techniques of Teaching.* San Francisco: Jossey-Bass, 1984.

Mac Committee, Social Science Computing. *The Impact of the Macintosh at Dartmouth.* Hanover, N.H.: Dartmouth College, n.d.

McCarthy, M. "Newsdesk." *InfoWorld,* Aug. 5, 1985, p. 13.

McCord, J. *Microcomputer Evaluation Study.* Philadelphia: Drexel University, n.d.

Mace, S. "Nationwide University Net Incorporates to Boost Growth." *InfoWorld,* July 20, 1987, p. 16.

McGrath, L. "Graphics Help People Who Cannot Draw." *InfoWorld,* Sept. 26, 1986, pp. 37-46.

McHenry, H., and Franklin, S. "Microcomputer In-Service Training for University Faculty and Staff: A Case Report." *Collegiate Microcomputer,* May 1986, pp. 173-178.

Manes, S. "The Oven of the Half-Baked Idea." *PC Magazine,* Feb. 24, 1987, p. 93.

Martinez, T. "Using the Bank Street Writer as an Aid for Freshman English Writing." *Collegiate Microcomputer,* Nov. 1985, pp. 291-294.

Meeks, B. N. "The Quiet Revolution—On-Line Education Becomes a Real Alternative." *Byte,* Feb. 1987, pp. 183-190.

Merrill, M. D. "An Expert System for Instructional Design." *IEEE Expert,* Summer 1987, pp. 25-37.

Meyers, C. *Teaching Students to Think Critically: A Guide for Faculty in All Disciplines.* San Francisco: Jossey-Bass, 1986.

*The Microcomputing Program at Drexel University: Organizing the Program.* Philadelphia: Drexel University, n.d.

*The Microcomputing Program at Drexel University: Preparing the Faculty.* Philadelphia: Drexel University, n.d.

"Microsoft Word." *Microsoft.* Microsoft Corp., 1986.

Miller, M. "Special Report: Database Management Software—IBM PC Programs Become Easier." *InfoWorld,* May 5, 1986, pp. 39–44.

Naiman, A. "A Hard Look at Educational Software." *Byte,* Feb. 1987, pp. 198–200.

Naisbitt, J. *Megatrends.* New York: Warner Books, 1982.

Needle, D. "Special Report: Graphics Software." *InfoWorld,* Sept. 22, 1986, pp. 35–40.

Needle, D. "Is This the Dawn of CD-ROM?" *Computer Currents,* Apr. 7–Apr. 20, 1987, pp. 24–25, 82.

Neff, R. K. "Merging Libraries and Computer Centers: Manifest Destiny or Manifestly Deranged?" *EDUCOM Bulletin,* Winter 1985, pp. 8–16.

Neff, R. K. "Quality of Engineering Education." Washington, D.C.: American Society for Engineering Education, 1986a.

Neff, R. K. *What We're Doing at U.C. Berkeley and Why.* Berkeley: Information Systems and Technology, University of California, Berkeley, 1986b.

O'Brien, L. M. *The Educational Software Project.* Providence, R.I.: Institute of Research in Information and Scholarship, Brown University, 1985.

Osgood, D. "The Difference in Higher Education." *Byte,* Feb. 1987, pp. 168–178.

"An Overview of the Different Kinds of Networks." *edu,* Winter 1985, pp. 37–39.

Pear, M. R. *A Plan for Creating a Network of Scholars' Workstations.* Providence, R.I.: Institute for Research in Information and Scholarship, Brown University, 1985.

"Personal Computing: The Challenge to Management." *Forbes* special supplement, 1985, pp. 1–34.

Phenix, P. *Realms of Meaning.* New York: McGraw-Hill, 1964.

Piaget, J. *Psychology of Intelligence.* 1947. Reprint. Totowa, N.J.: Littlefield Adams, 1976.

Plato. *Phaedrus.* W. C. Helmbold and W. G. Rabinowitz, trans. New York: Bobbs-Merrill, 1956.

Plummer, C. M., and others. "Evaluation of a Faculty Computer Literacy Education and Training System." In D. T. Bonnette (ed.), *NECC '84: Sixth Annual National Educational Computing Conference.* 1985.

*A Pocket Guide to the Hardest Working Software in the World.* Lotus Development Corp., n.d.

*Preliminary Report: The Future of Computing at Carnegie-Mellon University.* Pittsburgh: Carnegie-Mellon University, 1982.

Quarterman, J. S., and Hoskins, J. C. "Notable Computer Networks." *Correspondence of the Association for Computing Machinery,* Oct. 1986, pp. 1–50.

"Report from the Leading Edge." *The Tarrytown Letter,* 1981, 5, 4–5.

Richards, A. J. "Technology-Based Delivery System: Computer Conferencing and Distance Learning." Paper presented at Technological Issues in Higher Education Conference, Kansas State University, 1986.

Robinson, I. A. "Teaching Basic Concepts with the Microcomputer: A Study of the Effects on Learning in Introductory Sociology Courses." In D. T. Bonnette (ed.), *NECC '84: Sixth Annual National Education Computing Conference.* 1985.

Rogers, C. *Freedom to Learn.* Westerville, Ohio: Merrill, 1969.

Ryle, G. *The Concept of Mind.* London: Hutchinson, 1949.

Schwartz, L. "Teaching Writing in the Age of the Word Processor and Personal Computers." In D. O. Harper and J. H. Stewart (eds.), *Run: Computer Education.* (2nd ed.) Monterey, Calif.: Brooks/Cole, 1985.

Seymour, J. "Awaiting the CD-ROM Boom." *PC Magazine,* May 27, 1986, pp. 87–88.

Slatta, R. W. "Telecomputing Services, Teaching and Research." *Collegiate Microcomputer,* Feb. 1985, pp. 23–28.

Soltis, J. F. *An Introduction to the Analysis of Educational Concepts.* Reading, Mass.: Addison-Wesley, 1968.

Teichman, M. "What Does Word Processing Do for College Writers?" In *Proceedings of the Ninth IBM University Study Conference, 1984.* Milford, Conn.: IBM, 1984.

"Three-Year Bachelor Degree Predicted with Computer." *National Report for Training and Development,* July 5, 1984, p. 1.

"Trends in Computing—Systems and Services for the '80s." *Fortune,* July 2, 1984, p. 2.

Tross, G. "Thinking for Fun and Profit." *Teletrends—A League for Innovation Cable and Telecommunications Newsletter,* Winter 1986-87, pp. 6, 16.

Tucker, M. S. "The 'Star Wars' Universities: Carnegie-Mellon, Brown, and M.I.T." In M. S. Tucker (ed.), *Computers on Campus: Working Papers.* Current Issues in Higher Education. Washington, D.C.: American Association for Higher Education, 1983-84.

Turner, J. A. "Computers: Bentley College, N.J. Technology Institute Supplies Computers to Freshmen." *Chronicle of Higher Education,* Sept. 25, 1985, p. 34.

Turner, J. A. "Computers and Technology: At Berkeley, Computers Have to Work—Even If They're Donated." *Chronicle of Higher Education,* Apr. 2, 1986a, p. 27.

Turner, J. A. "Computers and Technology: Columbia U.'s Head Librarian Is Now Managing Academic Computing, Too." *Chronicle of Higher Education,* Apr. 9, 1986b, p. 39.

Turner, J. A. "Colleges Scramble for Money for Computing, Envious of Grants to Some Big Institutions." *Chronicle of Higher Education,* Apr. 30, 1986c, p. 1.

Turner, J. A. "NSF Launches Plan to Build National Computer Network for Researchers." *Chronicle of Higher Education,* May 21, 1986d, p. 28.

Turner, J. A. "The New Software: Math for Architects, Staging for 'Hamlet,' and Other Graphic Examples." *Chronicle of Higher Education,* July 2, 1986e, p. 4.

Turner, J. A. "Role of the Computing Director Is Increasingly Managerial." *Chronicle of Higher Education,* Sept. 17, 1986f, pp. 1, 13.

Turner, J. A. "Drive to Require Students to Buy Computers Slows." *Chronicle of Higher Education,* Feb. 4, 1987a, pp. 1, 28.

Turner, J. A. "Technology Consortium Raps Software Piracy, Backs Intellectual Rights." *Chronicle of Higher Education,* April 15, 1987b, p. 18.

Turner, J. A. "Microcomputers Found More Available—and

More Often Required—at Selective Colleges." *Chronicle of Higher Education,* April 29, 1987c, pp. 13, 17.

Turner, J. A. "Computer Industry Sees Higher Education as Tough but Lucrative Market for Products." *Chronicle of Higher Education,* June 10, 1987d, pp. 1, 18-19.

*Videodisc Science Laboratory Simulations.* Washington, D.C.: The Annenberg/CPB Project, 1985.

Warfield, A. "High Tech/High Touch Management Education." In B. Heermann (ed.), *Personal Computers and the Adult Learner.* New Directions for Continuing Education, no. 29. San Francisco: Jossey-Bass, 1986.

Watt, D. "Practical Teaching Tools." *Popular Computing,* Oct. 1984, pp. 58-59.

Whitney, G. G. "Business Strategy Simulation." *Collegiate Microcomputer,* Spring 1983, pp. 39-43.

Wilson, J. *Thinking with Concepts.* London: Cambridge University Press, 1969.

"A Wizard's Plan for an Electronic University." *Business Week,* March 19, 1984, p. 60.

Wresch, W. C., and Hieser, R. A. "Training Faculty for Computer Use Across the Curriculum." In D. T. Bonnette (ed.), *NECC '84: Sixth Annual National Educational Computing Conference.* 1985.

Yankelovich, N., and others. *The Sampler Companion.* Technical Report 85-1. Providence, R.I.: The Institute for Research in Information and Scholarship, Brown University, 1985.

# Index

Academic computing programs: analysis of organizing and managing, 168-184; associations, projects, and technological centers for, 217-218; budgets for, 139-141; centralization of control for, 174-178; choosing a structure for, 183-184; computer companies for, 220-221; control of, 173-178; examples of, 179-182; formal structure of, 168-169; indexes and directories to, 219-220; informal structure for, 169-173; information sources for, 217-223; line and staff authority for, 173-174; on-line sources and data bases for, 218-219; organizational structures for, 168-173; publications for, 221-222

ADAPSO, 143

Alverno College, competence-based program at, 25

Amador, S., 140

American Association for Higher Education, 218

American Medical Association, 58

Analytical skills: analysis of improving, 85-102; background on, 85-86; commercially available programs for, 97-100; concept of, 87; data base programs for, 91-93; evaluating software for, 100-102; importance of, 86-87; and intellectual development, 27; other tools for, 96-97; statistical and graphics programs for, 90-91; tool use for, 87-97; word processing programs for, 93-96

Anandam, K., 64, 107

Anders, V., 74

Andrews, D. C., 94

Annenberg Foundation, 6-7

Apple Computer, Inc., 220, 223

Apple Macintosh: operating system of, 39; programs for, 53, 65; and writing course, 121

Apple II, programs for, 54, 65, 66

Armington, N., 1

ARPANET, 78, 82

Art courses, network for, 80

Artificial intelligence, and teaching machines, 193

ASCII, 98, 199

Ashton-Tate, programs from, 91, 97, 98, 100

Assessment-centered programs, for teaching machines, 51-53

Assignments, computer use for, 35-38

Associated Press, 73, 81

Association for the Development of Computer-Based Instructional Systems, 218

235

Associations, listing of, 217-218
Atari, Inc., 220
Authoring systems: concept of, 199;
    and creating software, 107-108,
    109; learning objectives on, 155
Authority: centralization of, 174-
    178; decentralization of, 177-
    178; line and staff, 173-174
Automotive courses, software for,
    136

Badgett, T., 73, 81
Balestri, D., 8, 88
Baskin, C., 80, 81
Battin, P., 176-177
Baumol, W. J., 53
Bender, L. W., 133, 141
Bibliographic   Retrieval   Service
    (BRS), 73, 81
Biology courses: resource use for,
    33; simulation for, 61
BITNET, 78, 81
Bitnet Corporation, network from,
    81
Blinder, A. S., 53
Bloom, B. S., 23, 118
Bok, D. C., 2-3, 14, 188, 196, 197
Bologna, University of, 187
Bork, A., 109
Bourque, J. H., 72
Bowen, C., 73
Bowker, L. S., 91
Bowker, R. C., 91
Bowker, R. R., 219
Boyer, E. L., 137
Broker, as teaching style, 30-31
Broudy, H. S., 23, 24, 25
Brown University: academic com-
    puting development at, 134, 140;
    Education Software Project at,
    181; Institute for Research in
    Information   and   Scholarship
    (IRIS) at, 181-182, 183; instruc-
    tion-centered program at, 48-49;
    Intermedia Project at, 49; non-
    interactive simulations at, 59-61;
    practice-centered program at, 50
Browning, R., 49
Budgets: for academic computing,
    139-141; guidelines for, 146
Bulletin boards: for accessing peo-
    ple, 78; concept of, 200

Business   courses:   assessment-cen-
    tered   program   for,   52;   simula-
    tion for, 63; spreadsheets for, 89

California, Berkeley, University of:
    academic computing program at,
    179, 183; computing budget at,
    139, 192; libraries and comput-
    ers at, 176; network at, 71, 72
California, Irvine, University of:
    and authoring systems, 109; Edu-
    cational Technology Center at,
    217
California Polytechnic State Univer-
    sity, tool use at, 91
California State University, Long
    Beach, Learning Assistance Cen-
    ter at, 158-159
Capitol Publications, 222
Carnegie-Mellon   University:   aca-
    demic   computing   development
    at, 134-135, 140; and three-year
    degree, 3
Carter M., 156
Centaur Systems, program from, 54
Center for Learning and Telecom-
    munications, 218
Chemistry courses: simulations for,
    7; teaching machine programs
    for, 53; tool use for, 11
Clark Technical College, computer
    funding at, 136
Classroom work, computer use for,
    35-36
COBOL, 17
Cochrane, H., 8, 88-89
Collier, R. M., 96
Colorado School of Mines, graph-
    ing program at, 90
Colorado State University, spread-
    sheets at, 88-89
Columbia University, library and
    computer center at, 176-177
Compact   disk—interactive   (CD-I),
    190, 192, 193, 200
Compact   disk—read-only   memory
    (CD-ROM), 189-190, 192, 193,
    200
Compac, and PC compatibility, 39
COMPRESS, programs from, 53, 54
CompuServe: and accessing people,
    77; Forum of, 76; and informa-

tion retrieval, 112, 218; IQuest gateway of, 73, 75, 80

Computer-aided instruction (CAI). *See* Teaching machine, computer as

Computer-assisted design: simulation for, 66; tools for, 90

Computer literacy courses, examples of, 152-153

Computers: analysis of issues with, 1-19; background on, 1-3; companies for, 220-221; and delivery modes, 31-35; funding sources for, 135-136; future use of, 185-197; goals for using, 138-139; glossary of terms on, 199-216; and institutional concerns, 17-19, 125-184; institutionwide environment for, 125-147; and instructional delivery, 4-13, 46-102; for instructional design, 13-14, 103-124; for instructional enrichment, 20-124; and integrating with other teaching methods, 20-23, 41-45; and interpersonal aspects of learning, 14-17; needs assessment for, 130-134; pedagogical and technological forces on, 2-3; personal, 1-2, 154-155; planning integration of, 41-45; portability of, 191; promises and problems of, 3-19; purchase decisions for, 141-142; as resource, 8-10, 70-84; as simulator, 6-8, 57-69; support systems for, 148-167; as teaching machine, 4-6, 46-56; as tool, 10-13, 85-102; use assessment for, 126-129

Comware, program from, 107

CONDUIT, program from, 66

Conferences, computer: for accessing people, 77, 79-80, 82; concept of, 201

Conrad, L. P., 133, 141

Corporation for Public Broadcasting, 6-7

Costs, of resource use, 9-10, 76

CSG Press, 220

Cyert, R. M., 3, 134-135

Dartmouth College: computer as resource at, 8; grades at, 3; student use of computers at, 1

Data, accessing, 73-77

Data bases: for analytical skills, 91-93; concept of, 203; sources of, 218-219

Davis, B.R.H., 78

dBase III Plus, 91, 98-99

Decision Resources, program from, 98

Delaware, University of: Office of Computer-Based Instruction at, 158, 179-181, 183; word processing programs at, 94

Delivery: instructional, 4-13, 46-102; modes of, 31-35

DeLoughry, T., 143

Design courses, tool use for, 11

Dialog Information Services, 73, 80, 81, 112, 219

Dickinson College, incentives at, 156

Digital Equipment Corporation (DEC), 220, 221

Diversity, and future technology, 191

Divine, A. R., 78

Dodd, J., 74

Dougherty, B. N., 93-94

Dow Jones, 75

Drama courses, simulations for, 7, 62

Dressel, P. L., 2, 25, 28, 57-58, 70-71, 86

Drexel University: committees at, 171-173; computers required at, 2; computers as tools at, 11; extracurricular activities at, 16; organizational structure at, 169-170, 171-173; spreadsheets at, 89; student participation at, 172; support system at, 160-162, 172; technical support at, 157-158

Eastern Oregon State College, computing budget at, 134

Eble, K. E., 95-96

Ecology course, tool use for, 91

Economics courses: spreadsheets for, 88-89; teaching machine program for, 53-54; tool use for, 11, 34

Edison, T. A., 2-3

Education: in computer literacy, 152-153; future changes in structure of, 187-189; in support system, 150-156, 165; on teaching and learning with computers, 153-156

Educational Resources Information Center (ERIC), 80, 219

EDUCOM, 40, 143, 146, 158, 217

Einstein, A., 48

Electronic Communications, Inc., 222

Electronic Information Exchange System (EIES), 82

Electronic mail: for accessing people, 77, 79; concept of, 204; for learning teams, 113

Electronic University Network: and independent study, 37; as resource, 8-9, 77

Emery, J. C., 137, 138, 140-141

Engineering courses, tool use for, 11

English courses: resource use for, 74-75, 78; word processing program for, 94

Environment: action plan issues for, 137-138; action planning guidelines for, 144-147; actualizing vision for, 137-147; clarifying vision for, 125-134; flexibility of, 147; institutionwide planning for, 125-147; organizational factors in, 168-184; spreading vision for, 134-136; support systems in, 148-167

Environmental studies course, simulations for, 61-62

Epicurious, 220

Ericksen, S. C., 20, 21, 41, 47, 57, 58, 116

Evaluation, of student work, and software, 116-118

Ewens, T., 22, 23

Expert systems: concept of, 204; and teaching machines, 193

Exxon Foundation, 107

Facilitator, as teaching style, 29-30

Feature Writing, acquiring and implementing, 120-122

Ferris State College, assessment-centered program at, 52

Fields, C. M., 58

Figure-ground relationship, and informational skills, 47

Fisher, G., 112

Fisk, R. S., 90

Fiske, E. B., 1

FORTRAN, 17

Franklin, S., 152

Freud, S., 196

Fridlund, A. J., 98

Fund for the Improvement of Postsecondary Education (FIPSE) Technology Study Group, 8

Future: analysis of teaching and learning in, 185-197; background on, 185-187; and changes in structure of education, 187-189; and changes in technology, 189-192; and effects of technological change, 192-196; student in, 196-197

Gagne, R. M., 23

Gale, D., 72

Geography course, simulation for, 60

Geology course, data base program for, 92

German course, simulation for, 7

Gilbert, S., 151

Goals, for computer use, 138-139

GPO Publication Reference, 122

Grand Valley State College, competence-based program at, 25

Graphics programs: for analytical skills, 90-91; concept of, 205-206

Green, A. B., 11

Gueulette, D. G., 5

Haenicke, D. H., 139

Harcourt Brace Jovanovich, program from, 53

Hardware: availability of, 38-41; checklist for, 142; concept of, 206

Harvard University, 2-3, 14

Heermann, B., 188

Henderson, H., 82

Hesburgh, T. M., 139

Heuston, D., 15-16, 186, 188, 193

Hewett, T. T., 89

Hieser, R. A., 163
High Performance Systems, program from, 65
High tech, high touch, and software implementation, 112
Higher education, aim of, 46
Higher Education Management Institute, study by, 108
History courses: data base program for, 92; network for, 80; simulation for, 33, 67
Hofstetter, F. T., 4, 138, 158, 180, 181
Homework, computer use for, 36
Hoskins, J. C., 78, 82
Host computers: concept of, 206; for investigative skills, 71-72
Houston, University of, academic computing at, 134
Human service technician case studies, software for, 123-124
Hypertext: for analytical skills, 96-97; concept of, 206; future of, 194; in instruction-centered programs, 49; and simulation, 61

IBM Corporation, 135, 181, 220
IBM PC: and compatibility, 39; programs for, 53, 54, 65, 66
Idea generator programs: for analytical skills, 96; concept of, 207
Illinois, University of: pathology "textbook" at, 8; PLATO Project at, 217
Impact, learning objectives on, 155
IMSI Sales Division, program from, 54
Incentives, in support system, 156-157, 166
Independent study, computer use for, 37-38
INFOMASTER, 81
Informational skills: analysis of enhancing, 46-56; commercially available programs for, 53-54; concept of, 46-47; evaluating software for, 54-56; evaluation of, 117; importance of, 46-47; and intellectual development, 25-26; and teaching machine use, 47-53
Institutions: analysis of concerns of,

17-19, 125-184; computer environment at, 125-147; computer use at, 2; Star Wars type of, 134, 140
Instruction: acquiring and implementing software for, 103-124; analysis of computer use in, 20-45; and assignment types, 35-38; and availability of hardware and software, 38-41; and computer delivery modes, 31-35; delivery of, 4-13, 46-102; design of, 13-14, 103-124; enriching, 20-124; environment for computer-enriched, 125-184; factors related in, 22-23; and intellectual skills, 25-27; and learning objectives, 23-25; support for computer use in, 148-167; and teaching styles, 27-31
Instruction-centered programs, for teaching machines, 48-49
Integrative skills. See Problem-solving and integrative skills
Intellectual property rights, guidelines for, 143-144
Intellectual skills, computers for, 25-27
Investigative skills: analysis of fostering, 70-84; commercially available networks for, 80-82; for data access, 73-77; evaluating, 117; evaluating networks for, 82-84; importance of, 70-71; and intellectual development, 27; and people access, 77-80; resource use for, 71-80
Iowa, University of: Conduit at, 66, 218; simulation from, 66

Johns Hopkins University, 187
Johnson, L. G,, 100
Johnston, J., 119
Journalism course, resource use for, 75-76

Keeton, M. T., 23
Kemp, W., 79
King, K. M., 149
Kinko's Academic Courseware Exchange, programs from, 53, 65

Kinko's Service Corporation, program from, 66
Kinsey, T. G., 61
Knowing how: as learning objective, 24; and practice and evaluation-centered programs, 50
Knowing that: and analytical skills, 86; as learning objective, 24; and practice and evaluation-centered programs, 50
Knowing what: and analytical skills, 85, 86; as learning objective, 24-25
Knowing where, as learning objective, 24
Knowing why: and analytical skills, 85, 86; as learning objective, 24-25
Knowledge Index, 122
Knowles, M., 22

Land, G., 185-186, 188
La Salle University, and Philadelphia Area Computing Society (PACS), 159
Latin courses, teaching machine program for, 54
Leading Edge, and PC compatibility, 39
League for Innovations in the Community College, 107
Learning: applied and theoretical, 22-23; depersonalization of, 15, 17; interpersonal aspects of, 14-17; self- and other-directed, 22; stages of growth in, 151. See also Teaching and learning
Learning agreements, for software implementation, 114-115
Learning communities, support from, 113
Learning objectives: and computer use, 23-25; on teaching and learning with computers, 153-155
Learning Odyssey, 66
Learning styles, computers and, 5
Learning teams, for software implementation, 112-114
Lectures, and computer use, 21
Lennox, C., 157
Lewin, K., 149

Libraries, and academic computing programs, 176-177
Literature course, instruction-centered program for, 49
Living Videotext, program from, 99-100
Local area network (LAN): concept of, 208; for investigative skills, 71
Logical community, and networks, 72
Longo, S., 159
Lotus Development Corp., 97
Lotus 1-2-3, 97-98
Lowman, J., 20, 21, 88

Mac Committee, Social Science Computing, 3
McCarthy, M., 3
McCord, J., 16
Mace, S., 81
McGrath, L., 90
McGraw-Hill, programs from, 65-66, 107
McHenry, H., 152
Manes, S., 88
Marcus, D., 2, 28, 57-58, 70-71, 86
Marine biology course, data base program for, 92
Marlowe, C., 78
Martinez, T., 94
Mary Washington College, and computer conferencing, 79
Maryland, University of, spreadsheets at, 89
Massachusetts Institute of Technology (M.I.T.): academic computing development at, 134, 140; simulations at, 7
Mathematics courses: graphics program for, 90; network for, 80; simulation for, 6; teaching machines for, 5, 54
Mead Corporation, network from, 81
Medical schools: problem-solving skills in, 58; simulation for, 33
Meeks, B. N., 79
Memphis State University, computer literacy courses at, 152-153
Mentor, as teaching style, 30

Merrill, M. D., 193

Meyers, C., 21, 46, 85

Meyrowitz, N., 49

Miami-Dade Community College: simulation at, 64-65; software at, 107

Microsoft, program for, 99

Miller, M., 99

Mills College, incentives at, 156-157

Mindscape, 67

Missouri at Columbia, University of, resource use at, 75-76

Missouri Indexing, 219

Montclair State College, word processing program at, 95

MS-DOS, and PC compatibility, 39

Muller, S., 187

Music courses, teaching machine program for, 53

Naiman, A., 10

Naisbitt, J., 112

National Institute of Education, 219

National Science Foundation, 82

NCR Corporation, 136

Nebraska, University of: and networks, 72; and simulations, 6-7

Needle, D., 98, 190

Needs assessment, for computer use, 130-134

Neff, R. K., 71, 72, 108, 139, 176, 179, 190, 192, 196

Networks: for accessing people, 77-79; commercially available, 80-82; distributed, 78, 203-204; evaluating, 82-84; for investigative skills, 71-72

New Jersey Institute of Technology, network from, 82

NewsNet, 73, 81

NEXIS, 81

Nite Rider, 75

North Carolina Central University, practice programs at, 50-51

North Carolina State University, software program from, 54

Notre Dame University, computing budget at, 139

NTIS, 122

O'Brien, L. M., 181

Oregon, University of, Department of Computer and Information Science at, 221

Organizational structure: for academic computing programs, 168-184; choosing, 183-184; guidelines for, 144-145

Orwell, G., 14

Osgood, D., 49, 61, 62, 156

Paris, University of, 187

Pathology courses, resource use for, 8

Pear, M. R., 182

People, access to, 77-80

Performance, and future technology, 192

Personal computer: learning objectives on, 154-155; use of, 1-2

Peter Li, Inc., 221

Phenix, P., 25

Philadelphia Area Computing Society (PACS), 159

Physical facilities, guidelines for, 144

Physics courses: simulations for, 7, 65; spreadsheets for, 89

Piaget, J., 87

Piracy, issue of, 142-144

Plato, 185

PLATO, 4, 158, 179-180, 217

Plummer, C. M., 139, 152

Political science courses: as independent study, 37; instruction-centered programs in, 48-49; simulation for, 33, 66, 67; software for, 122

Portability, and future technology, 191

Practice and evaluation-centered programs, for teaching machines, 49-51

Problem-solving and integrative skills: analysis of developing, 57-69; commercially available programs for, 65-66; components of, 58; evaluating software for, 66-69; evaluation of, 117; importance of, 57-58; and intellectual development, 26-27; simulator use for, 58-65

Problem-solving course, simulation for, 64-65
Project on Information Technology and Education, 218
Projects out of class, computer use for, 36-37
Psychology courses: network for, 80; simulation for, 65-66; spreadsheets for, 89; tool use for, 11
Publications: for academic computing programs, 221-222; future for, 190-191

Quarterman, J. S., 78, 82

Resource, computer as: analysis of issues in, 8-10, 70-84; commercially available networks for, 80-82; concept of, 213; data access for, 73-77; as delivery mode, 33-34; evaluating networks for, 82-84; and evaluation of student work, 117; future of, 194-195; for investigative skills, 71-80; people access for, 77-80; training students for, 122
Richards, A. J., 30, 80
Robinson, I. A., 51
Rochester Institute of Technology (R.I.T.): computer literacy courses at, 152; goals at, 138-139
Rogers, C., 17, 196
Roosevelt, F. D., 48, 195
Rose-Hulman Institute of Technology, 221
Rosenberg, V., 142-143
Ryle, G., 23, 24

St. Louis Community College, electronic bulletin board at, 78
San Diego, University of, simulation at, 63
Schwartz, L., 95
Science courses: network for, 80; simulations for, 6, 33, 65
Scott, B. T., 75-76
SDC/Orbit, 73
Seymour, J., 190
Shareware: concept of, 213; in public domain, 40
Simulation with computers: analysis of issues in, 6-8; 57-69; commercially available programs for, 65-66; concept of, 213-214; as delivery mode, 33; evaluating software for, 66-69; and evaluation of student work, 117; forms of, 59; future of, 193-194; group competitive, 62-63; individual competitive, 64-65; interactive, 61-62; learning teams for, 113; noninteractive, 59-61; for problem-solving and integrative skills, 58-65; and spreadsheets, 89; training students for, 111
Sinclair Community College, Experience-Based Education (EBE) at, 188-189
Skills: analytical, 85-102; informational, 46-56; investigative, 70-84; problem-solving and integrative, 57-69
Slatta, R. W., 73
Social science courses: resource use for, 33-34; simulations for, 65, 66
Society for Applied Learning Technology (SALT), 218
Society for Manufacturing Engineers, 136
Sociology courses: practice program for, 51; tool use for, 11
Socrates, 185
Software: acquiring and implementing, 103-124; for analytical skills, 97-102; availability of, 38-41; checklist for, 105-107; concept of, 214; creating, 107-110; evaluating, 54-56, 66-69, 100-110, 118-120; and evaluation of student work, 116-118; examples of acquiring and implementing, 120-124; existing, 104-107; future, 194; implementing, 110-120; for information skills, 53-54; integrated packages of, 97; integrating with noncomputer materials, 112; and learning agreements, 114-115; learning objectives on, 155; and learning teams, 112-114; piracy of, 142-144; for problem-solving and integrative skills, 65-66; in public

domain, 39-40, 212; student feedback on, 116; training and preparing students for, 110-112

Software Publishers Association, 143

Soltis, J. F., 23, 24, 86

Source, The, 73, 75, 219

Southwestern College, computing budget at, 140

Spreadsheet programs: for analytical skills, 87-89; concept of, 214

Stanford University: Instruction and Research Information Systems (IRIS) at, 156; simulations at, 7, 62

State University of New York College at Buffalo, interactive simulations at, 61-62

Statistical programs: for analytical skills, 90-91; concept of, 214

Statistics course, teaching machine program for, 54

Strategic Simulations, 63

Students: autonomy of, 14-16; efficiency of, 16-17; feedback from, 116; future, 196-197; personal computer use by, 1-2; software for evaluating work of, 116-118; training, 110-112, 122

Support systems: analysis of building, 148-167; background on, 148; creating, 164-167; education in, 150-156, 165; examples of, 160-164; group, 158-160, 166-167; guidelines for, 145-146; incentives in, 156-157, 166; and learning communities, 113; need for, 149-150; technical, 157-158, 166

Synergy, future of, 189-190

Systat, 98

Tandy Corporation, 221

Tandy/Radio Shack, and PC compatibility, 39

Teacher, as teaching style, 28

Teaching and learning, with computers, 153-156; future computer use in, 185-197; learning objectives on, 154; person centeredness in, 17; phases in, 47-48; purpose of, 2

Teaching machine, computer as: analysis of issues with, 4-6, 46-56; and assessment-centered programs, 51-53; commercially available programs for, 53-54; concept of, 214; and creating software, 108; as delivery mode, 31; evaluating software for, 54-56; and evaluation of student work, 117; future of, 192-193; and informational skills, 47-53; instruction-centered programs for, 48-49; integration of, 112; learning agreements for, 114; learning teams for, 113; organizational structure for, 179, 183; practice and evaluation-centered programs for, 49-51; and resources, 9; support system for, 163-164; training students for, 111

Teaching styles, computers and, 6, 27-31

Technology: centers for, 217-218; changes in, 189-192; and diversity, 191; effects of change in, 192-196; and future of computer use, 185-197; and performance, 192; and portability, 191; for publication, 190-191; synergy of, 189-190; and transparency, 191

Teichman, M., 95

Telelearning, 8, 77

Texas A&M University, resource use at, 74-75

Texas at Austin, University of, Computation Center at, 2

Thoughtware, 52

Thursh, D., 8, 88

Tool, computer as: for analytical skills, 87-97; analysis of issues in, 10-13, 85-102; commercially available programs for, 97-100; concept of, 215; data base programs for, 91-93; as delivery mode, 34; evaluating software for, 100-102; and evaluation of student work, 117; future of, 195-196; and spreadsheet programs, 87-89; statistical and graphics programs for, 90-91; training students for, 111-112;

word processing programs for, 93-96
Transparency: concept of, 215; future of, 191
Tross, G., 64
Tucker, M. S., 135, 136
Turner, J. A., 1, 2, 7, 14, 19, 72, 93, 134, 139, 140, 144, 177, 179

Unertl, A., 61
United Press International, 73, 81
U.S. Army, and software implementation, 113
U.S. Department of Defense, network from, 82
UNIX, network from, 82
Use assessment, for computer use, 126-129
USENET, 78, 82

Van Horn, R. L., 134-135, 136
van Houweling, D., 135
Villanova University, word processing program at, 94-95

Warfield, A., 52
Wasch, K. A., 143
Watt, D., 92

Western civilization course, teaching machine program for, 54
Western Michigan University, computing budget at, 139
Western Union Telegraph Co., network from, 81
Western Washington University, Computer Center at, 218, 222
Whitney, G. G., 63
Wiesen, D., 61
Wilson, J., 86
Wisconsin at Milwaukee, University of, Educational Communications Division at, 219
Wisconsin Center in Marinette County, University of, support system at, 162-164
Word processing: acquiring and implementing, 121-122; for analytical skills, 93-96; concept of, 215
Wresch, W. C., 163
Writing courses: interpersonal aspects in, 16; practice-centered program for, 50; resource use for, 74; software for, 120-122; teaching machines for, 5, 50; word processing program for, 94-95

Yankelovich, N., 48, 50, 60